BACKGROUND PAPERS

**HUMAN
DEVELOPMENT
REPORT 1995**

Published
For the United Nations
Development Programme
New York

ISBN 92-1-126046-9
U.N. Sales Number E.96.III.B.3

Distribution and Sales: United Nations Publications
New York, New York 10017, USA

Printed in the United States of America on acid-free, recycled paper ✠

Cover and design: Gerald Quinn, Quinn Information Design, Cabin John, Maryland

Editing, desktop composition and production management: Knut Engedal and Renu D. Corea, all with the Human Development Report Office.

Foreword

In the past several years, an exciting debate has emerged world-wide on issues of human development. The Human Development Reports, commissioned by UNDP and prepared by an independent team, have made a significant contribution to this debate.

Many distinguished academics have contributed over the years to the central ideas explored by the Human Development Reports. Behind each annual report lies a rich body of background studies. These, in themselves, are valuable contributions to the debate on human development. We felt that these should be made accessible to a broader audience of academics, development professionals and policy makers. The Occasional Paper series was started in 1992 with this objective in mind, and so far, 20 papers have been published on a one-by-one basis.

Starting with this volume, it has been decided to combine the occasional papers for each annual report and publish a collection in a single volume. This first annual volume contains five of the papers commissioned for the 1995 Human Development Report which focussed on the theme of Gender Equality.

The paper by Sudhir Anand and Amartya Sen on "Gender Inequality in Human Development: Theories and Measurement" presents the full conceptual frame work and the methodology of the 'gender equity sensitive indicators'(GESI). This methodology is applied to the Gender-related Development Index (GDI) and the Gender Empowerment Measure (GEM) which were introduced in the Human Development Report 1995. These are pathbreaking measures which will be a permanent feature of future HDRs. GDI engenders the Human Development Index, thus measuring both progress in basic human capabilities and the extent of progress in gender equality. GEM is a composite measure of gender under empowerment. GEM encompasses women's role in decision making in the professional, economic and political arenas.

The other four papers address economic and political dimensions of gender and human development.

"Political Representation: Engendering Democracy" by Kathleen Staudt shows that in the historical legacies and lingering realities, men monopolize political space. Pointing out that such political monopolies are likely to produce policy outcomes that are neither gender-fair nor accountable to women, the paper submits that global sustainability in the twenty first century will require transformed, engendered politics. The paper analyzes women's political representation as a means towards an engendered policy agenda. A conceptual framework of engendering politics is introduced, and extensive quantitative evidence as well as exploratory efforts are presented in respect of women's political representation. The paper also contains 10 country studies highlighting successful and unsuccessful examples of women's participation as well as promising policy initiatives in various countries selected from all major regions of the world.

Jayati Gosh's paper on "Trends in Female Employment in Developing Countries: Emerging Issues" takes a holistic approach to women and work, examining women's employment within the framework of women's lives, which she points out is defined by work, as most women in developing countries are fully employed in productive work, paid and/or unpaid. The paper argues that the critical issues concern quality, remuneration and recognition as much as employment itself. The paper examines patterns of occupational segmentation and male-female wage disparities, as well as the impact of macroeconomic policies on women, particularly the negative impact of structural adjustment.

While Gosh's paper focuses on trends in female participation in the paid labour force, two other papers focus explicitly on unpaid work. Antonelia Picchio's paper on "The Analytical and Political Visibility of the Work of Social Reproduction" argues that work in the non-market household sector, is not recognized because it is invisible. This work of 'social reproduction' and the market production together form part of the economic system, conventional economic theory and concepts ignores the non-market sector. The functioning of these two parts in the total structure requires understanding of the non-market activities which remains unexplored. The case for a strategic policy of reversing the direction of the production-reproduction relationship is argued on the basis of a human development framework in which production and markets are made responsible and accountable institutions of human well-being.

The paper by Luisella Goldschmidt-Clermont and Elisabetta Pagnossis-Aligisakis addresses the issue of unpaid non-market work in a very concrete way. Their paper "Measures of Unrecorded Economic Activities in Fourteen Countries" documents available data on the non-market sector of economic activities in 14 countries. The paper demonstrates that non-monetized consumption and activities go unrecorded in labour statistics and in national accounts. The data presented in this paper show the order of magnitude of the unrecorded economic activity; over half as much and almost as much as recorded economic activities. These are therefore not just marginal contributions to the economy. The results suggest that concepts such as `labour'. 'employment', 'economically active', 'production', and 'economic contribution' need to be rethought as new concepts and systems of measurement are introduced.

Any comments and observations on the articles would be most welcome.

These papers reflect the views of the authors and not necessarily those of the Human Development Report Office, UNDP.

This publication was made possible by a generous grant from the governments of Sweden and Norway. We are very grateful for this contribution.

Richard Jolly
Special Adviser to the Administrator

Sakiko Fukuda-Parr
Director
Human Development Report Office

New York
June 1996

Table of Contents

Gender Inequality in Human Development: Theories and Measurement [1]

Sudhir Anand and Amartya Sen

Motivation

Over the past five years, a great deal has been achieved by the Human Development Report of the UNDP in shifting the focus of attention of the world community from such mechanical indicators of economic progress as GNP and GDP to indicators that come closer to reflecting the well-being and freedoms actually enjoyed by populations. Even though the Human Development Report has been influential primarily because of the extensive and detailed statistical analyses of achievements and limitations of living conditions of people in different parts of the contemporary world, the aggregative Human Development Index (**HDI**) also has played some part in bringing about this reorientation. Despite the obvious limitations of the **HDI** (arising in part from its attempt to capture a complex reality in a summary form with imperfect data), it has served as something of a rival to the other summary indicator — the aggregative GNP, which hitherto had been almost universally used as the premier index of the economic achievement of nations. The **HDI** has clearly been able to present some aspects of human development that the GNP tends to miss.

From the beginning, the Human Development Report has been concerned with inequalities in the opportunities and predicaments of women and men. Although this perspective has received some attention in past Reports, there is a strong case at this time for concentrating specifically on that issue for a more comprehensive investigation of gender inequality in economic and social arrangements in the contemporary world.

In performing this task, there is need for fresh economic and social analyses as well as careful and probing empirical research. Women and men share many aspects of living together, collaborate with each other in complex and ubiquitous ways, and yet end up — often enough — with very different rewards and deprivations. This note is specifically concerned with developing a framework for "gender-equity-sensitive indicators" of achievements and freedoms. The methodology for this is explored in the sections that follow, ending with specific recommendations to be put into practice.

While this exercise must be a crucial part of the important task that is now being undertaken by the programme of the Human Development Report, there are two other aspects of gender deprivation to which this Report must also pay some attention. First, aside from developing "gender-equity-sensitive indicators", the approach must also look at gender inequality per se. The investigation of such inequalities must have a close link with the development of equity-sensitive overall indicators, and it would be important to explore how the inequality measures should relate to the approach of using gender-equity-sensitive indicators (**GESI**).

Secondly, aside from looking at the state of advantages and deprivations that women and men respectively have, there is an important need to look at the contrast between (1) the efforts and sacrifices made by each, and (2) the rewards and benefits respectively enjoyed. This contrast is important for a better understanding of gender injustice in the contemporary world. The exacting nature of women's efforts and contributions, without commensurate rewards, is a particularly important subject to identify and explore.

Thus characterized, the new initiative in this Human Development Report has three distinct departures to make, concerning respectively:

(1)   the development and use of gender-equity-sensitive indicators;

(2)   the formulation and utilization of measures of gender equality and inequality; and

(3)   the identification of efforts and contributions made by women that go unrecognized in standard national income and employment statistics.

---

[1]   Paper prepared for the Human Development Report 1995. For helpful discussions, we are grateful to Mahbub ul Haq and to the other members of the "human development" team.

This paper is primarily concerned with the first two of these three fields, but some analysis of the last problem will also be presented.

Group Inequality and Aggregation: The Basic Structure

Aggregate indicators of life expectancy, literacy, and other advantages used in the UNDP's Human Development Report have tended to ignore distributional concerns, using a simple arithmetic average of achievement (or shortfall), in each dimension, over the entire population.[2] Such an average overlooks systematic and potentially large differences between distinct groups of people, in particular women and men, but there are disparities also between different classes, racial groups, regional populations, and so on. We focus here on gender differentials in achievement, but the issues discussed would, to a considerable extent, apply to other inequalities as well.

We may begin by examining the inequality between women and men in a dimension where the "potentials" of the two groups are not really different. Literacy is an obvious example. In contrast, in the case of life expectancy, we must take note of the evident biological advantage in survival of females over males (on this, see Waldron 1983, Sen 1992b, Anand 1993, and the references cited there). Given symmetric treatment in nutrition, health care, and other conditions of living (including the duration and intensity of work), women have systematically lower age-specific mortality rates than men, resulting in a life expectancy for women that is significantly higher than that for men — possibly by some five years or more. There is no corresponding difference in the potential for adult literacy (that is, in the percentage of the population aged 15 and above that is literate).

For a given level of mean achievement, relative inequality between groups has some obvious simplicity when there are just two groups. For example, if the first element of the pair (X_f, X_m) represents the female literacy rate for a country, and the second element the male literacy rate, the Human Development Report 1994 (Table 5, pp. 138-39)

shows three countries with the same mean or overall literacy rate of 80 percent distributed between females and males as follows: China (68, 92), Malaysia (72, 89), and Mauritius (75, 85). Comparing these three countries, it seems clear that gender inequality in literacy is highest in China and lowest in Mauritius. Similarly, at a higher level of mean achievement of 84 percent literacy rate, gender inequality in Indonesia (77, 91) is greater than in the Dominican Republic (83, 86).

The assessment of relative inequality in achievement can be reasonably perspicuous when there are only two groups — as in the case of gender. The larger the gender gap, holding the overall mean constant, the larger is inequality as measured by any index belonging to the Lorenz class (see Anand 1983, Appendix D); this class includes most commonly used inequality measures such as the Gini coefficient, the two Theil indices, the Atkinson index, and the squared coefficient of variation. A bigger gender gap, with the same overall mean (and the same population proportions of the two groups) is equivalent to a simple mean-preserving regressive transfer. (In terms of Lorenz curves, this would correspond to an unambiguously lower curve.) In the special 2-group case, disparity ratios or gaps will unambiguously reflect the inequality in achievement between the two groups. Given equality preference and the same overall mean, more relative inequality will indicate a worse social state of affairs, and this evaluative feature must be reflected in the gender-equity-sensitive indicators.

This simple recognition still leaves open the question of what would be appropriate standards of comparison when the overall or mean levels of achievement are different. In particular, how might we think about "trading off" more relative equality against a higher absolute achievement? Honduras, for example, has a total literacy rate of 75 percent divided between females and males as (73, 78).[3] Should this social outcome be judged worse or better than the case of China, which has a total literacy rate of 80 percent distributed as (68, 92) between females and males? Honduras has less gender inequality in literacy levels than China, but it also has a lower overall rate of literacy. A comparison between the two countries now calls for some way of assessing the comparative claims of more relative equality against higher absolute achievement. An explicit evaluative exercise on this "trade off" will be required in such situations.

We begin with the approach explored by A.B. Atkinson (1970) for the purposes of measuring relative income

---

2   The situation is slightly different in the case of adjusted income, which is based on a logarithmic transform of per capita GDP for the country as a whole (truncated at the official poverty line income for the richer, developed countries). See Anand and Sen (1993).

---

3   Human Development Report 1994, Table 5, p. 139.

inequality, and extend this analysis to fit our task.[4] Let X be the indicator of achievement, and let X_f and X_m refer to the corresponding female and male achievements. If n_f and n_m are the numbers of females and males in the population, respectively, then the overall or mean achievement $\overline{X}$ is given by

$$\overline{X} = (n_f X_f + n_m X_m) / (n_f + n_m).$$

We posit a social valuation function for achievement which is additively separable, symmetric, and of constant elasticity marginal valuation form

$$V(X) = \begin{cases} \dfrac{1}{1-e} X^{1-e} & e \geq 0, \ e \neq 1 \\[2mm] \log X & e = 1 \end{cases}$$

up to a positive affine transformation. Only values of $\epsilon \geq 0$ are considered so as to reflect a preference for equality in the social valuation function.

For any pair (X_f, X_m) of female and male achievements, we can construct an "equally distributed equivalent achievement" X_{ede}. This is defined to be the level of achievement which, if attained <u>equally</u> by women and men, as (X_{ede}, X_{ede}), would be judged to be <u>exactly</u> as valuable socially as the actually observed achievements (X_f, X_m). According to the formula for social valuation, for a given ϵ, X_{ede} is thus defined through the equation

$$(n_f + n_m) \frac{X_{ede}^{1-e}}{1-e} = n_f \frac{X_f^{1-e}}{1-e} + n_m \frac{X_m^{1-e}}{1-e},$$

which implies that

$$X_{ede} = (n_f X_f^{1-e} + n_m X_m^{1-e})^{\frac{1}{1-e}} / (n_f + n_m)^{\frac{1}{1-e}}$$

---

[4]   See also Kolm (1969), Sen (1973), Anand (1977, 1983), Blackorby and Donaldson (1978, 1984), Osmani (1982), and Foster (1984, 1985).

$$= (p_f X_f^{1-e} + p_m X_m^{1-e})^{1/(1-e)},$$

where we define the proportions $p_f = n_f/(n_f + n_m)$ and $p_m = n_m/(n_f + n_m)$. Hence X_{ede} is formed from (X_f, X_m) by taking what we shall call a "(1-ϵ)-average" of X_f and X_m rather than a simple arithmetic average of the female and maleachievements.[5] In the case when $\epsilon = 0$, X_{ede} reduces to $\overline{X}$, the simple arithmetic average; here there is no concern for equality, and the arithmetic mean indicates the social achievement. But when $\epsilon > 0$, there is a social preference for equality (or an aversion to inequality) which is measured by the magnitude of the parameter ϵ.

---

[5]   Considering X_{ede} as a function of ϵ, we can write

$$X_{ede}(\epsilon) = [p_f X_f^{1-e} + p_m X_m^{1-e}]^{1/(1-e)}.$$

For $X_f, X_m > 0$, $X_{ede}(\epsilon)$ is well-defined for all ϵ (positive or negative) except $\epsilon = 1$. As $\epsilon \to 1$, we can show that $\log X_{ede}(\epsilon) \to (p_f \log X_f + p_m \log X_m)$, i.e. the logarithm of the geometric mean of X_f and X_m; hence $X_{ede}(\epsilon)$ tends to the geometric mean of (X_f, X_m). If one of the X_i, say X_f, is equal to 0, then $X_{ede}(\epsilon)$ is well-defined for $\epsilon < 1$. But for $\epsilon > 1$, $X_f^{1-\epsilon} = 1/X_f^{(\epsilon-1)} \to \infty$ as $X_f \to 0$. In this case,

$$X_{ede}(\epsilon) = 1/[p_f/X_f^{(e-1)} + p_m/X_m^{(e-1)}]^{1/(e-1)},$$

so that

$$p_f / X_f^{(e-1)}$$

and the entire denominator of $X_{ede}(\epsilon)$ tends to infinity as $X_f \to 0$. Therefore for $\epsilon > 1$, $X_{ede}(\epsilon) \to 0$ as $X_f \to 0$. Putting together the cases $\epsilon = 1$ and $\epsilon > 1$, the limiting value of $X_{ede}(\epsilon)$ for $\epsilon \geq 1$ is zero as one of the X_i, e.g. X_f, tends to zero. Thus we may simply <u>define</u> $X_{ede}(\epsilon) = 0$ for $\epsilon \geq 1$ when X_f or X_m is equal to zero.

Assuming that female achievement falls short of male achievement, i.e. $(0 \leq) X_f < X_m$, the following results can be demonstrated for "$(1-\epsilon)$-averaging"[6]:

(1) $X_f \leq X_{ede} \leq X_m$.

(2)   The larger is ϵ, the smaller is X_{ede} (given X_f, $X_m > 0$).

(3) $X_{ede} \leq \overline{X}$ for $\epsilon \geq 0$ (with equality holding when $\epsilon = 0$).

(4) $X_{ede} \rightarrow X_f$ as $\epsilon \rightarrow \infty$.

Result (4) corresponds to the Rawlsian maximin situation where social achievement is judged purely by the achievement of the worst-off group, which in the case of gender may typically refer to women.[7] If $X_f < X_m$ in every country, and if $\epsilon \rightarrow \infty$ (equity preference tending to infinity), then social achievement across countries will be measured by female achievement alone: in the averaging, the weight given to male achievement in excess of female achievement will tend to zero. In this case, the equally distributed equivalent achievement index X_{ede} reduces to the index for the relatively deprived group (typically women), and countries are ranked according to the absolute achievement of women in those countries.

As mentioned earlier, X_{ede} is a "$(1-\epsilon)$-average" of X_f and X_m. When $\epsilon = 0$, $X_{ede} = \overline{X}$, the arithmetic average of X_f and X_m. When $\epsilon = 1$, X_{ede} is the geometric average; and when $\epsilon = 2$, X_{ede} is the harmonic mean of X_f and X_m.[8] When $\epsilon \rightarrow \infty$, $X_{ede} \rightarrow \text{Min} \{X_f , X_m \}$. The equally distributed equivalent achievement can be calculated for each country for different values of ϵ, the parameter of equity preference. Thus if the preference for equity is small (ϵ close to 0), China's literacy rates of (68, 92) for females and males, respectively, corresponding to an overall literacy rate of 80 percent, will be

judged to be better than Honduras's figures of (73, 78), corresponding to an overall rate of 75 percent. As the equity preference parameter ϵ is raised, Honduras's achievement will overtake that of China's; in the limit, as ϵ tends to infinity, Honduras's equally distributed equivalent achievement will be 73 while China's will be 68. For all values of ϵ above the critical cutoff 5.693, at which the two countries' achievements are the same, Honduras's achievement will be judged to be better than China's.

The equally distributed equivalent achievement X_{ede}, applied to gender differences, yields a measure that is, in fact, a gender-equity-sensitive indicator (**GESI**). This is, of course, an index of <u>overall</u> achievement which takes <u>note</u> of inequality, rather than a measure of gender <u>equality</u> as such. But it uses — explicitly or by implication — equity-sensitive weights on the achievements of the two groups, rather than the unweighted mean of the two sets of achievements that is more commonly used (including, hitherto, in the <u>Human Development Report</u>). It incorporates <u>implicitly</u> something like a gender equality index. The index of relative equality E that underlies X_{ede} can be defined simply as

$$E = X_{ede} / \overline{X} .$$

This can vary from 0 to 1 as equality is increased[9]; its properties are examined in Appendix A.3, "Properties of the Relative Gender- Equality Index E". Hence, the measure of social achievement $X_{ede} = E.\overline{X}$ is just the relative equality index E multiplied by the overall or mean achievement measure $\overline{X}$. Relative equality and mean absolute achievement are thus integrated into the Gender-Equity- Sensitive Indicators (**GESI**). Applying the correction for equality to <u>each</u> of the "human development" indicator (**HDI**) variables and aggregating them would yield a new gender-equity adjusted measure of "human development" — to be called the gender-related development index (**GDI**).

---

[6]   The Appendices contain a more general discussion and proofs of the major results.

[7]   There is some ambiguity as to whether this "extreme inequality aversion" leads to simple maximin, or to the lexicographic version of maximin (sometimes called "leximin"), on which see Hammond (1975).

[8]   By result (2) above, we have the following relationship between the three means when the two numbers X_f and X_m are positive and different: the harmonic mean is less than the geometric mean, and the geometric mean is less than the arithmetic mean.

---

[9]   The corresponding measure of relative <u>inequality</u> I is simply the Atkinson index

$$I = 1 - (X_{ede} / \overline{X}) .$$

Under the assumptions made on V(X) in the text, both E and I are <u>mean-independent</u> measures. Indeed, the constant elasticity marginal valuation form is both sufficient <u>and</u> necessary for E and I to be homogeneous of degree zero in (X_f , X_m).

Equity-Sensitive Aggregation and Life Expectancy

So far the analysis has been confined to achievements in which the "potentials" of women and men do not differ (for example, each group has the same range of achievable literacy, from 0 to 100 percent). The situation is different, however, when it comes to mortality rates and life expectancy (as was mentioned earlier). Given the evidence of biological differences in survival rates favouring women (with comparable care),[10] we are forced to address the question of the appropriate comparable scales of achievement of life expectancy respectively for women and men. And we have to integrate that differential scaling into the general evaluative scheme of gender-equity-sensitive indexes.

Letting (L_f, L_m) denote the life expectancy at birth of females and males, respectively, the Human Development Report 1994 shows the following comparisons for some advanced countries: Italy (81,74), Finland (80,72), France (81,73), United States (80,73), Japan (82,76). For all high-income countries together, the gender gap in life expectancy in 1992 was six years. The higher potential life expectancy of females relative to males is anticipated in demographic projections of the future as well. For the year 2050, for example, life expectancy projections of (87.5, 82.5) years for females and males, respectively, averaging to 85 years, have been made for the developed countries (Human Development Report 1993, p. 111).

In considering the disaggregation of the Human Development Index (HDI) by gender, in our paper (Anand and Sen 1993) for the Human Development Report 1993 we had suggested separate goalposts for maximal life expectancy of 87.5 and 82.5 years for females and males, respectively, that is, a five-year gender gap. The minimum life expectancy levels have been taken to be 37.5 and 32.5 years for women and men, respectively, giving the same range of variation (viz. 50 years) for both sexes. When no adjustment is made for gender inequality, this implies that a unit increase in longevity for either sex will contribute the same increment to the overall HDI.

In the corresponding disaggregation of HDI in Human Development Report 1993, female and male achievements in life expectancy, X_f and X_m respectively, have been assessed through

$$X_f = (L_f - 37.5)/50$$
$$X_m = (L_m - 32.5)/50.$$

The simple arithmetic average $\overline{X}$ of X_f and X_m, assuming female and male population proportions of ½ each, is then calculated as

$$\overline{X} = \frac{1}{2}X_m + \frac{1}{2}X_f$$
$$= (\overline{L} - 35)/50$$

where $\overline{L} = (L_f + L_m)/2$ is the average life expectancy attained in the population.

Equality between persons can be defined in two quite distinct ways, in terms of attainments, or in terms of the shortfalls from the maximal values that each can respectively attain. For "attainment equality" of achievements, we have to compare the absolute levels of achievement. For "shortfall equality", what must be compared are the shortfalls of actual achievement from the respective maximal achievements of each group. Each of the two approaches has some considerable interest of its own.[11] Shortfall equality takes us in the direction of equal use (relative or absolute) of the respective potentials. In contrast, attainment equality is concerned with equal absolute levels of achievement (irrespective of what the maximal potentials are).

In those cases in which human diversity is so powerful that it is impossible to equalize the maximal levels that are potentially achievable, there is a basic ambiguity in assessing achievement, and in judging equality of achievement (or of the freedom to achieve). If the maximal achievement of person 1 — under the most favourable circumstances — is, say, x, and that for person 2 is 2x, then equality of attainment would invariably leave person 2 below her potential achievement. Partly as a response to such issues, Aristotle had incorporated, in his Politics, a parametric consideration of what a person's "circumstances admit" and had seen his

---

[10]   There is indeed strong evidence that the maximal potential life expectancy for women is greater than for men -- given similar care, including health care and nutritional opportunities (see Holden 1987, Waldron 1983, and the references cited there). Indeed, in most of the "developed" countries, women tend to outlive men by typically six to eight years.

[11]   On this see Sen (1992a), Chapter 6.

"distributive conception" in that light. "For it is appropriate, if people are governed best that they should do best, <u>in so far as their circumstances admit</u> — unless something catastrophic happens."[12] It is possible to question this Aristotelian view in terms of the more rough-and-ready rationale of attainment equality, but there is force in the conception of shortfall equality as well, and it is that approach that is being used here for assessing gender equality in the context of life expectancy variations. The gender-equity-sensitive indicators can also be made to take note of the logic behind this approach.

Thus, the approach to adjusting for gender inequality in achievement in the case of life expectancy must first involve a re-scaling to take note of the potentially higher longevity of women. Such adjustments are, in fact, a part of the already used methodology of the <u>Human Development Report</u>, since these re-scalings have to be done whether or not we wish to take explicit note of gender inequality. However, instead of taking a simple arithmetic average $\bar{X}$ of the female and male achievements X_f and X_m, we take a "$(1-\epsilon)$-average" with $\epsilon >$ 0. As before, we form the average X_{ede}, given for $\epsilon \neq 1$ through

$$X_{ede}^{1-\epsilon} = \frac{1}{2}X_f^{1-\epsilon} + \frac{1}{2}X_m^{1-\epsilon},$$

which reduces to $\bar{X}$ when $\epsilon = 0$.[13] Thus we define L_{ede} through

$$[(L_{ede} - 35)/50]^{1-\epsilon} =$$
$$\frac{1}{2}[(L_f - 37.5)/50]^{1-\epsilon}$$
$$+ \frac{1}{2}[(L_m - 32.5)/50]^{1-\epsilon}.$$

---

12   The translation is from Nussbaum (1988), who also discusses the precise role that this qualification plays in Aristotle's "distributive conception" (pp. 146-15O; italics added).

13   On the other hand, for $\epsilon = 1$, X_{ede} is given through the logarithmic functional form. These formulations are based on the presumption that there are the same number of women as of men — hence the half-and-half division. When this does not hold, the gross mean and the gender-equity-sensitive measure involve weighting the achievements of each group by their respective population shares p_f and p_m (see Appendix A.1).

When $\epsilon = 0$, $L_{ede} = \bar{L}$. For $\epsilon > 0$, $L_{ede} < \bar{L}$.

Gender Differences in Earning and Rewarded Employment

The human development index H for a country has been defined to be

$$H = \frac{1}{3}\left[\frac{\bar{L} - 35}{50} + \frac{LIT}{100} + \frac{LPCY}{3.687}\right]$$

where $\bar{L}$ is the average life expectancy attained in the country, LIT is the average percentage literacy rate among adults, and LPCY is the logarithm of per capita GDP (in "purchasing power parity" dollars) truncated at the average official poverty line income in nine developed countries, with 3.687 being the-then value of the logarithm of the poverty level (Anand and Sen 1993).

For the gender-equity-sensitive **HDI**, we simply replace the arithmetic average attainments in each component by the equally distributed equivalent achievements. Thus the first component $(\bar{L} - 35)/50$ is replaced by $(L_{ede} - 35)/50$. The second component LIT/100 is replaced by $X_{ede}/100$, where X_{ede} is now the $(1-\epsilon)$-average of the female and male literacy rates. No <u>corresponding</u> correction can be made for the third component of **HDI**, because gender-specific attributions of income per head cannot be readily linked to the aggregate GDP per capita used in these calculations, and inequalities within the household are difficult to characterize and assess (Sen 1992a; Anand and Sen 1993).

It is important to distinguish between two different aspects of incomes, viz. <u>earning</u> and <u>use</u>. If we wish to concentrate on the <u>use</u> aspect, the within-family division of income use between women and men would have to be identified to assess income use by gender. But the empirical and conceptual problems in getting at these divisions within the family are formidable indeed.

In contrast, the earning aspect looks at women and men not as income users, but as people who <u>earn</u> incomes. The total gross national product can then be seen in terms of aggregate earnings of all women and all men, making up something like the total national income. An <u>approximate</u> idea of the income earnings of women and men can be obtained by looking at their respective employment ratios and their relative wages.

What significance can be attached to such income earning estimates? Indeed, there is some tension in concentrating on the earning aspect when the entire approach of the <u>Human Development Report</u> has been based on identifying what people get <u>out</u> of the means they can use, rather than on the means they <u>earn</u> — possibly to be used by their families. On the other hand, the earning contrasts between men and women do point to an important asymmetry between them in most — nearly all — existing societies. While women very often work as hard as — or harder than — men, much of their work is of the unpaid kind that does not yield remuneration.[14] There is also considerable evidence to indicate that earning explicitly recognized "incomes", and working in sectors that are treated as evidence of being "economically active", can significantly and favourably influence the "deal" that women tend to get in the division of benefits and chores within the family.[15]

There is, thus, a case for doing some gender division even for the "real income" component of **HDI**, trying to note the differences between the earnings of women and men. It would be hard to get anything like the degree of precision with earnings "allocated" between women and men on the basis of rough calculations that gender-specific measures of literacy or life expectancy can offer. But even some estimates of relative earnings of women and men would give the gender equity-sensitive indicator (**GESI**) another component with some bite. If this were to be done, then the total GDP per head can be notionally "split" between women and men in the ratio of the respective <u>products</u> of <u>employment rates</u> and <u>wage rates per unit of employment</u>. It would, however, be

necessary then to explain clearly that (1) this procedure looks at income from the "earning" perspective rather than the "use" perspective (even though gender inequalities seem to link the latter to the former), and (2) the evaluations of earnings of women and men are fairly "soft" estimates, to be interpreted with much caution.

Extent of Inequality Aversion ϵ

As was discussed earlier, the values of the parameter ϵ can be taken to range from zero to infinity, reflecting the extent of social preference for equality. In fact, ϵ as a parameter stands for the elasticity of the marginal social valuation of the respective achievement, and tells us how quickly the marginal value falls as the achievement level rises (that is, how strongly diminishing the marginal social returns are). ϵ can, in fact, be seen as a reflection of the extent of inequality aversion. When ϵ is taken to be zero, there is no decline in marginal values, so that the simple arithmetic mean does well enough. At the other extreme, when ϵ is taken to be infinity, the sensitivity is so great that we end up picking only the lower of the two numbers in a pair, ignoring the achievement of the better-off. It would be interesting to calculate the gender-equity-sensitive (**GESI**) adaptation of **HDI** for several parametric values of ϵ, such as 0, 1, 2, 3, 5, 10, ∞. We call this class of "corrected" **HDI** the gender-related development index, or **GDI** for short. Typically we will use the value $\epsilon = 2$.

The implications of different choices of ϵ can be gauged by examining the effects on X_{ede}, the equally distributed equivalent achievement. We can compare the relative increase in X_{ede} through a unit increase in female achievement X_f compared to a unit increase in male achievement X_m. From equation (2) in Appendix A.1, we have

$$\frac{\partial X_{ede} / \partial X_f}{\partial X_{ede} / \partial X_m} = \frac{p_f \ V'(X_f) / V'(X_{ede})}{p_m V'(X_m) / V'(X_{ede})}$$

$$= \frac{V'(X_f)}{V'(X_m)} \quad assuming \quad p_f = p_m = 1/2$$

---

[14]   See, for example, Goldschmidt-Clermont (1982, 1993), Folbre (1991), Folbre and Wagman (1993), Urdaneta-Ferrán (1993), and the references cited there. Many of the diverse underlying issues are discussed in Chen (1983), Bergmann (1986), Jayawardena (1986), Brannen and Wilson (1987), Sen and Grown (1987), Okin (1989), Goldin (1990), England (1992), Ferber and Nelson (1993), Folbre (1994), Agarwal (1995), and Nussbaum and Glover (1995).

[15]   For references to the literature on this, and an analysis of why this relationship is observed in situations of "cooperative conflict" (as family-living typically is), see Sen (1990). See also Anand (1979), Manser and Brown (1980), McElroy and Horney (1981), Lundberg and Pollak (1994), and the references cited there.

$$= X_f^{-e} / X_m^{-e} = (X_m / X_f)^e$$

if the social valuation function V(X) has a constant elasticity of marginal valuation ϵ.

According to this, if male achievement X_m is <u>twice</u> female achievement X_f, i.e. $(X_m/X_f) = 2$, and if $\epsilon = 1$ (i.e. we have the logarithmic form for V(X)), then a unit increase in female achievement will contribute <u>twice</u> as much to X_{ede} as a unit increase in male achievement (see Table 1). If (X_m/X_f) remains equal to 2, but $\epsilon = 2$, then a unit increase in female achievement contributes <u>four</u> times as much as a unit increase in male achievement. Holding (X_m/X_f) constant (at any value above 1), as ϵ is increased there is an <u>increase</u> in the relative contribution to X_{ede} from a unit increase in X_f compared to a unit increase in X_m.[16] Table 1 estimates the relative contribution to X_{ede} of a unit increase in female achievement compared to a unit increase in male achievement for different values of ϵ and different ratios of male-to-female achievement (X_m/X_f).

For particular values of ϵ, how different would **GDI** be from **HDI** (bearing in mind that **HDI** is, in fact, a special case of **GDI**, with $\epsilon = 0$)? Clearly, the distributional correction would tend to pull down the value of **HDI**, and we expect **GDI** to be quite significantly below the corresponding **HDI** values in a systematic way, for relatively high values of ϵ.

This does not, however, imply that the <u>rankings</u> would be necessarily much changed. That would depend on the <u>relative differences</u> in the extent of gender inequality. While there are often substantial differences between the gender inequality levels of the relevant parameters between high-achieving and low-achieving countries, the patterns of gender inequalities may often be quite close to each other for countries at similar

---

[16]   By partial differentiation with respect to ϵ, it is straightforward to show that

$$\frac{\partial}{\partial \epsilon} \left[\frac{\partial X_{ede} / \partial X_f}{\partial X_{ede} / \partial X_m} \right] > 0 \quad for \ (X_m / X_f) > 1,$$

and

$$\frac{\partial^2}{\partial \epsilon^2} \left[\frac{\partial X_{ede} / \partial X_f}{\partial X_{ede} / \partial X_m} \right] > 0 .$$

---

levels of human development. This would tend to make the rankings of **GDI** rather similar to those of **HDI**. However, some differences can be expected between low-achieving countries in Asia and low-achievers in Sub-Saharan Africa, since the extent of gender inequality in many fields has tended to be substantially less in the latter countries.[17]

Gender-Equality Measures and GESI

The Appendix A.3 ("Properties of the Relative Gender-Equality Index E") draws attention to the fact that the relative level of gender equality can be well captured by comparing the values of **GESI** with the uncorrected average measure. That average (gender-blind) measure is based on taking an <u>arithmetic</u> average (as with **HDI**) over the entire population, whereas the formula for **GESI** permits an entire class of "$(1-\epsilon)$-averaging" to take note of — and to weigh against — inequalities. In the special case in which ϵ is taken to be 2, the **GESI** formula corresponds to the <u>harmonic</u> mean. The equally distributed equivalent achievement corresponding to $\epsilon = 2$, i.e. $X_{ede}(2)$, is then given (for equal proportions of women and men) by the formula

$$X_{ede}(2)^{-1} = \frac{1}{2} X_f^{-1} + \frac{1}{2} X_m^{-1}.$$

Hence,

$$X_{ede}(2) = 2 [(1/X_f) + (1/X_m)]^{-1}$$

which is the harmonic mean of X_f and X_m. If we take the ratio of the harmonic mean to the arithmetic mean, we then get a measure of "gender equity" that has obvious interest.

For reasons discussed in the last section, the values of **GDI** and **HDI** may not diverge in a way that makes the respective rankings very different. When the values of **GDI** and **HDI** are shifted in similar ways — without much of a relative change — the ratios may not tell us very much either. It must, however, be remembered that the **GESI** formula can be applied to other variables as well, specifically chosen to highlight <u>differences</u> in gender disparities. We must, in general,

---

[17]   On this see Kynch (1985) and Sen (1988), and the references cited there.

Table 1

Relative Contributions to X_{ede} of Unit Increases in X_f and X_m, i.e. $\left[\dfrac{\partial X_{ede} / \partial X_f}{\partial X_{ede} / \partial X_m} \right]$,

for Alternative Values of ϵ and (X_m/X_f)

(X_m/X_f) \ ϵ	0.0	1.0	1.5	2.0	2.5	3.0	5.0	10.0	∞
1.0	1	1	1	1	1	1	1	1	1
1.5	1	1.5	1.8	2.3	2.8	3.4	7.6	57.7	∞
2.0	1	2.0	2.8	4.0	5.7	8.0	32.0	1,024.0	∞
2.5	1	2.5	4.0	6.3	9.9	15.6	97.7	9,536.7	∞
3.0	1	3.0	5.2	9.0	15.6	27.0	243.0	59,049.0	∞
4.0	1	4.0	8.0	16.0	32.0	64.0	1,024.0	1,048,576.0	∞

Note: The relative contributions to X_{ede} in this table are estimated under the assumptions that $p_f = p_m = 1/2$, and that $V(X)$ has a constant elasticity of marginal valuation ϵ.

distinguish between (1) the **GESI** formula of (1-ϵ)-averaging, and (2) the "space" on which it is applied (that is, the variables for which achievements and gender disparities are scrutinized).

It should be noted here that the procedure used for inequality correction in **GDI** involves the estimation of inequality-corrected achievements in terms of different focus variables, and then putting them together in one aggregate measure of inequality-adjusted performance. In some respects, this procedure is a little deceptive, since the different variables might, in principle, work in somewhat opposite directions, moderating the influence of each other in the inequality between individuals. For example, if person A has a higher achievement in longevity while person B does better in terms of education, it could be thought that these inequalities must, to some extent, counteract each other, so that in terms of a weighted average of achievements, A and B may be less unequal than in terms of each of the two variables. And this opposite-direction case would be different from the one in which one of the individuals, say A, is better off in terms of both the variables. In terms of the procedure used here, we cannot discriminate between these two types of cases, since the aggregation is done, first, in terms of specific variables, and then they are put together in an index of overall achievement.

This defect is, however, fairly inescapable at the individual level, given the data availability. There is no obvious way of relating the individual identities in the distribution of one variable with those for the other variable. There is, thus, no serious alternative to the kind of procedure we have used. As a matter of fact, this is not, however, a very serious limitation in the present context. This is partly because the individual deprivations very often go together and reinforce — rather than counteract — each other. For example, the educationally deprived person is often also the one with the lower longevity, as we know from statistical studies of development characteristics.

More importantly, it should be borne in mind that the exercise of gender-equity adjustment is being made here at a high level of aggregation, dealing with the mean positions of women and men. At this aggregated level, the inequalities almost always go together, with women being in a more deprived position, on the average, than men. The exceptions come from a handful of countries — such as the Scandinavian ones — where in terms of one variable, viz. life expectancy, women seem to have actually gone significantly ahead of men in terms of the standard correction for expected longevity (with five extra years expected in female longevity). In such cases, the disparity in life expectancy may go in the opposite direction to the disparity in education or income earning. If

note were to be taken of this connection, these countries would be placed higher in terms of overall achievement, since the inequality adjustments would have, to some extent, counteracted each other. But since these countries are, in any case, towards or at the top of the international "league tables", the effect of this correction would be only to reinforce that positional lead.

On Spaces and Formulas

This paper has been primarily concerned with proposing, explaining, and defending a particular approach to constructing gender-equity-sensitive measures of human development. It has not been directly concerned with the choice of variables, even though the argument has been developed in terms of the "classic" components of human development indicators, beginning with Human Development Report 1990.

The choices of variables — in particular, life expectancy and literacy — were primarily governed by the ability to discriminate among the relatively less affluent countries. For the high-achieving developed countries, there is relatively little sensitivity in the use of these variables, at least as far as the rankings are concerned. It is for this reason that we had earlier suggested (in Anand and Sen 1993) that different variables may be used in a supplementary way to discriminate between middle- and high-achieving countries, respectively. We stick to the logic behind that position, since the variables needed to discriminate between the advanced countries tend to dilute the importance of some of the basic features of human development that the "classic" variables capture, thereby turning a partially blind eye to the relative failures and successes of poorer countries in bringing about achievements in basic fields (such as literacy and life expectancy). However, it is not the purpose of this paper to insist that we must use only the classic **HDI** variables, or the pyramid structure proposed in Anand and Sen (1993). That is ultimately a question to be determined at the UNDP. But we would like to emphasize that even if we depart from the variables with which this note has been specifically concerned, there will be scope for using the methodology developed here. For example, replacing literacy by "total gross enrollment ratio" would not require any basic change in the methodological approach developed here. We have reasons to question the quality of these data and their perspicuity in "telling" between poorer countries in terms of what has been called "first things first" (on which see Streeten et al. 1981), but the methodology has enough catholicity to deal with that option if it were chosen. The ball should now be at the UNDP's court.

APPENDICES

Properties of the Gender-Equity-Sensitive Indicator X_{ede}

In this section we derive some properties of the gender-equity-sensitive indicator, X_{ede}. In particular, we examine X_{ede} as a function of the female and male achievements, X_f and X_m, respectively. To our knowledge, these properties of X_{ede} have not previously been derived in the literature on the measurement of inequality.

We begin with the general definition of X_{ede} with respect to a concave increasing social valuation function $V(X)$. We leave the functional form of $V(X)$ unspecified and require only that $V'(X) > 0$ and $V''(X) \leq 0$. Then X_{ede} is defined through the equation

$$(n_f + n_m)V(X_{ede}) = n_f V(X_f) + n_m V(X_m).$$

Henceforth, we denote p_f and p_m as the proportions of females and males in the total population, which is of size $(n_f + n_m)$. By definition,

$$p_f = n_f / (n_f + n_m) \quad \text{and} \quad p_m = n_m / (n_f + n_m).$$

It follows that $(p_f + p_m) = 1$, and

$$V(X_{ede}) = p_f V(X_f) + p_m V(X_m). \qquad (1)$$

Hence

$$X_{ede} = V^{-1}(p_f V(X_f) + p_m V(X_m))$$

subgroups, p_f and p_m. A rise in the population proportion of the subgroup with a higher level of with $V^{-1}(.)$ a convex increasing function. As X_{ede} is a monotonic increasing

function of a concave function, it will be at least quasi-concave in (X_f, X_m). But will it be concave? The answer to this question is of central interest in understanding the gender-equity-sensitive indicator (**GESI**).

The first property of X_{ede} that we wish to derive is simply that X_{ede} is monotonic increasing in both X_f and X_m. This follows directly from partial differentiation with respect to X_i of equation (1) above, for $i = f, m$:

$$V'(X_{ede}) \cdot \partial X_{ede}/\partial X_i = p_i V'(X_i).$$

Hence

$$\partial X_{ede}/\partial X_i = p_i V'(X_i)/V'(X_{ede}) \qquad (2)$$
$$> 0 \text{ for } i = f, m$$

because $V'(X) > 0$. Thus X_{ede} is monotonic increasing in both female and male achievements.[18]

Furthermore, if female achievement X_f is less than male achievement X_m, and the female population proportion p_f is greater than or equal to the male population proportion p_m, then a unit increase in female achievement will be more valuable socially than a unit increase in male achievement. This follows easily using equation (2). By assumption, $X_f < X_m$ and $V''(X) \leq 0$; hence $V'(X_f) \geq V'(X_m)$. Since also $p_f \geq p_m$, we have

$$\partial X_{ede}/\partial X_f = p_f V'(X_f)/V'(X_{ede})$$
$$\geq p_m V'(X_m)/V'(X_{ede})$$
$$\text{because } V'(X_f) \geq V'(X_m)$$
$$= \partial X_{ede}/\partial X_m.$$

Note finally the property of X_{ede} relating to changes in the population proportions of the two achievement will result in a higher value of X_{ede}. Thus if $X_m > X_f$, and since $p_f = 1 - p_m$, we have from equation (1) by partial differentiation with respect to p_m

$$\partial X_{ede}/\partial p_m = [V(X_m) - V(X_f)]/V'(X_{ede})$$
$$> 0 \text{ because } V'(X) > 0.$$

The results obtained hitherto are valid for any concave increasing social valuation function $V(X)$. But how precisely does X_{ede} depend on the "degree of concavity" of $V(X)$? We know that if $V(X)$ is linear then we have

---

[18]   Note that this property does not necessarily obtain with arbitrarily specified measures of gender equity, such as $(X_f/X_m)(p_f X_f + p_m X_m)$. The latter measure is equal to $[(p_f X_f^2/X_m) + p_m X_f]$, which is a strictly decreasing function of X_m.

$$X_{ede} = p_f X_f + p_m X_m = \overline{X}$$

where $\overline{X}$ is the simple arithmetic average of the individual achievements X_f and X_m. If $V(X)$ is <u>strictly</u> concave, then we will have

$$X_{ede} < \overline{X}.$$

This is because, by definition of X_{ede},

$$V(X_{ede}) = p_f V(X_f) + p_m V(X_m)$$

$$< V(p_f X_f + p_m X_m) \ \text{since } V(X) \text{ is strictly concave}$$

$$= V(\overline{X}).$$

Hence

$$X_{ede} < \overline{X}$$

because $V(X)$ is monotonic increasing in X. The analysis suggests that a "more concave" valuation function than $V(X)$ will imply a still lower value of X_{ede}. We define one monotonic increasing function to be <u>more concave</u> than another if the former can be expressed as a concave monotonic increasing transform of the latter.

It is indeed the case that a more concave valuation function will yield a <u>lower</u> value of X_{ede}. Thus, if an increasing concave transform $\phi(.)$ is applied to the concave function $V(X)$, then the equally distributed equivalent achievement corresponding to $\phi(V(X))$ will be <u>smaller</u> than that corresponding to $V(X)$. This is demonstrated by applying the function $\phi(.)$ to $(p_f V(X_f) + p_m V(X_m))$, and using concavity of $\phi(.)$ to prove the result.

Let X_{ede}^v and X_{ede}^ϕ be the equally distributed equivalent achievements corresponding to the functions $V(X)$ and $\phi(V(X))$, respectively. Then

$$(X_{ede}^v) = p_f V(X_f) + p_m V(X_m) \ \text{ by definition of } X_{ede}^v$$

Applying $\phi(.)$ to both sides of this equation gives

$$\phi(V(X_{ede}^v)) = \phi(p_f V(X_f) + p_m V(X_m))$$

$$\geq p_f \phi(V(X_f)) + p_m \phi(V(X_m))$$

because $\phi(.)$ is concave

$$= \phi(V(X_{ede}^\phi)) \ \text{ by definition of } X_{ede}^\phi$$

Hence,

$$X_{ede}^\phi \leq X_{ede}^v$$

because $\phi(V(X))$ is monotonic increasing in X.

This inference is analogous to the Arrow (1965)-Pratt (1964) result in the theory of uncertainty that a more risk-averse individual has a lower certainty equivalent income for any given risk.[19] It was also established as an inequality concerning convex functions in Hardy, Littlewood and Pólya (1952: 75-6).

The general proposition proven above on "more concave" functions can be applied to demonstrate result (2) in the text. This relates to <u>isoelastic</u> social valuation functions and states that the larger is the elasticity ϵ of the marginal valuation function $V'(X)$, the smaller will be X_{ede}. We let

$$V(X) = \frac{1}{1-\epsilon} X^{1-\epsilon}$$

and prove the result for $\epsilon \geq 0$, $\epsilon \neq 1$. Thus consider the function

$$W(X) = \frac{1}{1-\nu} X^{1-\nu} \ \text{ where } \ \nu > \epsilon.$$

To apply the general proposition we must be able to write so

$$W = \phi(V), \ \text{ where } \phi'(V) > 0 \ \text{ and } \ \phi''(V) < 0$$

that $\phi(.)$ is an increasin g concave function. We have

---

[19]   It is equivalent to saying that a more risk-averse individual is willing to pay more to eliminate any given risk — one of several characterizations of "greater risk aversion". See, inter alia, Arrow (1965), Pratt (1964), Rothschild and Stiglitz (1970), Diamond and Rothschild (1989).

$$X = [(1-\epsilon)V]^{1/(1-\epsilon)}$$

and hence

$$W = \frac{1}{1-\nu}X^{1-\nu} = \frac{1}{1-\nu}[(1-\epsilon)V]^{(1-\nu)/(1-\epsilon)}$$

$$= \phi(V),$$

say, which provides a definition of the required function $\phi(V)$. It turns out that $\phi(V)$ is indeed an increasing concave function of V provided that $\nu > \epsilon$. To show this, differentiate $\phi(V)$ with respect to V twice:

$$\phi'(V) = [(1-\epsilon)V]^{(\epsilon-\nu)/(1-\epsilon)} > 0,$$

and

$$\phi''(V) = (\epsilon-\nu)[(1-\epsilon)V]^{(2\epsilon-\nu-1)/(1-\epsilon)}$$

$$< 0 \quad \text{since} \quad \nu > \epsilon.$$

Note that whether $\epsilon < 1$ or $\epsilon > 1$, the quantity $(1-\epsilon)V$ is always _positive_ (and equal to $X^{1-\epsilon}$): when $0 \leq \epsilon < 1$ both $(1-\epsilon)$ and V are positive, and when $\epsilon > 1$ both $(1-\epsilon)$ and V are negative. Our definition of V(X) as $X^{1-\epsilon}$ divided by $(1-\epsilon)$ thus circumvents the need to prove separately results forpositiveand negative powers of X,i.e. separately for the cases $0 \leq \epsilon < 1$ and $\epsilon > 1$.[20]

---

[20]   For the case $V(X) = \log X$, which corresponds to an elasticity of marginal valuation $\epsilon = 1$, we have $X = e^V$. Now consider a more concave function, i.e. one with elasticity of marginal valuation $\nu > 1$. Then

$$W(X) = \frac{1}{1-\nu}X^{1-\nu} \quad \text{with} \quad \nu > 1$$

$$= \frac{1}{1-\nu}(e^V)^{1-\nu}$$

$$= \frac{1}{1-\nu}e^{(1-\nu)V}.$$

This is an increasing concave function for all values (positive and negative) of V, because $(1-\nu) < 0$. Hence we can apply the general proposition on "more concave" functions.

On the Concavity of X_{ede} with respect to (X_f, X_m)

Earlier we showed that X_{ede} was a monotonic increasing function of its arguments (X_f, X_m), demonstrated in equation (2). This is clearly a desirable property for a measure of social achievement, even once it has been adjusted for equity. Moreover, we saw that if $X_f < X_m$ (and $p_f \geq p_m$), then a unit increase in X_f adds _more_ to X_{ede} than a unit increase in X_m. But will there be "diminishing returns" to unit increases in X_f, and for that matter to unit increases in X_m? This might seem like an appealing property for the measure of social achievement X_{ede} to possess.

To address this question, we have to differentiate equation (2) partially with respect to X_i. This gives

$$V''(X_{ede}) \cdot (\partial X_{ede}/\partial X_i)^2 + V'(X_{ede}) \cdot (\partial^2 X_{ede}/\partial X_i^2) = p_i V''(X_i).$$

Hence,

$$V'(X_{ede}) \cdot (\partial^2 X_{ede}/\partial X_i^2) = p_i V''(X_i) - V''(X_{ede}) \cdot (\partial X_{ede}/\partial X_i)^2$$

$$= p_i V''(X_i) - V''(X_{ede}) \cdot [p_i V'(X_i)/V'(X_{ede})]^2$$

In general, therefore, the behaviour of $(\partial^2 X_{ede}/\partial X_i^2)$ will depend on both the first and second derivatives of the function V(X) at X_i and at X_{ede}.

Let us now consider two special cases of the function V(X): the constant elasticity marginal valuation (or constant _relative_ inequality aversion) form; and the constant _absolute_ inequality aversion form.[21] For the case

we have $V'(X) = X^{-\epsilon}$ and $V''(X) = -\epsilon X^{-\epsilon-1}$. Substituting into equation (3) above, we get

$$V(X) = \frac{1}{1-\epsilon}X^{1-\epsilon}$$

---

[21]   These two forms, named as such by Atkinson (1970) in the inequality literature, correspond in the risk literature to constant relative risk aversion and to constant absolute risk aversion, respectively (Arrow 1965, Pratt 1964).

we have $V'(X) = X^{-\epsilon}$ and $V''(X) = -\epsilon X^{-\epsilon-1}$. Substituting into equation (3) above, we get

$$X_{ede}^{-\epsilon}(\partial^2 X_{ede}/\partial X_i^2) = p_i(-\epsilon X_i^{-\epsilon-1}) - (-\epsilon X_{ede}^{-\epsilon-1}) \cdot [p_i X_i^{-\epsilon}/X_{ede}^{-\epsilon}]^2$$

$$= p_i^2 \epsilon X_{ede}^{\epsilon-1} \cdot X_i^{-2\epsilon} - p_i \epsilon X_i^{-\epsilon-1}$$

$$= p_i \epsilon X_{ede}^{\epsilon-1} \cdot X_i^{-\epsilon-1}(p_i X_i^{1-\epsilon} - X_{ede}^{1-\epsilon}). \quad (4)$$

But we know that for this functional form for V(X), X_{ede} satisfies

$$X_{ede}^{1-\epsilon} = p_f X_f^{1-\epsilon} + p_m X_m^{1-\epsilon}.$$

Hence the expression

$$(p_i X_i^{1-\epsilon} - X_{ede}^{1-\epsilon})$$

is equal either to

$$(-p_m X_m^{1-\epsilon})$$

or to

$$(-p_f X_f^{1-\epsilon})$$

depending on whether i = f or i = m. In any event, the expression

$$(p_i X_i^{1-\epsilon} - X_{ede}^{1-\epsilon})$$

in equation (4) will be negative[22], and therefore

$$(\partial^2 X_{ede}/\partial X_i^2) < 0 \quad for \ i = f, m.$$

For the isoelastic form for V(X), we have shown that X_{ede} does indeed increase at a <u>diminishing rate</u> in each of its arguments X_f and X_m.

---

[22]　　When there are more than two arguments, we will have

$$(p_i X_i^{1-\epsilon} - X_{ede}^{1-\epsilon}) = -\sum_{j\neq i} p_j X_j^{1-\epsilon} < 0.$$

The second special case we consider for the function V(X) is the constant absolute inequality aversion form:

$$V(X) = -e^{-\gamma X}$$

up to a positive affine transformation. Here γ is the (positive) parameter of absolute inequality aversion, which is defined in general as -V''(X)/V'(X). In this case,

$$V'(X) = \gamma e^{-\gamma X} > 0,$$

and

$$V''(X) = -\gamma^2 e^{-\gamma X} < 0.$$

Substituting into equation (3), we get

$$V'(X_{ede}) \cdot (\partial^2 X_{ede}/\partial X_i^2)$$
$$= p_i(-\gamma^2 e^{-\gamma X_i}) - (-\gamma^2 e^{-\gamma X_{ede}}) \cdot [p_i e^{-\gamma X_i}/e^{-\gamma X_{ede}}]^2$$

$$= p_i^2 \gamma^2 e^{\gamma X_{ede}} \cdot e^{-2\gamma X_i} - p_i \gamma^2 e^{-\gamma X_i}$$

$$= p_i \gamma^2 e^{\gamma(X_{ede} - X_i)} \cdot [p_i e^{-\gamma X_i} - e^{-\gamma X_{ede}}]. \quad (5)$$

But we know that for this functional form for V(X), X_{ede} satisfies

$$e^{-\gamma X_{ede}} = p_f e^{-\gamma X_f} + p_m e^{-\gamma X_m}.$$

Hence the expression

$$[p_i e^{-\gamma X_i} - e^{-\gamma X_{ede}}]$$

is equal either to

$$(-p_m e^{-\gamma X_m})$$

or to

$$(-p_f e^{-\gamma X_f})$$

depending on whether i = f or i = m. In any event, the expression

$$[p_i e^{-\gamma X_i} - e^{-\gamma X_{ede}}]$$

in equation (5) will be negative[23], and therefore

$$(\partial^2 X_{ede} / \partial X_i^2) < 0 \quad for \; i = f, m.$$

Thus in both the main cases of constant relative and of constant absolute inequality aversion, we have the result that X_{ede} increases at a diminishing rate with respect to the individual achievement X_i, for all i. But will this result be true of <u>any</u> concave function $V(X)$? An examination of equation (3) shows that $(\partial^2 X_{ede}/\partial X_i^2)$ can fail to be negative if $V''(X_i)$ is close to zero and $V''(X_{ede})$ and $(\partial X_{ede}/\partial X_i)$ are large in absolute terms.[24]

To construct a counterexample, we choose $V''(X) = 0$ in the neighbourhood of variation of X_i, and $V''(X) < 0$ in the range around X_{ede}, while noting that X_{ede} depends both on X_f and on X_m. Let $X_f < X_m$, and let us here evaluate $(\partial^2 X_{ede} / \partial X_m^2)$. Take $X_f = 0$ and let X_m lie on a linear segment of the function $V(X)$. Thus consider the function

$$V(X) = \begin{cases} X^{1/2} & for \; 0 \le X \le 1 \\ \dfrac{X}{2} + \dfrac{1}{2} & for \; X \ge 1. \end{cases}$$

Then $V'(X) = 1/2$ for $X \ge 1$.

Now we choose $X_m \ge 1$, but not so large that X_{ede} will also lie on the linear segment containing X_m. For simplicity, assume that $p_f = p_m = \dfrac{1}{2}$. Then

$$2V(X_{ede}) = V(0) + V(X_m) \quad by \; definition \; of \; X_{ede}$$
$$= 0 + (X_m + 1)/2$$

so that

$$V(X_{ede}) = (X_m + 1)/4.$$

For $V(X_{ede}) < 1$, i.e. for $X_m < 3$, we have

$$V(X_{ede}) = X_{ede}^{1/2}.$$

Therefore,

$$X_{ede}^{1/2} = (X_m + 1)/4 \quad for \; 1 \le X_m < 3$$

and

$$X_{ede} = (X_m + 1)^2/16$$

which is strictly <u>convex</u> in X_m. Hence

$$\partial^2 X_{ede} / \partial X_m^2 = 1/8 > 0$$

for the parameters and ranges of the variables we have chosen.

It is easy to see that the result will still hold if a small curvature were added to the function $V(X)$ along its linear segment, so that $V''(X) < 0$ throughout. If the function were made slightly strictly concave in this range, we would still get

$$(\partial^2 X_{ede} / \partial X_m^2) > 0.$$

---

[23]   When there are more than two arguments X_f and X_m, we will have

$$[p_i \, e^{-\gamma X_i} - e^{-\gamma X_{ede}}] = -\sum_{j \ne i} p_j \, e^{-\gamma X_j} < 0.$$

[24] $(\partial X_{ede} / \partial X_i)$ is always less than unity for the case of constant absolute inequality aversion. Here

$$(\partial X_{ede} / \partial X_i) = p_i \, e^{-\gamma X_i}/e^{-\gamma X_{ede}}$$

$$= p_i \, e^{-\gamma X_i}/(\sum_j p_j \, e^{-\gamma X_j})$$

$$< 1.$$

But for the case of constant relative inequality aversion, we can make $(\partial X_{ede} / \partial X_i)$ as large as we like. For example, let $(X_m / X_f) = \lambda$, $p_m = p_f = 1/2$, and $\epsilon = 1/2$. Then

$$\partial X_{ede} / \partial X_f = \frac{1}{2} [\frac{1}{2} (1 + \lambda^{1-\epsilon})]^{\epsilon/(1-\epsilon)}$$

$$= \frac{1}{4} (1 + \lambda^{1/2}) \quad for \; \epsilon = 1/2$$

$$\to \infty \quad as \; \lambda \to \infty.$$

Moreover, using smoother splines, we could make higher-order derivatives of the function continuous at X = 1. (In our example, the second derivative of the function V(X) is not continuous at X = 1; it is equal to (-1/4) just to the left of X = 1, and to 0 just to the right of X = 1.)

The basic intuition behind the counterexample is that if social value from increasing an individual achievement goes up (essentially) linearly, then to bring about equal unit increases in V(X) we will have to raise X_{ede} at an <u>increasing</u> rate if X_{ede} lies on a diminishing marginal returns segment of the function.

Properties of the Relative Gender-Equality Index E

In this subsection we examine the properties of the relative gender-equality index E, defined as $X_{ede}/\overline{X}$, for the isoelastic social valuation function V(X). We have

$$X_{ede} = [p_f X_f^{1-e} + p_m X_m^{1-e}]^{1/(1-e)}$$

and

$$\overline{X} = [p_f X_f + p_m X_m].$$

Hence

$$E = X_{ede}/\overline{X}$$

$$= [p_f X_f^{1-e} + p_m X_m^{1-e}]^{1/(1-e)}/[p_f X_f + p_m X_m]$$

$$= p_f^{e/(1-e)}[(p_m/p_f) + (X_f/X_m)^{1-e}]^{1/(1-e)}/[(p_m/p_f) + (X_f/X_m)]$$

From now on we assume that $p_f = p_m = \frac{1}{2}$, and we define z = (X_f/X_m) as the <u>ratio</u> of female to male achievement. Then

$$E(z) = (1/2)^{e/(1-e)}[1 + z^{1-e}]^{1/(1-e)}/[1 + z].$$

It is not difficult to check that, for any $\epsilon > 0$, the index of relative equality E is maximized at z = 1, and its maximum value is E = 1. In general, we have $0 \leq E(z) \leq 1$ for $z \geq 0$.

By differentiating E(z) with respect to z, and simplifying, we obtain

$$E'(z) = (1/2)^{e/(1-e)}(1 + z^{1-e})^{e/(1-e)}(z^{-e} - 1)/(1 + z)^2.$$

Given $\epsilon > 0$, it follows that E'(z) > 0 for z < 1, E'(z) = 0 for z = 1, and E'(z) < 0 for z > 1. By further differentiation with respect to z we can show that E"(1) < 0, i.e. z = 1 maximizes E(z).

Manipulating the second derivative of E(z), it can be seen that E"(z) = 0 when

$$-e(1 + z)^2 = 2z(1 - z^e)(1 + z^{1-e}).$$

Inspecting the left- and right-hand sides of this equation, it is evident that its solution must occur at a value of z > 1.[25] To the left of this point of inflection in E(z) the second derivative E"(z) will be negative, and to the right of this point the second derivative E"(z) will be positive. The shape of E(z) for different values of ϵ is shown in the figure below.

For $\epsilon = 0$, there is no concern for equality and E = 1 for all values of z.

For $0 < \epsilon < 1$, we have E → $(1/2)^{\epsilon/(1-\epsilon)}$ both as z → 0 and as z → ∞.

For $\epsilon = 1$, we have X_{ede} as the geometric mean of X_f and X_m, and

$$E = 2z^{1/2}/[1 + z] = 2/[z^{-1/2} + z^{1/2}]$$

$$→ 0 \text{ as } z → 0 \text{ and as } z → ∞.$$

For $\epsilon > 1$, we can again check from equation (6) that E → 0 both as z → 0 and as z → ∞.

For $\epsilon = 2$, in particular, we have X_{ede} as the harmonic mean of X_f and X_m, and

$$E = 4/[1 + z][1 + (1/z)]$$
$$→ 0 \text{ as } z → 0 \text{ and as } z → ∞.$$

---

[25]   For certain parameter values of ϵ, this equation can be solved immediately. Thus the solution is z = 2 for ϵ = 2, and z = 2.1547 for both ϵ = 1/2 and ϵ = 1. (For these parameter values, the equation is a quadratic.)

Irrespective of ϵ, the value of E(z) will obviously be the same as $z \to 0$ and as $z \to \infty$; the index of relative equality E is clearly _symmetric_ (given $p_f = p_m = \frac{1}{2}$) in z and (1/z). From equation (6) it is easy to verify that $E(z) = E(1/z)$ for all $z \geq 0$. For any $\epsilon \geq 0$, E as a function of z must therefore always satisfy the following properties:

(1) $E(z) = E(1/z) \geq 0$ for all $z \geq 0$.
(2)   E(z) is maximized at $z = 1$, and $E(1) = 1$.

Thus within this framework we cannot impose arbitrary functional forms for E(z) for $z \geq 0$, such as $E(z) = z$ or $E(z) = 1 - |1 - z|$, which violate properties (1) and (2).

REFERENCES

Agarwal, Bina (1995): <u>A Field of One's Own: Gender and Land Rights in South Asia</u>. Cambridge: Cambridge University Press.

Anand, Sudhir (1977): "Aspects of Poverty in Malaysia", <u>Review of Income and Wealth</u>, Series 23, No. 1, March, 1-16.

_____ (1979): "Models of the Farm Household in Less Developed Countries", mimeographed, St. Catherine's College, Oxford, July.

_____ (1983): <u>Inequality and Poverty in Malaysia: Measurement and Decomposition</u>. New York: Oxford University Press.

_____ (1993): "Inequality Between and Within Nations", mimeographed, Center for Population and Development Studies, Harvard University, Cambridge, MA.

_____ and Amartya K. Sen (1993): "Human Development Index: Methodology and Measurement", Human Development Report Office Occasional Paper 12. New York: United Nations Development Programme.

Arrow, Kenneth J. (1965): <u>Aspects of the Theory of Risk-Bearing</u>, Yrjö Jahnsson Lectures. Helsinki: Yrjö Jahnssonin Säätiö.

Atkinson, Anthony B. (1970): "On the Measurement of Inequality", <u>Journal of Economic Theory</u>, Vol. 2, No. 3, September, 244-263.

_____ (1973): "How Progressive Should Income-Tax Be?" in (ed.) M. Parkin, <u>Essays on Modern Economics</u>, Longman. Reprinted in (ed.) E.S. Phelps, <u>Economic Justice</u>, Penguin Education, Harmondsworth, Middlesex, 386-408.

Bergmann, Barbara (1986): <u>The Economic Emergence of Women</u>. New York: Basic Books.

Blackorby, C. and D. Donaldson (1978): "Measures of Relative Equality and their Meaning in Terms of Social Welfare", <u>Journal of Economic Theory</u>, Vol. 18.

_____ (1984): "Ethically Significant Ordinal Indexes of Relative Inequality", <u>Advances in Econometrics</u>, Vol. 3.

Brannen, Julia and Gail Wilson (1987): <u>Give and Take in Families: Studies in Resource Distribution</u>. London: Allen and Unwin.

Chen, Martha A. (1983): <u>A Quiet Revolution: Women in Transition in Rural Bangladesh</u>. Cambridge, MA: Schenkman Publishing Inc.

Desai, Meghnad J. (1991): "Human Development: Concepts and Measurement", <u>European Economic Review</u>, Vol. 35, 350-357.

Diamond, Peter A. and Michael Rothschild (eds). (1989): <u>Uncertainty in Economics: Readings and Exercises</u>, Revised Edition. New York: Academic Press.

Edgeworth, F.Y. (1922): "Equal Pay to Men and Women for Equal Work", <u>Economic Journal</u>, Vol. 32, 431-457.

_____ (1923): "Women's Wages in Relation to Economic Welfare", <u>Economic Journal</u>, Vol. 33, 487-495.

Elson, Diane (ed.) (1991): <u>Male Bias in the Development Process</u>. Manchester, UK: Manchester University Press.

England, Paula (1992): <u>Comparable Worth: Theories and Evidence</u>. New York: Aldine.

Ferber, Marianne A. and Julie A. Nelson (eds) (1993): <u>Beyond Economic Man: Feminist Theory and Economics</u>. Chicago: University of Chicago Press.

Folbre, Nancy (1991): "The Unproductive Housewife: Her Evolution in Nineteenth Century Economic Thought", <u>Signs: Journal of Women in Culture and Society</u>, Vol. 16, No. 3, 463-484.

_____ (1994): <u>Who Pays for the Kids? Gender and the Structures of Constraint</u>. London and New York: Routledge.

_____ and Barnet Wagman (1993): "Counting Housework: Revised Estimates of Real Product in the United States, 1800-1860", <u>The Journal of Economic History</u>, Vol. 53, No. 2, 275-288.

Foster, James E. (1984): "On Economic Poverty: A Survey of Aggregate Measures", <u>Advances in Econometrics</u>, Vol. 3.

_____ (1985): "Inequality Measurement", in (ed.) H.P. Young, <u>Fair Allocation</u>. Providence, RI: American Mathematical Society.

Glendon, Mary Ann (1989): <u>The Transformation of Family Law: State, Law, and Family in the United States and Western Europe</u>. Chicago: University of Chicago Press.

Goldin, Claudia (1990): <u>Understanding the Gender Gap</u>. Oxford: Oxford University Press.

Goldschmidt-Clermont, Luisella (1982): <u>Unpaid Work in the Household</u>. Geneva: International Labour Office.

_____ (1993): "Monetary Valuation of Unpaid Work", paper presented at the International Conference on the Measurement and Valuation of Unpaid Work, Statistics Canada, Ottawa, April 28-30.

Hammond, Peter J. (1975): "A Note on Extreme Inequality Aversion", <u>Journal of Economic Theory</u>, Vol. 11, 465-467.

Hardy, G.H., J.E. Littlewood and G. Pólya (1952): <u>Inequalities</u>, Second Edition. Cambridge: Cambridge University Press.

Hartmann, B. (1987): <u>Reproductive Rights and Wrongs: The Global Politics of Population Control and Reproductive Choice</u>. New York: Harper and Row.

Holden, Constance (1987): "Why do Women Live Longer than Men?", <u>Science</u>, Vol. 238, 158-160.

Jayawardena, Kumari (1986): <u>Feminism and Nationalism in the Third World</u>. London: Zed Books.

Kolm, Serge Ch. (1969): "The Optimal Production of Social Justice", in (eds.) J. Margolis and H. Guitton, <u>Public Economics</u>. Lontdon: Macmillan.

Kynch, Jocelyn (1985): "How Many Women are Enough? Sex Ratios and the Right to Life", <u>Third World Affairs 1985</u>. London: Third World Foundation.

Lundberg, Shelly and Robert A. Pollak (1994): "Noncooperative Bargaining Models of Marriage", <u>American Economic Review</u> (Papers and Proceedings), Vol. 84, No. 2, 132-137.

McElroy, Marjorie and Mary Jean Horney (1981): "Nash-Bargained Household Decisions: Toward a Generalization of the Theory of Demand", <u>International Economic Review</u>, Vol. 22, No. 2, 333-349.

Manser, Marilyn and Murray Brown (1980): "Marriage and Household Decision Making: A Bargaining Analysis", <u>International Economic Review</u>, Vol. 21, No. 1, 31-44.

Moen, P. (1989): <u>Working Parents: Transformations in Gender Roles and Public Policies in Sweden</u>. Madison, Wisconsin: University of Wisconsin Press.

Nussbaum, Martha C. (1988): "Nature, Function, and Capability: Aristotle on Political Distribution",

Oxford Studies in Ancient Philosophy (supplementary volume).

_____ and Jonathan Glover (eds.) (1995): Women, Culture, and Development. Oxford: Clarendon Press.

Okin, S.M. (1989): Justice, Gender and the Family. New York: Basic Books.

Osmani, Siddiq R. (1982): Economic Inequality and Group Welfare. Oxford: Clarendon Press.

Pratt, John W. (1964): "Risk Aversion in the Small and in the Large", Econometrica, Vol. 32, 122-136.

Rothschild, Michael and Joseph E. Stiglitz (1970): "Increasing Risk: I. A Definition", Journal of Economic Theory, Vol. 2, No. 3, September, 225-243.

Sen, Amartya K. (1973): On Economic Inequality. Oxford: Clarendon Press.

_____ (1988): "Africa and India: What Do We Have to Learn from Each Other?", C.N. Vakil Memorial Lecture, 8th World Congress of the International Economic Association; published in (ed.) K. J. Arrow, The Balance Between Industry and Agriculture in Economic Development. London: Macmillan.

_____ (1990): "Gender and Cooperative Conflicts", in (ed.) Irene Tinker, Persistent Inequalities: Women and World Development. New York: Oxford University Press.

_____ (1992a): Inequality Reexamined. Oxford: Clarendon Press; and Cambridge, MA: Harvard University Press.

_____ (1992b): "Missing Women", British Medical Journal, Vol. 304, 587-588.

_____ (1993): "Life Expectancy and Inequality: Some Conceptual Issues", in (eds.) P.K. Bardhan, M. Datta-Chaudhuri and T.N. Krishnan, Development and Change. Bombay: Oxford University Press.

Sen, Gita and Caren Grown (1987): Development, Crises, and Alternative Visions: Third World Women's Perspectives. New York: Monthly Review Press.

Stern, Nicholas H. (1977): "Welfare Weights and the Elasticity of the Marginal Valuation of Income", in (eds.) M. Artis and R. Nobay, Current Economic Problems. Oxford: Basil Blackwell.

Streeten, Paul, with Shahid J. Burki, Mahbub ul Haq, Norman Hicks, and Frances Stewart (1981): First Things First: Meeting Basic Human Needs in the Developing Countries. New York: Oxford University Press.

United Nations Development Programme (UNDP) (1993): Human Development Report 1993. New York: Oxford University Press.

_____ (1994): Human Development Report 1994. New York: Oxford University Press.

Urdaneta-Ferrán, Lourdes (1993): "Measuring Women's and Men's Economic Contribution", in Proceedings of the ISI 49th Session, Firenze.

Waldron, Ingrid (1983): "The Role of Genetic and Biological Factors in Sex Differences in Mortality", in (eds.) Alan D. Lopez and Lado T. Ruzicka, Sex Differentials in Mortality: Trends, Determinants and Consequences, 141-164. Canberra: Department of Demography, Australian National University, 1983.

"Political Representation: Engendering Politics"*

"Political space belongs to all citizens"

Kathleen Staudt

With this eloquent statement, an Inter-Parliamentary Symposium synthesized its 1989 conference. Democracies <u>ought</u> to draw on the voices and participation of both women and men, in balanced, shared, and partnered ways. Yet in the historical legacies and lingering realities in most countries, men monopolize political space. Political monopolies are likely to produce policy results that are neither gender-fair nor accountable to women. Generally speaking, male monopoly reproduces politics that militarize relationships, devalue human development, and destroy the environment. In the twenty-first century, global sustainability will require transformed, engendered politics.

Until transformation occurs, how can women get a fairer share of development benefits? Over the last twenty years, people have pursued a variety of strategies. They have encouraged women's participation in the formal labor force, promoted equitable education, passed resolutions in numerous international meetings, passed anti-discrimination laws (only some of which are enforced and accessible to ordinary people), and established "women's machinery" in international agencies and governments.

In contrast to those approaches, this paper analyzes women's political representation as a means toward a gendered policy agenda. It first discusses, in Part I, a conceptual framework on engendering politics. In Part II, the paper presents quantitative data on women's political representation, organized around three explanatory themes: 1) human development priority; 2) culture, including gender differentiation, egalitarianism, and women's movements; and 3) political institutions, parties, and procedures. Following that, Part III of the paper provides the five most and the five least successful examples of women's participation and promising policy initiatives in democratic or partially democratic countries,[1] organized into five world regions. The conclusion, Part IV, assesses the critical factors which contribute to engendering democracy, based on the quantitative and country studies.

Engendering Politics: a Conceptual Model

Will more women's participation make a difference? The question is answerable for both **women's movements and groups** and **official representation**, for which this paper will cite evidence in subsequent pages. Women's movements and groups attempt, sometimes successfully, to broaden and transform the policy agenda; they also create a climate of expectations that male and female political officials be accountable to their needs.

Women representatives behave in more complex ways, depending on their career pathways into politics, their gender ideologies, and their sources of support. In the best-case scenario, women representatives are connected to interests and ideas supportive of gender fairness (U.S. evidence is strong [CAWP 1990;94]). When working under the condition of "critical mass" numbers, beginning with 15% "skewed representation" toward balanced representation (Kanter 1993: Ch 8), women are able to build coalitions with other women and men to accomplish those goals. In the worst case scenario, women representatives are appointed to and beholden to men who seek to perpetuate the status quo. Figure 1 below posits pathways toward engendered political outcomes, drawing on socio-economic factors that feed conventional politics and are in turn affected by political outcomes.

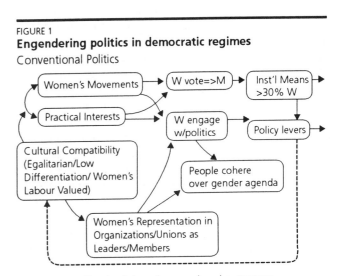

FIGURE 1
Engendering politics in democratic regimes
Conventional Politics

Gender-fair and engendered outcomes

Moving from the left, **cultural compatibility** establishes the ease by which women organize for change both in women's movements and in mainstream organizations such as unions. Compatibility emerges in societies which stress egalitarianism (see explanation # 1, culture, below); with traditions which value public female labor, (Southeast Asia, parts of Africa) or in industrial/post-industrial societies and their high female labor force participation rates; and/or with changes which render the construction of gender "difference" less meaningful. Low fertility is assumed to link with less differentiation. In societies that lack cultural compatibility, women's organizational activities can promote increased value for female labor, thus fostering compatibility.

Moving to conventional politics, women's (W in model) voices and choices are connected to public decision-making. Female voter turnout is nearly equal to and/or surpasses male turnout. Importantly, this turnout must be visible to the electorate, to candidates, and to elected officials. But more than voting must occur. Women's movements and groups must opt to **engage with** the political process rather than avoid it, as is quite common in many countries (Charlton, et al 1989; Parpart and Staudt 1988) and among the more radical factions of women's movements as European examples will later detail. Voting and organizational engagement are assumed to invoke a gendered policy agenda around which people--men and women--will cohere. Gendered policy agendas address the ways that tax, economic, land, health, and other mainstream policies differently serve or burden men and women (along with female household heads who may live in poverty).

Representatives and officials act on a coherent gendered policy agenda, especially when built upon critical mass numbers of women's voices. These actions will provide policy levers, such as equality laws and women's machinery (such as women's bureaus or ministries), which feed back to strengthen voting and organizational engagement.

The outcomes of these pathways are expected to lead to engendered policy outcomes. Few examples exist of engendered politics, save Nordic countries, with egalitarian values, high female labor force participation, and women's extensive involvement in civic, women's, and union groups. Among the earliest of countries to enfranchise women, strong unions subsequently collaborated with the state to establish policies which encouraged egalitarianism and support for female labor force participation (Adams and Winston 1980; Ruggie 1987; Gelb 1989). Only with the rise of new women's movements did the policy agenda broaden, including a concerted agenda to change politics with more female representation through use of institutional levers in parties and appointment processes. Achievements like these occurred

through a combination of strong women's movements and skewed female representation (around 15%). They created conditions under which women's representation would rise to world-record levels in the current era, of a third or more.

Globally, Low Female Participation: Why?

From an eligible electorate of half or more, women's representation withers to 16% in local legislatures, 10% in national legislatures, 7% in national cabinets, and 4% of chief executives, presidents and prime ministers. Women's pyramid is shown aside men's inverted pryamid below.

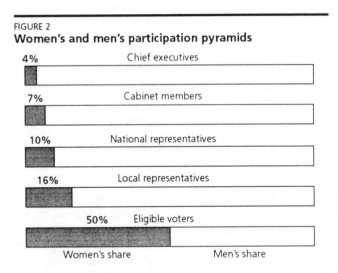

FIGURE 2
Women's and men's participation pyramids

4% Chief executives
7% Cabinet members
10% National representatives
16% Local representatives
50% Eligible voters

Women's share   Men's share

National Legislatures

Table 1a lists countries in alphabetical order, positioning those under the 10% global norm for female representation in national legislatures (referred to as parliaments by the Inter-Parliamentary Union (IPU) on the left and those above the 10% norm on the right. The table also highlights countries with provisions for appointments to their legislative bodies, some in unicameral systems and others in bicameral systems, usually the upper house. For the majority of countries with appointee provisions, the procedure elevates female representation above the global norm. (More on this under Explanation #3, institutions.) Table 1b shows variation over the last two decades, and Table 1c, regional variation.

Table 1a: Women's Representation Above/Below the Global 10% Norm

Below	Norm	Above
Albania 6%		
Algeria 7%		
Andorra 4%		
	Angola 10%	
		Ant&Bar 12%*
Argentina 9%		
Armenia 3%		
		Australia 15%
		Austria 21%
Azerbaidjan 2%		
		Bahamas 15%*
	Bangladesh 10%	
		Barbados 16%*
Belarus 4%		
	Belgium 10%	
		Belize 13%
Benin 6%		
Bhutan 0%		
Bolivia 6%		
Bosnia & Herz 5%		
Botswana 5%		
Brazil 4%		
		Bulgaria 13%
Burkina Faso 6%		
	Burundi 10%	
Cambodia 4%		
		Cameroon 12%
		Canada 17%*
CapeVerde 8%		
Cent African Rep 4%		
		Chad 16%
Chile 7%		
		China 21%
Colombia 9%		
Comoros 2%		
Congo 3%		
		Costa Rica 14%
Cote d'Ivoire 5%		
Croatia 5%		
		Cuba 23%
Cyprus 5%		
	Czech 10%	
		Dem PeoRep Korea 20%
		Denmark 33%
Djibouti 0%		
		Dominica 13%
Dominican Rep?		
Ecuador 5%		
Egypt 2%		
		El Salvador 11%
Eq Guinea 9%		
		Eritrea 16%
		Estonia 14%
Ethiopia 1%		
		Finland 39%
France 6%		
Gabon 6%		
Gambia 8%		
Georgia 6%		
		Germany 18%
Ghana 8%		
Greece 6%		
		Grenada 14%*
Guatemala 5%		
		Guinea-Bissau 13%
		Guyana 20%

Table 1A: Continued

<u>Below</u>	<u>Norm</u>	<u>Above</u>
Haiti 4%		
Honduras 8%		
		Hungary 11%
		Iceland 24$
India 7%		
		Indonesia 12%
Iran 4%		
		Iraq 11%
		Ireland 13%*
Israel 9%		
		Italy 12%
		Jamaica13%*
Japan 9%		
Jordan 6%*		
		Kazakhstan 11%
Kenya 3%**		
Kiribati 0%		
Kuwait 0%**		
Kyrghyzstan 6%		
Lao PeoDem Rep 9%		
		Latvia 15%
Lebanon 2%		
Lesotho 2%		
Liberia 6%		
Liechtenstein 8%		
Lithuania 7%		
		Luxembourg 20%
Madagascar 4%		
Malawi 6%**		
		Malaysia 13%*
Maldives 4%**		
Mali 2%		
Malta 2%		
Marshall Islands 3%		
Mauritania 0%		
Mauritius 3%*		
Mexico 6%*		
Micronesia 0%		
Moldova 5% Monaco 6%		
Mongolia 4%		
Morocco 1%		
		Mozambique 16%
Namibia 7%*		
Nauru 6%		
Nepal 2%*		
		Netherlands 28%
		New Zealand 21%
		Nicaragua 16%
Niger 6%		
		Norway 39%
Pakistan 2%*		
Panama 8%		
Papua New Guinea 0%		
Paraguay 7%		
Peru 9%		
		Philippines 14%*
		Poland 13%
Portugal 9%		
Rep Korea 1%		
Romania 3%		
		Rwanda 17%
Russian Fed 8%		
Saint Kitts & Nevis 6%*		
		Saint Lucia18%*
		SaintVin&Gren13%*
		San Marino 12%
		SaoTome&Prin 11%
		Senegal 12%
		Seychelles 27%*
Singapore 4%		
		Slovak Rep 18%

Table 1A: Continued

Below	Norm	Above
		Slovenia 14%
Solomon Isds 2%		
		South Africa16%
		Spain 14%
Sri Lanka 5%		
Sudan 5%		
Suriname 6%		
		Swaziland 12%
		Sweden 34%
		Switzerland 13%
Syrian Arab Rep 8%		
Tajikistan 3%		
Thailand 4%*		
(former) Macedonia 4%		
Togo 1%		
Tonga 3%		
		Trin&Tobago18%*
Tunisia 7%		
Turkey 2%		
Turkmenistan 5%		
Tuvalu 8%		
		Uganda 17%* Ukraine 4%
UnArabEmir 0%		
UK 9%		
		UnRepTanzania11%*
USA 9%		
Uruguay 3%		
	Uzbekistan 10%	
Venezuela 7%		
		Viet Nam 19%
WesternSamoa 4%		
Yemen 1%*		
Yugoslavia 3%		
Zaire 4%		
Zambia 7%		
		Zimbabwe 12%*

Source: IPU 1994, covering elections from 1990-94
*averaged %s for bicameral system, w/appointees

**unicameral system, w/some or all appointees

all other bicameral systems, averaged %s

FIGURE 3
Womens Representation, 1975–94

Percentage of positions held by women

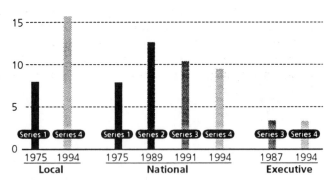

Sources: IPU, WW, Nuss

FIGURE 4
Womens representation by region, 1991–94

Percentage of positions in National legislatures held by women

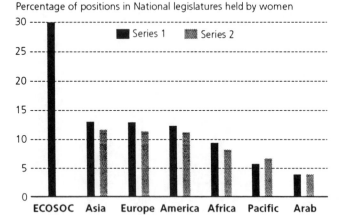

Source: IPU 1991, 1994

As Figure 3 shows, women's representation in legislative bodies has been growing, peaking in 1989 at 12.7%, and then dropping to approximately a tenth of members in 1994. The source for this fall, ironically, is the transition from one party to multi-party systems in Eastern Europe and the former Soviet Union. In 1987, the average for those countries was 27.5%, but in 1991, it had fallen to 10.9%. In 1994, it fell further to 7.8%.

"Where have all the women gone?" asks Einhorn in her thorough analysis of women's politics in central and eastern Europe (1993). Women were active in the democratic transition, as were women in Latin American transitions also bypassed on the whole (Jaquette 1989; 1994; Frohmann and Valdes 1995). While women are still recovering from their exclusion, and analysts, grappling for explanations, the most commonly cited reasons follow. First, women's organizations lacked strength and independence under socialism, belied by their inflated representation during that era (an explanation Wolchik stresses, 1989). Second, right-wing nationalists were particularly active in the new democratic space, playing the "ethnic card" as a priority over other political issues. Third, conservative religious forces became active and/or associated with the democratic opposition. Poland's active Catholic church is a most compelling example, with its support for criminalizing abortion. Finally, women's "double day" was particularly challenging under socialism, with high labor force participation, incomplete family-support policies, and limited consumer conveniences. In the post-socialist era, women face rapid increases in the cost of living and government austerity programs which impel desperate income-generating activities.

Regional variation is considerable, as Figure 4 demonstrates. IPU figures from 1991, with a world average of 11%, show Asia at 12.6%, Europe at 12.5%, the Americas at 12%, Africa at 9.2%, the Pacific at 5.6%, and Arab States at 3.7% (1991:26-27). By 1994, drops were evident in Asia (11.5%), Europe (due to more decline in Eastern Europe/Russia) (11.3%), the Americas (11.1%), and Africa (8%). Only the Pacific region was up. At the bottom, the Arab states held steady at 4%. At a subregional level, the Nordic countries have the highest average, surpassing the 30% goal the U.N. Economic and Social Council set for 1995.

Local Legislatures

When data are available, they show a higher percentage of women representatives in local governments than at national levels. This participation provides an experienced pool of women available to serve at national levels. Based on

CEDAW reports, women's representation at local levels is becoming more substantial in some countries, and growing at dramatic rates. Recent constitutional changes in India reserve a third of <u>Panchayat</u> (local council) seats for women. At least 800,000 women will consequently be in a local political pool (IPSA 1994).

Significant, even life or death decisions, are made at local and state levels. This is documented in one of India's states, Kerala. Besides its high female literacy and health rates, Kerala is the only state with favorable sex ratios (Jeffery 1987). In Germany, more than 1,200 equal-rights offices operate at local levels (Lemke: 1994:277). In the U.S. approximately 83,000 subfederal jurisdictions (counties, cities, school boards) operate with taxing and spending authority.

Women's local representation levels usually surpass that at the national level (in approximately two-thirds of 47 countries for which there are data), demonstrating the possibility that a strengthened pipeline might develop from local to national recruitment. In constructing women's proportional representation in local bodies from CEDAW reports, developed regions (N=28) show 18.5% women. In nine of these cases, or 32%, women's local representation is LESS than their national representation. Of 19 developing countries, women have an average of 11.7% representation at the local level. In eight of these cases, or 42%, this level is less than at their national levels. Figure 5 illustrates some promising and less promising cases.

These data do not differentiate between state, county, city, and other levels of government. Considerable range may exist by region and subfederal political culture. In the U.S., southern states, with their traditional political cultures, demonstrate low female representation rates, below 10% (Louisiana is lowest, at 2%), while Northeastern states surpass 30% (Clark 1994).

Cabinet-Level Representation

Table 3 shows a country-by-country breakdown on the proportion of women in cabinets, from high to low participation. Countries with female chief executives, noted on the table, fall above the global norm for a majority of cases, though not by huge margins. Second to Norway's striking 37% is Ireland, at 11%.

FIGURE 5
Womens local representation

Percentage of positions in local government held by women

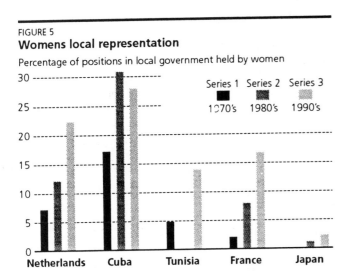

Constructed from CEDAW reports

Table 3: % Female Cabinet Representation, High to Low

Finland 44%	xxxxxxxxxxxxxxxxxxxxxxxxxxxxxxxxxxxxxxxxxxxx
*Norway 37%	xxxxxxxxxxxxxxxxxxxxxxxxxxxxxxxxxxxxx
Sweden 35%	xxxxxxxxxxxxxxxxxxxxxxxxxxxxxxxxxxx
Seychelles 33%	xxxxxxxxxxxxxxxxxxxxxxxxxxxxxxxxx
Netherlands 29%	xxxxxxxxxxxxxxxxxxxxxxxxxxxxx
Denmark 29%	xxxxxxxxxxxxxxxxxxxxxxxxxxxxx
Bahamas 23%	xxxxxxxxxxxxxxxxxxxxxxx
Guatemala 20%	xxxxxxxxxxxxxxxxxxxx
Haiti 20%	xxxxxxxxxxxxxxxxxxxx
Trin&Tobago 19%	xxxxxxxxxxxxxxxxxxx
Switzerland 17%	xxxxxxxxxxxxxxxxx
Germany 16%	xxxxxxxxxxxxxxxx
Austria 16%	xxxxxxxxxxxxxxxx
USA 15%	xxxxxxxxxxxxxxx
Estonia 15%	xxxxxxxxxxxxxxx
Ghana 14%	xxxxxxxxxxxxxx
Spain 14%	xxxxxxxxxxxxxx
Benin 14%	xxxxxxxxxxxxxx
Canada 14%	xxxxxxxxxxxxxx
Malawi 14%	xxxxxxxxxxxxxx
Australia 14%	xxxxxxxxxxxxxx
Uzbekistan 13%	xxxxxxxxxxxxx
Cape Verde 13%	xxxxxxxxxxxxx
Bhutan 13%	xxxxxxxxxxxxx
Italy 12%	xxxxxxxxxxxx
Belgium 11%	xxxxxxxxxxx
Burkina Faso 11%	xxxxxxxxxxx
Colombia 11%	xxxxxxxxxxx
Venezuela 11%	xxxxxxxxxxx
*Ireland 11%	xxxxxxxxxxx
Honduras 11%	xxxxxxxxxxx
El Salvador 10%	xxxxxxxxxx
Ethiopia 10%	xxxxxxxxxx
Uganda 10%	xxxxxxxxxx
Grenada 10%	xxxxxxxxxx
Namibia 10%	xxxxxxxxxx
Costa Rica 10%	xxxxxxxxxx
*Nicaragua 10%	xxxxxxxxxx
Fiji 10%	xxxxxxxxxx
UnRepTanzania 9%	xxxxxxxxx
Slovakia 9%	xxxxxxxxx
Rwanda 9/%	xxxxxxxxx
Luxembourg 9%	xxxxxxxxx
Chile9%	xxxxxxxxx
Industrial Country Average 8.7%	
UK 9%	xxxxxxxxx
*Bangladesh 8%	xxxxxxxx
New Zealand 8%	xxxxxxxx
St. Lucia 8%	xxxxxxxx
Korea,PeoDemRep8%	xxxxxxxx
*Dominica 8%	xxxxxxxx
*Iceland 8%	xxxxxxxx
Macedonia 8%	xxxxxxxx
Philippines 8%	xxxxxxxx
Burundi 7%	xxxxxxx
Gabon 7%	xxxxxxx
Panama 7%	xxxxxxx

28

France 7%	xxxxxxx
World Average 6.7%	
Poland 7%	xxxxxxx
Cyprus 7%	xxxxxxx
Angola 7%	xxxxxxx
Belize 6%	xxxxxx
Congo 6%	xxxxxx
China 6%	xxxxxx
Botswana 6%	xxxxxx
India 6%	xxxxxx
Indonesia 6%	xxxxxx
Zambia 6%	xxxxxx
South Africa 6%	xxxxxx
Yugoslavia 6%	xxxxxx
Lesotho 6%	xxxxxx
Peru 6%	xxxxxx
*Turkey 5%	xxxxx
Solomon Isds 5%	xxxxx
CentAfrican Rep 5%	xxxxx
Liberia 5%	xxxxx
Mexico 5%	xxxxx
Maldives 5%	xxxxx
Chad 5%	xxxxx
Niger 5%	xxxxx
Togo 5%	xxxxx
Azerbaijan 5%	xxxxx
Portugal 5%	xxxxx
Brazil 5%	xxxxx
Developing Country Average 4.5%	
Greece 5%	xxxxx
Ecuador 5%	xxxxx
Guinea 5%	xxxxx
Zaire 5%	xxxxx
Cuba 4%	xxxx
DominicanRep 4%	xxxx
GuineaBissau 4%	xxxx
Eq Guinea 4%	xxxx
Croatia 4%	xxxx
Korea, Rep 4%	xxxx
Algeria 4%	xxxx
Kenya 4%	xxxx
*Pakistan 4%	xxxx
Tunisia 4%	xxxx
Mauritius 3%	xxx
Senegal 3%	xxx
Tajikistan 3%	xxx
*Sri Lanka 3%	xxx
Jordan 3%	xxx
Sudan 3%	xxx
Zimbabwe 3%	xxx
Armenia 3%	xxx
Belarus 3%	xxx
Kazakhstan 3%	xxx
Cameroon 3%	xxx
Russian Fed 3%	xxx

Below: 0% in Alpha Order by Dev, then Ind Countries
Afghanistan
Antigua & Barbuda
Argentina
Bahrain
Barbados

Bolivia
Brunei Darussalam
Cambodia
Comoros
Djibouti
Egypt
Gambia
Iran
Iraq
Kuwait
Lao PeoDemRep
Lebanon
Libyan Arab Jamahiriya
Madagascar
Malaysia
Mali
Mauritania
Mongolia
Morocco
Moambique
Myanmar
Nepal
Nigeria
Oman
Papua New Guinea
Paraguay
Qatar
Sao Tome & Principe
Saudi Arabia
Sierra Leone
Singapore
Somalia
St Vincent/Grenadines
Suriname
Swaziland
Thailand
United ArabEmirates
Uruguay
Viet Nam
Yemen
Albania
Bosnia-Herzegovina
Bulgaria
Czech Rep
Georgia
Hungary
Japan
Kyrgyzstan Latvia
Lithuania
Malta
Moldova
Romania
Slovenia
Turkmenistan
Ukraine

Source: UN/DAW 1994 (averaged figures, as of January.
*Countries with a female prime minister or president

Women's participation in cabinets reached 4% world-wide in 1991 and inched upward to 7% in 1994. Figures are rarely stable: cabinet positions undergo constant reshuffling, fluctuating not just with elections but in between elections.

Cabinet work, which spans both legislative and executive/bureaucratic branches of government in parliamentary systems, is a special strategic location from which to exercise decision-making power. In presidential forms of government, appointed cabinet members work primarily in the executive branch departments; they represent their agencies to the legislature and thus engage in sustained contact with those representatives.

One of the most revealing figures about this strategic, inner sanctum of power is the number of countries with no women at ministerial levels. In 1987, 100 countries had no women, a majority figure which was reduced to 77 in 1991 (WOM/619) and to 61 in 1994 (using UN/DAW 1994 figures). (Only in the last decade have global breakdowns been available on cabinets.) Figure 6 shows this exclusion quite graphically.

breakdown, Table 4 shows the number of countries with male monopolies (0 women's representation), token female representation (1 seat; 2 seats), and those with 3 or more. The proportions, of course, reflect the total number of cabinet seats at the highest level, from 50 (China and North Korea, with 3 and 4 women respectively) to 8 (Bhutan, with 1 woman).

Table 4. Women's Cabinet Seats

DEVELOPING COUNTRIES

Male Monopolies (0 women)	45 countries/36%
One woman only	38 countries/31%
2 women	24 countries/19%
3+ women	17 countries/14%

INDUSTRIALIZED COUNTRIES

Male Monopolies (0 women)	16 countries/40%
One woman only	4 countries/10%
2 women	8 countries/20%
3+ women	12 countries/30%

(note:12 industrialized countried had no data--not in %)

In a 1991 ministerial count of 170 countries (179 in 1994), only seven seat more than 20% women cabinet members, as follows.

Both the tables above and below show that few countries have a "critical mass" of women (3+ or proportionality).

Table 5. Less than 5% of Governments Seat >20% Cabinet Women

1991	1994
Bhutan: 28%	Bahamas 23%
Denmark: 21%	Guatemala 20%
Finland: 29%	Haiti 20%
Guyana: 23%	Seychelles 33%
Norway: 47%	Finland 44%
Seychelles:30%	Norway 37%
Sweden: 36%	Sweden 35%
	Denmark 29%
	Netherlands 29%

Source: Lloyd, 1991; UN/DAW 1994.

FIGURE 6
Countries with no cabinet women
Number of countries

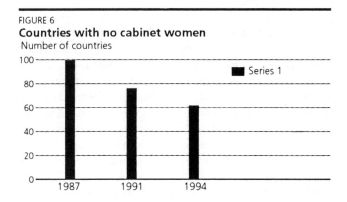

The regional group of countries with highest average ministerial levels is the Western European and Other States (Canada, U.S.A., New Zealand, Australia), with 9.3% in 1991, up from 9% in 1987. The next highest level is found in Latin America and the Caribbean, at 5.6% in 1991, up from 2.7% in 1987 (WOM/619). In a UN/DAW 1994 list, with different categorical labels, industrial countries show a 8.7% figure while developing countries show 4.7%. Using that same

While the number of countries jumped from 7 to 9, the countries differed, with the exception of European democracies. The remaining countries are partially democratic or nondemocratic. The lack of electoral choices and freedoms make one question whetherthese percentages have any significance at all.

Whatever the proportional female participation, the portfolios to which women are assigned fall generally in the areas of social welfare, women's affairs, education, and culture. These are seldom considered to be the more powerful ministries. Ministries like foreign affairs, defense, and finance generally rest in male hands alone. A world exception exists in Finland with a woman Minister of Defence and a woman Central Bank Director.

In a count of women cabinet officials (Staudt 1989), ministries in which women served were divided by type. Totals equal more than the number of countries due to ministry combinations across categories, such as labor and social. The results below show women most often serve in "social" affairs. As sociologist Kanter analyzes (1993), the lone or few pioneers in dominant (all male) groups are assigned tasks that seem fitting with the interests or perceptions of their group, however stereotyped that might be.

Table 6. Women's Cabinet Assignments, 1989

Social	84
(education, arts, community development, health, sports, culture, consumer affairs, etc.)	
Economic Production	45
(labor, employment, agriculture, industry, commerce, finance)	
Law	21
(justice, local government, environmental regulation)	
Distribution	19
(public works, transportation, housing, urban affairs, public enterprise)	
Defense/Foreign Affairs	16
Undetermined (without Portfolio)	26

Source: Staudt 1989

Heads of Government and of State

Women heads of state and government have been a few drops in the bucket of history. Among them are women who have rose through party and citizen organization ranks as well as those from famous political families, a South Asian pattern (now matched in Nicaragua). Only a few of these women

identify with and/or pursue pathways through women's organizations: Norway's Brundtland; Iceland's Finnbogadottir; and Ireland's Robinson. Additionally, Edith Cresson (France) fell within that category (Kelber 1994). In all of world history, through 1993, only 20 women have been elected Head of State or Government of independent countries (CSDHA 1992). By late 1994, 9 women were still in office, and their names and countries are found below.

Presidents	Prime Ministers
NICARAGUA Violeta Chamorro	NORWAY Gro Harlem Brundtland
ICELAND Vigdis Finnbogadottir	DOMINICA Eugenia Charles
IRELAND Mary Robinson	PAKISTAN Benazir Bhutto
TURKEY Tansu Ciller	BANGLADESH Khaleda Zia
SRI LANKA Chandrika Bandaranaike Kumaratunga	

While the symbolism of a female head of state or government is to be applauded, in no case has a single woman transformed political process and outcome. Nor do all women executives put gender-fairness at the top of their policy priorities. Margaret Thatcher, dubbed the "Iron Lady," cut milk subsidies to children (thus, the refrain, "Margaret Thatcher, the milk snatcher"). After detailing a grim reality for the majority of Indian women, from uneven sex ratios to enormous gender gaps in literacy, D'Souza and Natarajan conclude "these are sobering thoughts for a country that had a woman prime minister [Indira Gandhi] for 16 years" (1986).

Working toward gender-fairness is viewed as threatening where inequalities have long been institutionalized. Whether woman executives can expend political capital to work toward fairness is questionable in such systems, which include Pakistan and Turkey. President Aquino's record on poverty alleviation (wherein many women are concentrated) was mixed, but she signed the Executive Order to create and implement a Development Plan for Women developed under the direction of the women's commission, with 60 staff members, augmented by a "sisters sorority" of focal points in government agencies, and fully accountable to women's organizations (see case).

In democratic systems, women chief executives work with representative bodies and potentially entrenched bureaucracies. The presence of women must be understood in this context, as well as the probable lack of critical mass numbers of women in the national legislature. In the presidential systems listed with women at the helm, 18% of representatives are women, while in the parliamentary systems with women at the helm, 12%. Both are above the global average, but far from the U.N. goal for 1995. A base of support, with women and men, provides the foundation from which women chief executives can proceed.

Moreover, those representative bodies operate differently in parliamentary versus presidential systems. In parliamentary systems, the fusion of executive and legislature means more efficient, concentrated decisionmaking, whereas the fragmentation of presidential systems into separate branches means much political energy is expended for naught. In the U.S. Congress, one of ten to twenty bills introduced are passed into laws. Most die in committees and subcommittees. In the twentieth century, the high point for introducing and passing "women's bills" was the late 1960s and early 1970s, the height of the women's movement: in 1969-70, 289 women's bills, of 26,301 bills introduced (or 1.1% of the total); and in 1973-74, 17 "women's laws" of 649 laws passed (or 2.6% of the total) (Costain 1988). The introduction and passage of women's measures are fostered with a cross-partisan Congressional Caucus for Women, the renamed women's caucus which recruits men and women into its fold.

Why Such Low Representation?

Extensive scholarship on the question of women's low representation is barely two decades old, focused mainly on the U.S. and Europe. Mainstream scholars of government routinely ignore the topic, still.[2] This paper focuses on three explanations, all with implications for policy and political action and discussed in the conclusion.

EXPLANATION #1: Low Human Development Priority

Using the Human Development Index (HDI) 1994 rankings below (UNDP), the top and bottom ten countries show differences in the proportion of women both in parliaments (IPU 1994 data) and in cabinets (UN/DAW 1994 data).

Table 7. HDI and Women's Representation

Rank/Country	%Parl	%Cabinet
HIGHEST		
1.Canada	17	14
2.Switzerland	13	17
3.Japan	3 (lower house)	0
4.Sweden	34	35
5.Norway	39	37
6.France	6	7
7.Australia	15	13
8.USA	9	15
9.Netherlands	28	29
10.UK	8	9
LOWEST		
164.Guinea-Bissau	13	4
165.Somalia	--	0
166.Gambia	8	0
167.Mali	2	0
168.Chad	16	5
169.Niger	6	5
170.Sierra Leone	--	0
171.Afghanistan	--	0
172.Burkina Faso	6	11
173.Guinea	--	5

Source: IPU 1994 on parliamentary representation, averaged if bicameral, unless specified. (In parliamentary systems, the upper house tends to be marginal, a reversed tendency In presidential systems.) UN/DAW 1994 on cabinets.

These figures show a tendency toward greater representation in countries with high priority for human development, countries which are widely viewed as democracies. However, the relationship is far from perfect as the Japan, France, UK, and US figures show. In the lowest HDI ranked countries, The Gambia, Guinea, Burkina Faso, Mali, and Guinea-Bissau are considered democratic or partly democratic based on criteria like fair elections, press freedom, and individual and group rights (Freedom House 1994; Africa Demos 1994 (quarterly reports). None of the low HDI countries have the striking representation of northern European democracies, but several surpass high-HDI countries in female representation.

EXPLANATION #2: Culture

Cultural explanations fall into several categories, focused on gender differentiation, including prejudice; egalitarianism that values class equity, power-sharing, and less hierarchy; and women's movements which frequently rise out of a women's culture. Cultural explanations share in common a focus on enduring values and norms that guide behavior, or what Dutch theorist Hofstede Calls collective mental programming (1984).

Gender Differentiation in Cultural Context

The social construction of gender, although different from one society or nation to the next, tends to encourage more interest and background preparation thought suitable for politics among men. First, then, women's **human capital** is underdeveloped for politics. Gender educational gaps are commonplace worldwide, both in terms of schooling years completed and of professional training commonly linked to politics, like law and the military. The earliest of female chief executives pursued traditionally male professions, equipping them with political skills or perhaps survival skills as pioneers in a male world: Thatcher and Pintasilgo (chemistry, chemical engineering), Charles and Bhutto (law, diplomacy) (pathways discussed in Staudt 1989). If politics is to be transformed, political recruitment would draw on a wider range of work backgrounds, including teaching and service wherein women so often specialize.

Gendered wage inequalities, still chronic worldwide (even in Nordic countries) also provide women with less money to run campaigns or to donate to candidates of their choice. In strong party systems, or in those with public financing or subsidized campaigns, this is less relevant. In countries where money is crucial to political success, like the U.S., this is a serious problem for women. In the U.S., women's groups emerged to raise funds specifically for women. The most famous is EMILY, an acronym for Early Money is Like Yeast (...it makes the dough rise)[3]

Second, **cultural values** are conveyed during childhood ("socialization") that encourage more males to develop traits that translate into political leadership and females, dependency and domesticity. Voters, male and female alike, acquiesce to this cultural tradition, and prejudice forms. Governments perpetuate these values with tax, welfare, and pension policies. Until recently, the Netherlands Government family policies perpetuated a "motherhood ideology" (Leijenaar and Niemoller 1994) and traditional male "breadwinner ideology" (Sainsbury 1994) that set it apart from other welfare states in perpetuating female dependency.

Media often feed on prejudices, mocking female candidates' dress, face, among other characteristics. In the many regional and global meetings wherein women representatives speak about obstacles they have faced, they cite headlines on their physique and dress and pictures situating them in kitchens, discussing recipes. Also, media overemphases on female sexuality does not inspire voter confidence in women leaders.

To cite one of many possible countries, Mexican newspapers are replete with pictures of scantily clad girls and women.

Political recruitment often occurs through men's networks in the social- or work-segregated professional worlds (Kanter 1993 on "homosocial recruitment"). Slang advertises just how commonplace this is ("old boys network," U.S.; "chaps [look] after other chaps" Lovenduski 1994 on Britain). In some countries, term limits aim to expand the recruitment pool.

Third, **role conflict** between mothering/domestic responsibilities and the rigors of political life discourages female participation. Women's extensive, unpaid household responsibilities are popularly known as the "double day," translated into many languages. When women enter politics, it is often through the "widow route," stepping in for deceased husbands who served in representative or executive positions. (Widow routes are common in South Asia, and the U.S. historically.)

Of course, politics is compatible with motherhood: Who can forget the vivid pictures of Pakistan's pregnant Prime Minister, Benazir Bhutto? Bhutto is the exception rather than the rule, however, for many empirical studies cite women's late entry into politics, once their children have grown, or their unmarried status (see examples on Europe and the U.S. in Epstein 1981).

Yet for the few women who manage to overcome conflicts with household responsibilities, there are numerous others who are deterred by religious and other cultural traditions which treat female public leadership as suspect. Arat sampled all those 40 women ever elected to national office in Turkey, most with impeccable educational credentials; among the 18 of this universe who were alive and agreed to interviews, respondents revealed the difficulty of overcoming resistance to the idea that they were deserting responsibilities to their husbands (1989).

Interviews with successful female candidates in India reveal the difficulty of acquiring public voice for campaigning after being reared in strict purdah (Everett 1984:212). An extensive review of biographical and autobiographic data shows the unique characteristics of women elites who develop impeccable credentials, often in nontraditionally female fields, and grapple with the "double day" (Staudt, 1989; Leijenaar and Niemoller 1994; Thomas on U.S. states 1993). The Latin American proverb, "whereas a man may be made of silver, a woman must be made of gold," (Chaney 1979) rings true in many countries, with women politicians' educational achievements surpassing men's.

Women's differing human capital has become an asset in some national politics, sometimes only temporarily. Voters, disgusted with political corruption and scandals, turn to women who (rightly or wrongly) are identified with honesty and morality (see Chaney on perceptions of women as "supermadres" (1979)). Women's gains in Japan's 1989 election occurred this way, quickly lost thereafter (see country case). Neither women nor men can transform politics in a year or two, so voters' expectations may be dashed after a few women "had their chance." President Corazon Aquino of the Philippines capitalized on her pure image, a marked contrast with the Dictator Marcos. Norway's voters actively sought a wider policy agenda which they judged women would bring. Voters chose women <u>because</u> they were women (Skard 1981:87), a pattern sustained there but unmatched in most countries.

The above discussions are predicated on the idea that women are in fact "different" from men, an idea that may derive from socially constructed difference from childhood on, biological factors, or some combination of both which rests on still-lingering work differentiation during adulthood. On the other hand, women's human capital, viewed in terms of temperament and personality, may be similar to men's generally, or specifically for the few women who occupy top positions who may differ from ordinary women by economic class and other factors.

But are women really different from men? For social, biological, or experiential reasons? The world is replete with anecdotes about women "who act more like men" once at the helm. Male cabinet members said publicly, about Indira Gandhi and Golda Meir (neither of whom appointed other women to the cabinets): they are the only men on the cabinet! Few outside the western world have systematically studied the extent to which women leaders behave like men. Moreover, the methodological tools we have for such study may be questionable for they may derive from the U.S., incorrectly assumed to tap universal feminine-masculine characteristics.

Turkey provides an example of one rare study. In her interviews with 18 former female representatives, with a matched sample of 10 comparable men, Arat scored Turkish respondents using the Bem Sex Role Inventory (a list of "masculine" and "feminine" self-descriptive adjectives, developed in the U.S.). Arat puts the scores in an appendix, without analysis or interpretation. Curiously, these female political elites score more "masculine" than males for half the adjectives (1989). Women have never occupied more than 5% of the parliament in Turkey, a figure now at 2%. How, then, do we interpret this? That highly educated elite men and women are alike? That U.S. sex-role adjectives make little sense in Turkey?

Egalitarianism in Cultural Context

Hofstede's quantification of cultures represents the best and largest effort to compare nations, based on 116,000 interviews in forty countries. Although dated (perhaps unproblematic, for cultures do not change instantly), it is the only study available of this type with such a large sample (1984). He plots countries on scattergrams along four dimensions (rated from 0-100), two of which are relevant to this analysis: high power distance ("accept the fact that power in institutions and organizations is distributed unequally") and masculinity ("dominant values...[involve] assertiveness, the acquisition of money and things and not caring for others, the quality of life, or people." (Elsewhere, he reduces masculinity to high male-female differentiation, cultural programming which decreases in low-fertility, complex economies.) As Table 8 below reveals, a stronger relationship exists between high power distance countries and low female representation than masculinity.

Table 8. Cultural Values & Women's Representation

Value	% Parl	% Cabinet
High Power Distance (50-100)	7	7
Low Power Distance (0-49)	16	20
High Masculinity (50-100)	11	10
Low Masculinity (0-49)	10	15

(Source on Cultural Values: Hofstede 1984. Source on Representation: IPU 1994; on Cabinets: UN/DAW 1994)

Those countries which score low on power distance, and are presumably more egalitarian, include the "stars" on gender balance such as Finland (33), Norway (31), Sweden (31), and Denmark (18). Those same stars have low masculinity, i.e. less differentiated, scores (Finland (26), Norway (8), Sweden (5), and Denmark (16)). Hofstede's indicators lend support to the idea in the conceptual model of this analysis: cultural compatibility is linked to gender-fair political process.

Lacking cultural compatibility, just how long will gender balancing strategies take? Even Nordic countries experienced a half-century delay between female suffrage and female representation above the ten percent mark at which it is stuck worldwide. It took sixty years before U.S. women gained suffrage in 1920 and a "gender gap" appeared in voting preferences that affected electoral campaigns.[4] The most consistent gaps appear in women's preference for social spending and for peace rather than war options (Mueller 1988). (The particular character of the gender gap is likely to vary from country to country, to the extent social rather than biological factors produce cultural values.)

However, the world now is far different than it was over a half-century ago, to mention just U.N. machinery, global communication, and new women's movements. Switzerland only granted women the right to vote in 1971 (some male voters in conservative canons delayed local franchise even longer), yet it now has 9% women in its Council of States and 18% women in its National Council. Furthermore, a synergy exists between policies and women's movements in cultural contexts.

Women's Movements in Cultural Contexts

Historical processes are further telescoped with strong women's organizations. Hardly an egalitarian culture, South Africa's free elections of 1994 produced substantial female representation, totalling a quarter in one legislative body. Women of the African National Congress pushed their party to nominate a third women among candidates (Kelber 1994: xii). Women were among delegates in negotiations for a post-apartheid government. The Women's National Coalition sought to build a Women's Charter in the new constitution. Few new constitutions have been established with such awareness and organization among women (Africa Report 1993). Women occupied enough political space to put gender on the policy agenda (Kemp, Madlala, Moodley, Salo, 1995).

The South Africa example demonstrates the importance of examining women's movements as they influence cultures. Such movements can be divided into **old and new**, with older movements focused on suffrage, welfare, nationalism and civil rights.

Over the twentieth century, women achieved the right to vote and to be elected to office in virtually all countries of the world with representative institutions.[5] These rights are usually, but not always granted simultaneously. New Zealand, then Australia, were the pioneer countries to recognize female citizenship through voting at the national level, beginning in 1893.

Women's suffrage struggle builds leadership and organization which can translate into empowerment once rights are achieved. The visibility of "womenpower" demonstrates to the male political establishment the potential strength of a new constituency. When women's rights are granted without women's struggles or demands, leadership and organizational opportunities are lost. The various rights and benefits

accorded women in former socialist countries pre-empted women's own struggle. In transition to market economies and democracies, women's rights were tainted through connection to illegitimate regimes which people opposed (Wolchik 1989; Einhorn 1993).

When the franchise is granted equally to men and women near or at the time of independence or revolutionary change, we have to ask whether women's participation in the nationalist movements and/or guerrilla struggles served as equivalents for the kind of "womenpower" that suffrage movements have gained. Women organized, fought, struck, and petitioned for change, with men and in separate women's organizations (selections in Basu 1995). Historical literature analyzes such change all over Africa and Asia (Latin American countries delayed female suffrage until well after independence, though women always participated in revolutionary movements). The "Founding Fathers" often recognized women's contributions, thereafter granting them concessions, appointments, and symbolic changes. In India, curiously, higher percentages of women were jailed during nationalist struggles (10%) than percentages serving in the national parliament (8%) (Swarup et al 1994:368).

Zimbabwe, one of the most recent examples of independence to emerge from nationalist-revolutionary struggle, has a track record of research which paints complex pictures of women's struggles. Women's motivations to join guerrilla movements were mixed, with some pursuing a gender struggle and others being forced into participation (Kriger 1991). One scholar analyzes Zimbabwe as engaged in "simultaneous revolutions" with contradictory implications for policy (Sylvester 1991). Women's parliamentary representation (12% in 1994) rises barely above global norms, but cabinet participation (3%) is below those norms. Ex-guerrilla fighter and cabinet member Joyce Mujuru (nom de guerre "spill blood") said she struggled more in the bureaucracy than in the war. Her former ministry, which served women through community development and cooperative support, confronted the practice of lobola (bridewealth exchange), but backed off after charges of this supposed imperialist project (analyzed in Staudt 1990:21).

The advantages of women's struggles are not always sustained after they achieve their goals, such as the voting franchise or national independence. In the U.S., advocates used the argument that more female voters would clean up, moralize, and transform politics. After women achieved the vote in 1920, politics went untransformed. Women's initial voter turnout was low, estimated at a third, and what remained of the exhausted women's movement had divided into two factions: equal rights and social reform, factions working at cross-purposes with one another over such principles as protective laws for women, inherently contradictory to equal rights (two classic studies, among many, are Flexner 1974; Kraditor 1965). Only a second-stage women's movement of the late 1960s, and a different workplace and legal environment, stimulated some convergence (Freeman 1975).

Worldwide, women began organizing formally and informally in what some refer to as the new women's movement in the 1960s and 1970s. Many adherents pursue high-visibility protests and lobbying activities and low-visibility self-help and consciousness-raising activities, but few are counted and totalled in nationally comparable ways. Women's studies courses flourish in many countries (Rao 1991), to which wide readerships of feminist magazines and publishing houses must be added in speculating the impossible task of tabulating women's movement supporters. Even the state-controlled press in China legitimizes issues usually associated with women's movements. Below are some headlines and titles (from Honig & Hershatter 1988):

*"Why Such a Wide Gap in the Proportions of Boys and Girls Entering the Upper Grades?"
*"It is Not Permissible to Defame Woman's Image."
*"I Mistakenly Blamed Her" (husband repents after abusing wife who gave birth to a girl)
*"Is it Right to Refuse Someone a Job Just Because She is Female?"
*"To Discriminate Against Women is to Discriminate Against Your own Mother"

Gender consciousness is more widespread in the U.S than western Europe, perceptable to male and female representatives alike in this weak party/presidential system, but women's integration into the strong party/parliamentary systems of western Europe is more likely to produce gender-fair outcomes (Klein 1994).

Women's activists are a diverse and diffuse populace, with some suspicious of the state, political representatives (including women), and state-subsidized women's bureaus; others are reformers who are willing to engage with the establishment (Katzenstein on the U.S. and western Europe 1987; many of the 43 selections and overview in Nelson and Chowdhury 1994). According to Lovenduski, writing about party politics, many of those once identified as radical and/or leftist

feminists saw the importance of engagement in order to transform policy agendas in the last decade (1993). Canada has a wide variety of non-partisan NGOs which educate and motivate women to political action through conferences, training, and guidebooks (Canada's response to IPU questionnaire 1992:38-39). Can activities like these (a "new girls' network"?) one day be equivalent to those of the "boys?"

Under Latin American authoritarian regimes, women's and mothers' groups (the latter, seeking disappeared family members) had good reason to be suspicious of the state. Their willingness to use whatever political space existed, at great risk, helped create the mass base for mobilizing opposition and making transitions to more democratic regimes. Yet in these presidential regimes, few women were elected and appointed to office (selections in Jaquette 1994; Frohmann and Valdes 1995). Brazil's Councils on the Status of Women went to great lengths to retain connections with women's organizations, though ultimately their dependence on state budgets during economic crisis led to demise (Alvarez 1990; Soares, et.al. 1995). Engagement with the state, done at great cost and energy, produces paltry returns or overcompromised solutions, as women in Mexico found on the topic of violence (Lamas, et.al. 1995; also see country case).

Men may simply remove feisty women, to name just a few of many examples: Women's Rights Minister Yvette Roudy (France), (dubbed "Madame Ayatollah" by her enemies) with her vigorous, action-oriented, and anti-sexism policy agenda (analyzed in Staudt 1990:20); appointee Bella Abzug (U.S.), who dared move beyond women's issues to critize President Carter's economic policy; and Poland's Subcabinet Minister Anna Popowicz who supported reproductive rights, at odds with President Walesa's efforts to criminalize abortion (he prayed publicly in "solidarity" with the unborn) (Einhorn 1993).

Women's groups have attempted to use their country's endorsement of principles in the Convention on the Elimination of All Forms of Discrimination Against Women as leverage to promote gender-fair laws and policies. This opportunity was a catalyst to mobilize women in Japan, as the country case outlines. Figure 7 shows some difference between countries which have acted on CEDAW versus those which have not, in terms of proportional women's representation in national parliaments. Once Nordic countries are removed from the ratified group, little difference exists between those that have ratified and those that have signed. Both democratic and nondemocratic countries have signed and/or ratified, and those which have not acted are generally nondemocratic or partially democratic.

FIGURF 7
CEDAW action
Number of countries

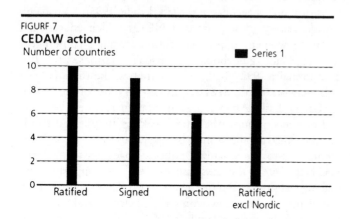

The enforcement of CEDAW ratification could provide a golden opportunity for women to hold governments accountable to them, as Box 1 suggests.

Box 1 CEDAW Ratification: What Next?

"When governments ratify the Convention, they agree to report periodically on process and obstacles to improving the status of women in their country. Under the Convention, a twenty-three member expert committee--CEDAW--reviews a number of government reports each year and then produces a report for the U.N. General Assembly and the Public based on that year's reviews. Under the Convention, governments are obligated to report to CEDAW within one year of ratification and every four years thereafter. Government reports are submitted in writing to the U.N. but are usually not reviewed for a year or more after receipt. When the report is reviewed a government representative appears before the committee to officially submit the report and add any new information that may be relevant."

Excerpt from the International Women's Rights Action Watch (IWRAW), <u>IWRAW to CEDAW Country Reports</u> (1994:1). CEDAW seeks information from NGOs on the legal and practical situation of women; IWRAW and other human rights organizations serve as conduits to pass on this information.

right to be elected?   Table 10 below graphically illustrates the span between women's right to be elected and their election. When a lapse exists between both, the range is from 1 to 66 years, with Lebanon holding the world record. In nearby country Jordan, Toujan Faisal's first candidacy resulted in religious leaders calling for her assassination, though she was finally victorious in 1993 (in Kelber 1994).

To what extent might old and new women's movementshelp propel women into office, once achieving the

Table 10. Time Lapse: Right to Vote and Female Representation

	Yr.Vote	FemaleRepr	Lapse
Afghanistan	1965	1965	
Albania	1945	1945	
Algeria	1962	1962	
Angola	1975	1980	xxxxx
Antigua&Bar	1951	1980	xxxxxxxxxxxxxxxxxx
Argentina	1947	1952	xxxxx
Australia	1901	1943	xxxxxxxxxxxxxxxxxxxxxxxxxxxxxx42yrs
Austria	1918	1919	x
Bahamas	1962-4	1977	xxxxxxxxxxxxxx
Bangladesh	1947	1975	xxxxxxxxxxxxxxxxxxxxxxxxxxx
Barbados	1951	1951	
Belgium	1918	1921	xxx
Belize	1945	1984	xxxxxxxxxxxxxxxxxxxxxxxxxxxxx39yrs
Benin	1956	1979	xxxxxxxxxxxxxxxxxxxxxx
Bhutan	1953	1975	xxxxxxxxxxxxxxxxxxxxxx
Bolivia	1938	1966	xxxxxxxxxxxxxxxxxxxxxxxxxxxx
Botswana	1965	1979	xxxxxxxxxxxxxx
Brazil	1934	1934	
Bulgaria	1944	1945	x
Cameroon	1946	1962	xxxxxxxxxxxxxx
Canada	1917	1921	xxxx
CapeVerde	1975	1975	
CentAfRep	1986	1987	x
Chile	1949	1951	xx
China	1949	1954	xxxxx
Colombia	1957	1958	x
Comoros	1956	1993	xxxxxxxxxxxxxxxxxxxxxxxxxxxxxx37rs.
Congo	1963	1970	xxxxxxx
CostaRica	1949	1953	xxxx
Côte D'Ivoire	1952	1965	xxxxxxxxxxxxx
Cuba	1934	1940	xxxxxx
Cyprus	1960	1963	xxx
Czechoslovakia	1920	1920	
Dem Rep Korea	1946	1948	xx
Denmark	1915	1918	xxx
Djibouti	1946	NO WOMAN EVER ELECTED	
Dominica	1951	1980	xxxxxxxxxxxxxxxxxxxxxxxxxxxxx
DomRep	1942	1946	xxxx
Ecuador	1946	1957	xxxxxxxxxxx
Egypt	1956	1957	x
El Salvador	1961	?	
EqGuinea	1963	1968	xxxxx
Ethiopia	n.d.	n.d.	
Estonia	n.d.	n.d.	
Finland	1906	1906	
France	1944	1945	x
Gabon	1956	1961	xxxxx
Gambia	1960	?	
Germany	1918	1919	x
Greece	1952	1952	
Grenada	1951	1976	xxxxxxxxxxxxxxx
Guatemala	1945	1954	xxxxxxxxx
Guinea-Bissau	1977	?	
Guyana	1953	1953	
Haiti	1950	?	
Honduras	1957	1967	xxxxxxxxxx
Hungary	1945	1945	

Iceland	1915	?	
India	1950	1952	xx
Indonesia	1945	1945appt	
		1955elec	xxxxxxxxxx
Iran	1963	1963	
Iraq	1980	1980	
Ireland	1918	?	
Israel	1948	1948	
Italy	1945	1946	x
Jamaica	1944	?	
Japan	1945	1946	x
Jordan	1974	1993	xxxxxxxxxxxxxxxxx
Kenya	1963	1969	xxxxxx
Kiribati	1971	NO WOMAN EVER ELECTED	
Kuwait	No	No	
Laos	1948	?	
Latvia	n.d.		
Lebanon	1926	1992	xxxxxxxxxxxxxxxxxxxxxxxxxxxxxxx66yrs
Liberia	1946	1964	xxxxxxxxxxxxxxxx
Libya	1969	?	
Liech	1984	1986	xx
Lithuania	n.d.		
Luxembourg	1919	1919	
Madagascar	1959	1965	xxxxxx
Malawi	1964	1964	
Malaysia	1957	1959	
Maldives	1932	?	
Malta	1947	1947	
Mauritius	1956	?	
Mexico	1947	1952nom.	xxxxx
Monaco	1962	1963	x
Mongolia	1923-4	1923-4	
Morocco	1963	1993	xxxxxxxxxxxxxxxxxxxxxxxxxxxxxx
Mozambique	1975	1977	xx
Namibia	1989	1989	
Nauru	1968	1986	xxxxxxxxxxxxxxxxx
Nepal	1951	?	
Netherlands	1919*		
NewZealand	1893	1933	xxxxxxxxxxxxxxxxxxxxxxxxxxxxxx40yrs
Nicaragua	1955	1957	xx
Niger	1948	1989	xxxxxxxxxxxxxxxxxxxxxxxxxxxxxxx41yrs
Norway	1907	1911proxy	xxxx
		1921	xxxxxxxxxxxxxx
Pakistan	1937	1947	xxxxxxxxxx
Panama	1941	1946	xxxxx
PapuaNewGu	1975	1977	xx
Paraguay	1961	1963	xx
Peru	1950	1956	xxxxxx
Philippines	1937	1941	xxxx
Poland	1918	1919	x
Portugal	1931	1934	xxx
Rep Korea	1948	1948	
Romania	1929	1946	xxxxxxxxxxxxxxxx
Rwanda	1961	1965	xxxx
SaintKitts&N	1951	1984	xxxxxxxxxxxxxxxxxxxxxxxxxxxxxxxxxxx
Saint Lucia	1951	1951appt	
		1979	xxxxxxxxxxxxxxxxxxxxxxxxxxx
SaintVin&G	1951	1979	xxxxxxxxxxxxxxxxxxxxxxxxxxx
SanMoreno	1960	1974	xxxxxxxxxxxxxx
SaoTome&Pr	1975	1975	
Senegal	1945	1963	xxxxxxxxxxxxxxxxx

Seychelles	1948	1976	xxxxxxxxxxxxxxxxxxxxxxxxxx
SierraLeone	1951	?	
Singapore	1948	1984	xxxxxxxxxxxxxxxxxxxxxxxxxxxxxxxx
SolomonIsds	1945	?	
SouthAfrica	1930Wh	1933	xxx
	1994Bl	1994	
Spain	1931	1931	
SriLanka	1931	1931	
Suriname	1953	?	
Swaziland	1968	?	
Sweden	1918-21	1921	xxx
Switzerland	1971	1971	
Syria	1949	1958	xxxxxxxxx
Thailand	1932	1949	xxxxxxxxxxxxxxx
Togo	1956	?	
Tonga	1960	1993	xxxxxxxxxxxxxxxxxxxxxxxxxxxxxxxxxx
Trin&Tobago	1946	1971	xxxxxxxxxxxxxxxxxxxxxxx
Tunisia	1959	1959	
Turkey	1930-4	1930-4	
Tuvalu	?	1989	
Uganda	1962	1962nom	
USSR	1918	1922	xxxx
UnArabEm	NO	NO	
UK	1918	1919	x
UnRepTanzania	1959	?	
USA	1920 *		
Uruguay	1932	1942	xxxxxxxxxx
Vanuatu	1980	?	
Venezuela	1947	1948	x
VietNam	1946	?	
W Samoa	1990	?	
Yemen	1967-70	1970	xxx
Yugoslavia	1949*		
Zaire	1962	1964	xx
Zambia	1962	1964	xx
Zimbabwe	1957	?	

*Eligible to Represent before Voting Franchise
Source: IPU,1992 (updated w/IPU 1994)

Analyzing the lapse data further, Figure 8 divides the female franchise into three historic eras, presumably watersheds in notions about adult self-determination and socio-economic/cultural change. The first era goes through 1920 and the conclusion of first World War. The second goes from 1921 through 1945 and the conclusion of World War II. The third covers the rise of the United Nations, national self-determination, and decolonization for vast regions of the globe, presumably the era in which women's civic adulthood would be recognized.

FIGURE 8

Average years, vote to representation by era

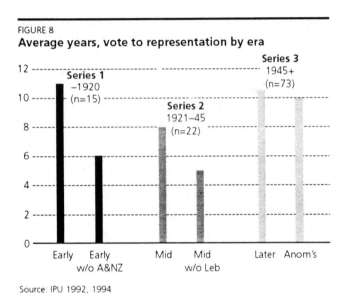

Source: IPU 1992, 1994

Curiously, Table 11 does not bear out expectations of shorter lapse times between franchise and elected women in later eras. Early franchise-granting countries, with over a 10-year lapse, drop down to a 6-year lapse when excluding the two pioneering franchise granters, New Zealand and Australia.[6] The middle era displays the smallest lapse time, almost 8 years but down to just over 5 when Lebanon is excluded (Lebanon's extremely lengthy lapse would distort this overall pattern.) In the later era, the lapse surpasses 10 years, dropping down slightly when anomolous countries (granting franchise in 1980+) are excluded.

The explanation for these inconclusive findings is probably found in the organizational empowerment that emerges from

a women's suffrage struggle. The fallout of struggle produces a shorter lapse time than the kind of struggle and empowerment derived from participation in nationalist movements. Yet mixed in the later group are countries both compatible with and hostile to gender egalitarianism, based on religious grounds. This complicates the picture still further.

To what extent do women vote, or turn out to vote at rates comparable or larger than men? The right to vote does not produce instantaneously high female turnout rates.[7]

Few countries regularly report and tabulate turnout by gender. A recent collection of 43 country studies sought, but could not obtain findings for all but a few countries (Nelson and Chowdhury 1994:50-51). In the Costa Rica and Philippines best case countries, as well as in France (Jenson & Sineau 1994:248) women's turnout rates equalize and surpass men's in most elections. In Japan and the U.S., women's turnout initially lagged but then surpassed male turnout. Larger <u>absolute</u> numbers of women add potentially huge numbers of female votes, even with a seemingly small <u>proportional</u> turnout difference. In India, turnout gaps halved by 1984 to a 9.6% difference (Swarup 1994:368), comparable to Switzerland's turnout gap in 1987 (Stampfli 1994: 701).

Turnout alone does not work miracles, as demonstrated in the Japan and U.S. cases. (See Japan case later.) In the U.S., women's energetic participation in movement and establishment politics has yet to produce high payoffs in representation (9%, nationally) or policy outcomes, where numerous competing civil organizations compete and undermine each others' possible gains. Moreover, the gender gap since 1980 has been to some extent a liberal-conservative gap; the conservative party used this gap to mobilize a male backlash in successful off-year 1994 elections.

Thus, high female turnout does not necessarily predict balanced political representation or gender-fair policies. Important factors that mediate that connection include <u>awareness of the "gender gap."</u> (to candidates and to voters, through the media) and a <u>gendered policy agenda</u>, around which voters can cohere. High female turnout can sustain this agenda. Mexico's 1994 Presidential electoral campaigns were filled with numerous surveys that broke down data by gender and other demographic characteristics. While many doubted the accuracy of surveys in this political culture, highly suspicious of establishment politics, widespread reporting made gender difference visible. The next step will involve speculation and strategizing about the likely partisan winners and losers of such difference.

In some countries, official bodies and/or NGOs take steps

to promote civic education or to make women's citizenship as fully real as men's. The IPU reports responses from 81 countries (of 150 countries with representative bodies) which have official bodies concerned with women, 24 of them ministry-level and 57 of them with other bodies. Of these 81, 34 devote staff and budgetary resources toward promoting political participation (1992: 37). Women's activists who are wary of state initiatives wonder: whose partisan and policy interests will be thereby served? What are the costs of cooptation and dependency? (see various chapters in Staudt 1990).

Sorting out the explanations of women's representation by human development priority and culture is difficult, as they interact on each other. We have yet to discuss institutions, the following explanation, with promising prospects for change. Using multiple regression analysis, Norris examined culture and institutions with data from two decades ago in 24 economically developed democracies (18 of which were in Europe). She constructed an index on political egalitarianism from a 1977 Euro-barometer survey (N=8,791), measured strength of Catholicism versus Protestantism, (hypothesizing less traditionalism for the latter), and used UNESCO educational data. The results showed that **institutional factors (specifically, proportional representation) were most significant for explaining women's representation,** followed by the egalitarianism index. Catholicism was relatively insignificant (Norris 1985). Given the strong showing for institutional factors, we turn to those below.

EXPLANATION #3: Institutional Factors

Institutional change is commonplace, inducing potentially speedy changes in human development priorities and reconstructing culture. For women, the optimal institutions provide ideological choices in multi-party systems, wherein women have established an organizational base to support female candidates, to connect with women's organizations, and to transform party policy agendas.

Parties in Different Electoral Systems

Parties, weak and strong, come in all sorts of ideological stripes and types. At their most basic level, parties nominate and support candidates for office. Strong parties cohere around policy areas and ideologies, a coherence that guides the behavior of political representatives, both executive and legislative. Parties frequently provide a machine-like grid to which organized sectors of the population affiliate and through which patronage is delivered during campaigns and in

between elections. When women are absent from decision-making positions in parties, their voices go unheard in setting policy agendas and in receiving patronage benefits and jobs.

The strength and coherence of parties depend heavily on the type of electoral system in which they compete. Proportional representation (PR) systems promote multiple parties along a left-right ideological spectrum. In single-member (SM), winner-take-all ("first past the pole") systems, fewer parties (two or three large parties) compete for the ideological center.

Scholarly studies consistently show that women's representation is higher in proportional representation in which parties develop lists of potential winners (Rule 1987; 1994). Rule conducted multivariate analyses in established democracies and found electoral system to be the most important predictor of women's representation, exlaining 30% of the variance (other, lesser factors were cultural, socioeconomic (including education) and political) (consistent with Norris' earlier data, 1985).

Figure 9 below enlarges the sample to democracies and nondemocracies in all world regions.

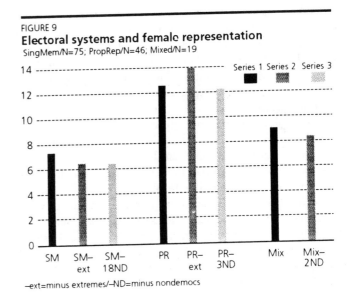

FIGURE 9
Electoral systems and female representation
SingMem/N=75; PropRep/N=46; Mixed/N=19

Series 1 Series 2 Series 3

SM   SM–ext   SM–18ND   PR   PR–ext   PR–3ND   Mix   Mix–2ND

–ext=minus extremes/–ND=minus nondemocs

The data show striking differences between SM and PR systems. Among the 74 SM systems, women's national representation falls below the global norm, worsened by removing three high extremes (which are double the global average) and then reduced slightly with the removal of 18 nondemocratic (as defined by Freedom House, 1994) countries. Among the PR systems, representation rates surpass global norms, approaching the critical mass, "skewed participation" so crucial to building a base of support for coalition building. The average jumps to 14% with removal of the five low extremes (mostly Mediterranean countries, including Turkey, which show PR produces no miracles). With the removal of 3 nondemocratic countries (as defined by Freedom House 1994), women's representation under PR still surpasses 12%. Interestingly, about a fourth of SM systems (18/74) are nondemocratic, compared to just a fraction of PR systems (3/46).

The PR advantage over SM is vividly conveyed as well through contrasts within nations with mixed systems, (which do better overall than pure SM), specifying PR for one and SM for another group of seats. Germany's women received 12.2% of seats from SM vote and 28.4% of seats from PR (Rule's 1987-1991 count, 1994:17); Japan's upper house contains some PR seats, and women obtained 24% of those seats versus 2.3% in the lower, more powerful house in Rule's same count. Japan's lower house in IPU's 1994 data shows 2.7% women and 14.7%, upper. In 1979, France elected 4% women to its National Assembly with its two-ballot SM system, but 21% of the French delegation to the EEC Parlaiament with a PR system (Norris 1985:99). Germany's latest election in 1994 produced even more dramatic gains for women in PR seats:39%. One legacy of British and French colonialism in Africa was SM; interestingly, Senegal adopted both SM and PR and its 12% female representation rate surpasses the 8% continental norm.

PR displays better chances for women for several reasons. Once women have a toe-hold inside party machinery, they can use leverage to promote female candidacy goals, targets, and quotas (on the success of this strategy in the Netherlands, see Leijenaar and Niemoller 1994). Green parties typically take the approach, "every other name a woman" on lists. Without women's action, female candidates may find themselves on the bottom of lists, in unwinnable slots as is common in Peru. A woman generally does better without head-on-head competition with a man. Finally, gender-conscious voters seek a diverse list. In a "closed list" internal process, parties make placement choices, but in other PR voter-preference formats, voters rank candidates. This has worked to women's advantage in Norway, when women mobilize voters to support women candidates.

Exit from Established Parties: Women's Parties

In frustration with exclusion or meaningless policy platforms, women have formed their own parties. Countries which have, or once had, such parties are listed below (from IPU 1992:63-65, responses from 150 countries with representative bodies and other sources).

Canada
Chile
Egypt
Finland
Iceland
Norway
Philipppines
Republic of Korea
Russia
Sweden
United States
(former) Yugoslavia

Women's parties win few seats, particularly in single-member systems. However, women's exit from established parties can pressure those parties to change procedures and policies in order to entice their return. Women's parties produce mixed results, as examples show. Iceland's Women's Alliance (the women's party) formed in 1983, concerned over the inadequate number of women on established party lists. It mobilized women to vote for women's lists in two municipal councils, where they received 12% and 18% of the vote; subsequently women M.P.s increased from 4 to 15 percent of the national parliament as other parties made overtures to them (Dominelli and Jonsdottir 1988). Iceland also has a favorable electoral system (party list, and rules which permit small party representation); results under SM would not be the same. The early twentieth century U.S. women's party helped institutionalize the division between equal rights and social feminists. Just after women obtained the vote in Norway, in 1901, they proposed women's lists "becoming parties in all but name" (Norderval 1985:75). Karlsson also reports on the Association for Women's Slates in Sweden, formed in the 1920s and acting like a party, which proposed women candidates (1994). Russia's women's party won 23 of 450 seats in the 1993 elections.

Balanced Parties: Ideology Makes a Difference

Parties with the best gender balance are "Green" (environmental) parties, followed with leftist parties. Rightist parties take the least action on balanced representation. While women do not vote as a bloc (the same is true for men), women were once thought to be more conservative and religious. However, beginning in the 1970s, conservative parties' edge with women no longer held in Britain, France, and Germany (Walker 1994). This electoral loss may prompt conservative parties to win back more women. Germany's conservative Christain Democratic Union instituted 30% female quotas in 1994, an action which may be interpreted as such.

Female Party Leadership

Women's presence in party governing bodies is an obvious indicator of commitment to balance. Ranging from 0 to half, a typical level of female representation is 10%, based on responses to IPU 1992 surveys. In the largest country of the world, women represent 5.7% of Central Committee members of the Chinese Communist Party (a contrast to its 21% female representation in the 2,978-person legislature).

Once inside parties, through what Leijenaar calls "infiltration" in her review of national reports at a European Commision conference (1994), women and supportive men take steps to increase female representation. Among these are goals and quotas for representation within parties and candidate lists. Political parties in 34 countries have established quotas, binding and voluntary for governing bodies and for legislative elections. Of course, not all parties within countries adopt such quotas, and some countries spawn multitudes of parties, many of which will not survive in subsequent elections (i.e. 150 are registered in Romania, and 70 in Poland [1991 figures]). Finland, with 38.5% women parliamentarians, has no party-based quota system (IPU 1992:98).

Attempts to do quantitative analysis of party quotas for legislative elections and their effects on female representation are fraught with difficulty. This is because some, but not all parties generally establish a quota, and the figures we have for female representation are for the whole parliament. Moreover, not all reports to IPU are complete in, for example, the numeric figure for the quota. Some countries fail to establish quotas that rise above the global norm of 10%, at which female representation is stuck. Perhaps those parties would be even less representative without quotas. Generally, though, Table 11 shows that party quotas favor greater female representation and that and centrist, left, and opposition parties are the usual adopters of quotas (bicameral systems are averaged).

Table 11. Legislative Quotas and Female Representation

Angola 10% (?%)
Belgium 10% (CVP;20%PS;20%PVV **only**)
Colombia 9% (**all** ?%)
Denmark 33% (40%: SocDemo & Soc People's **only**)
Germany 18% (40% SoDemo & 50% Greens **only**)
Morocco 1% (Istiqlal, 10% **only**)
Netherlands 28% (33% PvdA; 40% GroenLink; 26% CDA **only**)
Norway 39% (40%: Lab,SocLeft; others have 40% "objectives")
Portugal 9% (25%, Soc **only**)
Switzerland 13% (35% ChDemo; 50% Greens **only**)
Turkey 2% (25% SoDemoPop **only**)
UK 8% (Lab; 33% LibDemo **only**)
Venezuela 10% (20% AcDemo;COPEI;20% Soc **only**)

Although rare, women lead parties: in several South Asian countries, they control as many as two parties. Four women lead parties in Finland, two for the parliamentary group. Maria de los Angeles Moreno assumed leadership in Mexico's largest party, but was ousted within a year. Leaders are poised in positions with the opportunity to divide women or to build cross-partisan women's coalitions. In Germany, Federal Parliamentary leader Rita Sussmuth successfully supported a cross-partisan compromise that put women in greater control over reproductive decisions about their bodies than the Women's Minister (a law subsequently overturned in 1993 by the court) (Lempke 1994). In Poland, one reason former Prime Minister Hanna Suchocka was an acceptable appointee was that she did not support women's groups' stance against criminalizing abortion.

Increasing Female Membership

Parties typically include few involved, card-carrying members. How do they increase membership among women, thereby improving the future pipeline of women into party leadership and possible candidacies? To facilitate attendance at party events, many parties worldwide schedule meetings at family-friendly times and provided nurseries for children. Parties train the underrepresented and subsidize their campaigns. Parties have also set targets and timetables for increased female representation at conventions. Such strategies were pursued in the U.S., even as state primary election results--not convention attendees--drove presidential nominations, thereby undermining the significance of this achievement. Women's branches have the potential to empower women in parties, but they can have quite the opposite effect when isolated, marginalized, and simply used as cheap labor to mobilize the vote. The few scholarly studies on women's branches (on Zambia, Tanzania, the U.S., Mexico, Malaysia), paint a mixed picture on their effectiveness

45

(see review in Staudt 1989; Geisler, 1995), as do responses to the IPU questionnaire (1992).

FIGURE 10
Party building blocks

Quotas toward parity, legislative
Quotas toward parity, appointive
Quotas toward parity, governance
Women's branches
Targeted objectives
Campaign subsidies
Training candidates
Nurseries/family-friendly space
Family-friendly meeting times

State-Driven Institutional Reforms

Besides parties, states take steps to increase female representation though quotas, reservations, and appointments for candidacies or results (seats in a representative body). In the responses of 150 countries to IPU questionnaires, five countries identified quotas to ensure female presence in their representative bodies. (IPU says such devices probably exist in more countries.) IPU identifies two countries in transition (Namibia and Russia (the quota law was "USSR 1988"), so comparisons with representation results are inappropriate. Results below provide mixed signals on quotas for improving representation.

*In 1991, the Congress in Argentina passed the Ley de Cupos with strong support from the President, the national women's council, and the President's Gabinete de Consejeras Presidenciales (cabinet of women presidential advisors). The law requires that all parties list 30% women on winnable seats. Some parties resisted, but the law was enforced with the threat and action of lawsuits. For the decade before the law, women's representation was stuck below 4%; after the law, it rose to 21% (1993) and 29% (1995) (Jones forthcoming, who also reports "contagion effects," as 17 of 23 provinces subsequently implemented quota laws).

*Nepal's 1990 Constitution required that 5% of party and organizational candidates be women. IPU reports that the 1991 elections produced 0 women in the National Council,

and 3.4% women in the House of Representatives. (UN's WW reports 5.7% for 1987).

*The Philippines Constitution of 1987 addresses class, gender, indigenous and age targets for list-based selection in three subsequent legislative periods. The mixed group of representatives and the 20% figure for list seats makes percentage comparisons irrelevant for the Philippines.

The review of this small group of countries with government-imposed quotas reveals the promising opportunities that quotas have for rapid increases in female representation. Of course, quotas have no meaning when they go unenforced. Also, some quotas are set at levels too low to move women near or above the global, imbalanced norm.

Women occupy reserved seats in only four countries: Bangladesh, Nepal, Pakistan, and Tanzania. Women are seated through election and appointment, and therefore, connections with and accountability to women and women-friendly organizations are unknown or questionable. Egypt abandoned its 1979 reservation system for the People's Assembly and municipal councils when the term of reserving women's seats ended in 1990. The pre-reservation figure of 2% (national) went up to 4% with reservation, then subsequently down again to 2%, post-reservation.

Table 12: Reserved Seats: Floor or Ceiling for Women?

Bangladesh:10% (30 of 330 reserved; total women 34/330)
Nepal:3% (10 of 205 appointed; 7 are women)
Pakistan:2% (20 seats reserved for women, but IPU reports 1/87 in Senate and 4/217 in Nat'l Assembly 1994)
Tanzania:11% (15 seats reserved for women; total 28)

Of these IPU-reported cases, only Tanzania represents an unambiguous success for reserved seats, with almost double the number of women than reserved seats. Bangladesh has just four more. In Pakistan, reserved seats go unfilled, and the law, unenforced.

Another unambiguous success exists, however invisible its record in UN and IPU lists. Taiwan established its reserved seat system which not only encouraged women to run, but encouraged parties to nominate women to avoid wasting the seats. The system was installed in 1953 (women received voting rights in 1937) at national, provincial, and local levels. Initially, during the 1950s, women surpassed their minimum number, but this improved in the 1970s and 1980s, when women jumped to 11% and finally 13% at the national level. The results at the local level were even more dramatic, moving women from .002% of seats in 1952 township and village councils to 15% more recently. Importantly, though, no reserved seats exist for executive positions (Chou and Clark 1994).

Far more widespread is the practice of <u>appointment</u> to representative bodies. "First-time women" entered via this route in Dominica, Indonesia, Mexico, Norway, Saint Lucia, and Uganda. A full 44 countries appoint women to their representative bodies. In the United Arab Emirates, where all parliamentarians are appointed, a woman has never been appointed. Table 13 shows those countries, with percent female representation in the body, the number of appointed seats of the total seats, and the number of women in that selected group shown in parentheses.

Table 13: Appointments for Women to Parliament

Afghanistan (3%1991) 64/192 Senate (0 women)
Antigua & Barbuda 18% all-appointee Senate of 17 (3)
Bahamas 19% all-appointee Senate of 16 (3)
Barbados 29% of all-appointee Senate of 21 (6)
Belgium (11%) 27/184 Senate (?)
Belize 22% all-appointee Senate of 9 (2)
Botswana (5%) 4/40 Nat'l Assy (?)
Canada (15%) all-appointee Senate of 104 (elsewhere 110)(16)
Chile (7%) 9/48 Senate (l)
Dominica (13%) 9/31 unicameral (?)
Egypt (2%) 10/454 unicameral ("a number of"the 10=women)
Equitorial Guinea (9%) 25% of 60 men and women (?)
Gabon (6) 9/120 unicameral (?)
Gambia (8%) 9/51 (?)
Germany (15%) all appointee Fed Council (?)
Grenada (15%) all-appointee Senate (?)
India (7%) 12/245 Council of States (?)
Indonesia (12%) 100/500 unicameral (?)
Ireland (13%) 11/60 Senate (?)
Jamaica (14%) all-appointee Senate (4)
Jordan (5%) all-appointee Senate (1)
Kenya (3%) 12/202 unicameral (0)
Kiribati (0%) 1/41 (0)
Kuwait (0%) 25/75 unicameral (0)
Malawi (6%) unlimited #/112 unicameral (7)
Malaysia (20%) 43/69 Senate (?)
Maldives (4%) 8/48 unicameral (?)

Mauritius (3%) 8/70 unicameral (?)
Namibia (7%) 6/72 unicameral (?)
Nepal (0%) 10/60 Natl Council (0)
Philippines (11%) 13/200 (1)
Saint Kitts and Nevis(6%) 3/15 (?)
Saint Lucia (36%) all-appointee Senate (2)
Saint Vincent and the Grenadines (13%) 6/21 unicameral (?)
Seychelles (27%) 2/25 (?)
Sierre Leone (?) 10/27 unicameral (?)
Swaziland (20%) 10/20 Senate (?); (3%) House 10/50 (?)
Thailand (3%) 292/292 (elsewhere 360) House (15, or ?)
Trinidad and Tobago (23%)all-appointee Senate (4)
Uganda(17%) 68/270 unicameral (?)
United Arab Emirates (0%) all appointee Council (0)
Tanzania (11%) 15/255 (15 reserved for women)
Yemen(1%) 31/301 unicameral (?)
Zimbabwe (12%) 30/150 unicameral (4)

This table shows a large number of countries with one body of a bicameral system which is an all-appointee body. Particularly in Caribbean countries, appointments have gone to more than a single, token woman, up to six (Barbados) and over a third (numbering just 2 women) in Saint Lucia. Appointment procedures like these inflate figures for parliamentary representation in what are usually the less powerful, upper houses. Few women are actually involved due to the small size of the upper body. The overall message conveyed in this list is the generally stinginess of appointers (the positions of whom are unknown in the IPU list). With 12, 30, 43, 60, 68, 100, or 292 slots, how else do we interpret just 0 to 7 women (save Tanzania, at 15)? Of course, just as with reservation systems, questions might be raised about female appointees' accountability to women.

Special measures like these are controversial. Little dispute exists that they open doors for women and provide valuable experience both to women AND to recalcitrant men who learn that women can do representative work. Without established connections to women's organizations, we know little about women's willingness to invest political capital into gender-fair policies. Regimes that lack political will to be accountable to women either display little energy into enforcing special measures or appoint women in minimal numbers.

Appointments can falsely inflate the real representation of women's interests. Eastern European countries, once exhibiting high rates of female representation, experienced drastic drops in the transition to multi-party elections in the

1980s and thereafter, as discussed. While this is cause for concern, single-party appointments did not guarantee quality, accountable representative but rather "quantitative decoration" in some instances (Poland's response, IPU 1992:101; Siemienska in Jaquette and Wolchik 1992:7).

SUCCESSFUL AND UNSUCCESSFUL CASES: TEN COUNTRIES

We now turn to country cases, by world region. These ten countries contain distinctive features, sometimes comparable to neighboring countries, which add considerable insight to the largely quantitative analysis above. Readers should evaluate these cases in regional context, for a "best" case in one region may appear unsuccessful in another region.

How was the pool of nearly two hundred country cases narrowed? Four criteria were used. First, only **civilian democratic or partially democratic regimes** were used. Military control is incompatible with democracy. Also excluded were nondemocratic countries, even from the unsuccessful case list. Thus, these unsuccessful countries do not represent the worst abuses.

Second, **relative stability** was a criterion, excluding those with ethnic strife, ongoing and/or recent civil war. Several South Asian countries were excluded for this reason. South Africa, with its promising 1994 election, was also considered too recent a democracy with too many deep-seated problems to make a "success" call at this point. Uganda has a strong representation record for women, but its post civil war transition is under nonparty leadership highly dependent on a single leader. In such circumstances, succession could provoke political crisis.

Third, countries were chosen **with sufficient research** studies, optimally conducted by nationals from those countries. Fourth, success cases required documentation of **women's organizational activities**. This criterion aided in making judgements about relatively promising cases in a single region. For example, both Turkey and Tunisia have adopted secular law with Turkey confronting the challenge of a national rather than religious identity well before Tunisia. Tunisia has a higher female representation rate (7% versus 2%), though no female executive. Turkey, however, has flourishing women's organizations which are actively engaged in politics.

A F R I C A

Unsuccessful Case:

"Kenya: Male Political Machinery"

In terms of the conceptual model, Kenya's socio-economic conditions are incompatible with engendered politics. While women join many groups to address their practical interests, these and a fledgling women's movement are not engaged with conventional politics in ways to advance their concerns. Socioeconomic development is such that men and women are highly differentiated from one another; fertility, once highest in Africa, has only recently begun to decline somewhat. The trade union movement is small and male dominated, as nonagricultural female labor generates income largely in the informal sector. Civil organizations are registered and suspect, for many are presumed to cause ethnic tension. Gendered voter turnout data are unavailable. Women's voices are too weak in conventional politics to be heard, and policy levers such as the women's bureau are minuscule.

History and Culture

Frequently touted as a continental success story, Kenya has good economic potential and reasonable growth rates. Its recent history involved a violent nationalist struggle over land: European settlers, who occupied great expanses of ranch and farmland, had deep stakes in this former British colony. Kenyans achieved their independence in 1963 and enjoyed a seemingly multi-party parliamentary democracy. Quickly it became evident to opposition party members that power, patronage, and political survival lie with loyalty to the single party, the Kenya African National Union (KANU). Power and authority revolved personally around the Founding Father Jomo Kenyatta, succeeded after his death by current President Daniel arap Moi.

Governance in Kenya involves the complex management of forty ethnic groups, which coincide with region, through the distribution of patronage. Ethnicity is politicized, due to real and perceived disparities in the distribution process. Through regular parliamentary elections every five years, voters choose among competing candidates within KANU. Cynicism grew over widespread allegations of corruption and a queueing system for primary elections, whereby voters exposed the nominee of their choice publicly and at political risk to themselves. Mounting pressure to restore multi-party democracy led to elections in 1992, wherein KANU emerged victorious amid a divided opposition.

Women, the backbone of the agricultural economy and trade, participate extensively in formal and informal women's groups. Some of these groups receive support for income-generating activities from the government Women's Bureau, established in 1975, and subsumed in the Ministry of Culture and Social Services. Women's programs account for a fraction of a percent of government spending. Public subsidies and patronage flow overwhelmingly through the political machinery that men monopolize more thoroughly than any other country on the continent. Some male politicians voice the same kinds of stereotyped comments about women whose proportional participation is highly skewed, as did some Europeans about Africans (men) when their participation was similarly skewed during the colonial era.

Politics and Policy

Women, whose parliamentary representation hovers below 2% on average, never occupied more than 4% of seats. In 1994, women occupy 6 of 202 seats, or 3% of the parliament. One woman currently sits in the 27-person cabinet. Before that, not a single woman had served on the cabinet since independence, though women have served in subcabinet posts. Legal pluralism prevails, making women vulnerable in matters of marriage, divorce, and inheritance. This legal vulnerability was personified in the famous case of Wambui Otieno, denied the right to bury her deceased husband according to their wishes.

The Maendeleo ya Wanawake (Progress of Women), formed under tainted colonial conditions during nationalist struggle in 1952, grew after independence to become the oldest and largest women's organization. By the mid 1980s, it claimed a third of a million members. KANU moved to take political control of the organization in 1987, to strengthen its political hold over larger segments of society, on the pretext of financial mismanagement (the organization has been courted by international organizations and donors). This dealt a major blow to a civil organization. Another large umbrella organization, the National Council of Women of Kenya, had uneasy relations with the independent Maendeleo; its willingness to take positions sometimes contrary to government has led to intimidation of its leaders.

Women's inability to engage the male political machinery with independence and leverage helps explain their paltry access to political goods, such as credit and patronage employment. As or more significantly, women's silence over policies which acknowledge their significance for the economy, but aim to extract maximal labor from them, do not bode well for growing gender disparities in income,

opportunities, and control.

Outside the official development agenda, women continue to face problems of personal security and safety from male violence. The mass rape and death of secondary school girls in the St. Kizito tragedy in 1991 represents Kenya's infamy in this regard. Nineteen girls died and 79 were raped.

Sources:

Maria Nzomo and Kathleen Staudt, "Man-Made Political Machinery in Kenya: Political Space for Women?" in Barbara Nelson and Najma Chowdhury, eds. Women and Politics Worldwide (Yale University Press 1994), pp. 416-435. This chapter contains 79 footnotes, many of them with multiple citations. Noteworthy among them is:

Mary Adhiambo Mbeo and Oki Ooko-Ombaka, eds. Women and Law in Kenya: Perspectives and Emerging Issues (Nairobi: Public Law Institute 1989).

Patricia Stamp, "Burying Otieno: The Politics of Gender and Ethnicity in Kenya," Signs 16, 4 (1991), 808-845.

Successful Case

"Ghana: Women's Cultural and Economic Resources"

In terms of the conceptual model, socio-economic conditions are compatibile with engendered politics. Although hierarchical, indigenous sources of authority accorded political voices to women (queens) who spoke for and adjudicated women's interests. Women's public labor is valued in famous markets and trading networks, from coast to upcountry. Women's practical interest groups interact with formal women's movements to articulate concerns in the so-called Rawlings populist democracy which established local institutional machinery and revenue generation that prioritized markets and to a lesser extent, child-care centers. No gender data on turnout exist, but women are visibly engaged with the political process. Women are weakly represented in institutions, but at rates that are growing.

History and Culture

Ghana, considered a disaster case economically and politically during part of the post-independence period, survived structural adjustment and multiple military coups. It held multi-party elections in early 1993, after local elections five years before. Incumbent leader Jerry Rawlings and his organization emerged victorious, and although irregularities were alleged, election results appear credible.

Ghana achieved independence after more than a half century of British rule. Prime Minister Kwame Nkrumah, prominent in the Organization of African Unity, enshrined the significance of politics in his famous remark: Seek ye first the political kingdom. Six years after victory, single-party rule, coupled with economic difficulties and corruption, was replaced with a series of military rulers alternating with civilian rule. In 1979, Flight Lt. Rawlings intervened in politics temporarily, then permanently in 1981.

Parliamentary and military rule have been imposed upon communal, but hierarchical monarchies and other indigenous political structures. Among the Akan people, whose traditions affect nearly half the population, kings AND queens had significant authority. Although hierarchical, decision-making aimed to settle conflict through seeking consensus. Women traditionally exercised rights over their income and property amid many female responsibilities. They participated in women's organizations and mutual aid societies, on which Nkrumah capitalized in the nationalist movement and through the women's wing of his Convention People's Party. During economic downturn, women traders joined those calling for change. Military rule drew less on female representation, a change under Rawlings.

Politics and Policy

A variety of boards and commissions, through military rule, maintained visibility for women and children. The National Council on Women and Development, represented on other boards and seating women and men to represent women, has high stature. The National Commission on Children is another such body. Rawlings' Provisional National Defence Council (PNDC), a military-civilian body, was initially all male, but it added prominent women members with links to women's constituencies. Ghana had the largest number of women cabinet members for Africa in 1989 (including a man on the PNDC to represent women and development); a tenth of 84 government appointees were women.

In the 1989 district elections, comprised of two-thirds elected posts and one-third appointees, women secured 7% of seats. Four percent of candidates were female, but 3% of seats were won by women; government appointments inflated female representation. In the 1993 national elections, the 31st December Women's Movement (DWM), led by Rawlings' wife but representing a wide base of female support, helped

bring victory to Rawlings. Women won 7.5% of seats in the parliament, and secured 4 of 24 seats on the cabinet, or 14.3% The DWM receives government subsidies to construct markets and day care centers through the district assemblies, responsible for development projects.

Structural adjustment programs bear heavily on women, with cuts in human development spending such as education and health. Ghana was one of the ten countries featured in UNESCO's two-volume Adjustment with a Human Face. New user fees for health and other state services frequently come out of women's pockets. With economic collapse, women cocoa farmers were unable to hire labor, thereby augmenting other women in state-neglected food farming. Man y joined migrant husbands in urban areas, becoming isolated from traditional assistance from their kinship groups and from the income-generating activities off land.

Economic collapse was also devastating for women traders in urban areas. During the mid-1980s, the PNDC developed new laws to encourage men to support their children which formerly relatively autonomous wives in this largely matrilineal area increasingly could not do with hard economic times. The 1985 legislation emphasized male-female "interdependence." Cases brought before family tribunals in the 1980s demonstrated that women could use the courts to their advantage. However, courts and statutes neither acknowledge nor protect women from commonplace domestic violence.

Five years after its Structural Adjustment Program, Ghana received multi-donor support in a Programme of Actions to Mitigate the Social Costs of Adjustment (PAMSCAD), totalling US$90 million. Such efforts helped cushion adjustment burdens for women. The PNDC's political survival through democratic transition may also be linked to this effort.

Sources:

Crook, Richard C. "Four Years of the Ghana District Assemblies in Operation," Public Administration & Development 14 (1994)339-364.

Haynes, Jeff, "Sustainable Democracy in Ghana? Problems and Prospects," Third World Quarterly 14, 3 (1993) 451-468.

Mikell, Gwendolyn, "Women and Economic Development in Ghana: Fluctuating Fortunes," Sage VII, 1 (1990), 24-27.

Ofei-Aboagye, Rosemary Ofeibea, "Altering the Strands of the Fabric: A Preliminary Look at Domestic Violence in Ghana,"

Signs 19, 4 (1994), 925-938.

Pepera, J. Sandra, "Political Parties and Social Representation: The Case of Women," in Political Parties and Democracy in Ghana's Fourth Republic, eds Kwame Ninsin & F. K. Drah (Acra: Woeli Publishing 1993, pp. 133-148.

Kamene Okonjo, "Women and the Evolution of a Ghanaian Political Synthesis," in Barbara Nelson and Najma Chowdhury, eds. Women and Politics Worldwide (Yale University Press 1994), 285-297.

A S I A

Unsuccessful Case

"Japan: Has the Mountain Moved?"*

Little in Japan's culture is compatible with increased female representation. Egalitarian traditions do not prevail (Japan is, in Hofstede's analysis a high-power distance country, and THE most masculine (95) of all countries he sampled.). Women dutifully turn out to vote, but only occasionally make an impact such as the 1989 elections about which outrage was expressed over consumer taxes. Women's representation levels are minuscule, even at local levels. However, women made notable efforts to ratify CEDAW, which government took seriously for the necessary legal changes to be made.

History and Culture

Japan embarked upon its rapid modernization project in 1868, establishing a partially democratic parliamentary regime in 1890. Militarism and war were setbacks to this partial democracy. After World War II, a foreign-imposed constitution reestablished a parliamentary form of government (the bi-cameral Diet), with a more powerful lower house. Men have monopolized political and governmental decision-making positions until the post-war constitution granted women suffrage and the right to serve in public office in 1945. Yet the percentage of women in office puts Japan at the lowest rank of industrialized countries (Nuita, citing InterParliamentary Union, 1994: 409).

As a late feudal regime, Japan's steeply hierarchical status relations and elements of Confucian ideology permeated culture and society well into the twentieth century. Confucian legacies emphasize harmony, making it difficult and rare to articulate grievances. Those groups marked as status inferiors, including women, youth, and burakumin (hereditary members of outcaste status, officially emancipated in 1871), DO seek change, but their protests encounter government strategies to pre-empt, contain and/or marginalize efforts in ways that make sustained organization difficult. Japan's political culture stresses conflict avoidance, harmony, and deference to authority--all factors which limit criticism and protest (Pharr 1990: Chs 1-2).

Despite the existence of laws and abstract principles, decision-making vaguely drifts in search of quiescent consensus, making it difficult to establish accountability and responsibility (Pye 1985:174ff).

Amid this hierarchical, nonconfrontational political culture exists a gendered culture which puts special obstacles in front of women as public representatives or of those seeking male-female equality. Japanese society exhibits high gender polarity, assigning women to valued domestic and men to public domains in relatively rigid, time-consuming, and segregated ways. The Labor Ministry conducted a survey of working couples' housework in 1990; wives spent an average of 210 minutes daily, and husbands, 8 minutes (reported in Reingold 1992:119). In a 1989 study of 20,000 housewives and female labor force participants, women averaged six hours housework daily (Iwao 1993:33). Although the birth rate is low, women invest considerable time and labor in child-rearing, especially in encouraging children to excel in school (as the widely known term, "Education Mothers," suggests). Women work outside the home in large numbers, but often in parttime or temporary positions. Their significant household duties compete with the long hours necessary for professional and political careers. As important, many women are indifferent to and/or disgusted with politics (Iwao, 1993; Lebra 1984).

Politics and Policies

Despite voter turnout rates in national elections that surpass 70%, and female turnout that surpasses male, women's representation in public office is minimal. In 1993, women represented less than 3% of the lower House of Representatives, and 14.7% of the celebrity-filled upper House of Councillors (the latter, selected through proportional representation). At the local level, where women are more active in neighborhood organizations and schools, the number of women who have stood for local assemblies has nearly tripled since 1983, but they still represent less than 2% of representatives (Abe, et.al, 1994:70,222). The virtual silence of female voices is reflected in near genderless party agendas and limited policy action to alleviate social and economic inequalities.

In Japan's multi-party system, faction-ridden parties make no goals to improve representation for women. In only the Social Democratic Party of Japan (former Socialist Party) are quotas set for the national convention. Women's party sections, which do exist in major parties, have sought subsidies for campaigns in this money-ridden electoral process. Party governing parties reflect minuscule female leadership; the Liberal Democratic Party, with a female membership of 38%, has 1% women on its governing body. Party measures to facilitate women's participation are minimal; several parties set up nurseries or time meetings in line with women's schedules. The Liberal Democratic Party, learning from late 1980s experience, focuses on themes such as prices, taxes, and the environment, but also on the "wise use of hobbies." (Mortier, from party secretariats, 1994).

Nor do parties promote coherent policy or ideological agendas, with the exception of those on the left. Proportional representation, however, DOES improve women's representation, though this electoral method is limited to some seats in the less powerful upper house. Only after corruption and sex scandals of the 1980s did parties try to capitalize on the idea of change through supporting several high-visibility women. Women's grassroots activities peaked at that time, over issues like the consumption tax (women manage household budgets) and environmental pollution. Liberal Democratic Party M.P. Moriyama Mayumi, former labor vice minister, was given full cabinet status to improve public confidence in the party until it made a strong showing in a subsequent election when she was dropped. No woman currently sits on the cabinet.

The most highly visible political woman of recent years has been Doi Takako, who became leader of the Japan Socialist Party in 1986, a party which made major gains in 1989 (which were lost by 1991). In 1989, the Agricultural Minister questioned whether women had the right "instincts" for politics. He criticized Doi because she was unmarried and without children, thereby unproven in traditional roles (Iwao 1993: 223). He was thought to echo the thoughts of many men; female victories for other seats evoked male politicians' comments about the "stupid obasan" (aunts). After five years leading the party, Doi since went on to the Speakership in the House of Representatives. Her life-long poltical agenda has been linked to women's and citizens' movements, to foreign affairs and environmental policy, and to the human rights of Koreans in Japan (Stockwin 1994).

With frequent change and corruption in politics, govern-

ment bureaucracy brings stability to governance. Bureaucracy is also the chief institution from which politicians and cabinet members are recruited (Pye 1985: 175). Therefore, bureaucracy is crucial to women's representation and gender-fair policies. The chief advocates for women inside government are found in the Women's Bureau of the Labor Ministry and the Women's Section of the Prime Minister's Office. They have commissioned many studies on the discrepancies between male and female achievements. Women's managerial participation in other parts of the public sector is extremely limited. Public sector laws about hiring and promotion, however, are stricter and more carefully enforced.

While Japan adopted the CEDAW in 1979, it was reluctant to ratify, for officials found at least 150 laws that would require change. An International Women's Year Liaison Group, representing fifty organizations and many millions of members (not all of which view women's issues a priority), promoted ratification. The Government then ratified, and the Liaison Group works toward full implementation by the year 2000 (Nuita, et.al. 1994:402-3).

Women make up over two-fifths of the labor force, but equal employment opportunity is not part of their experience and gender wage gaps are wide. Only 2% of managers are female; strikingly, studies report the percentage of firms with ANY women managers (Steinhoff and Tanaka 1994:32-34), showing the widespread resistance to female leadership. An equal employment opportunity law, in effect since 1986, replaced protective labor laws for women which prohibited night work and provided menstrual leave. The new law lacks enforcement mechanisms. Combined with the nonconfrontational culture and the non-litigious nature of society, few complaints are resolved through the administration of justice.

The "revolt of the tea pourers" has now become a famous study on the micro-politics of work (Pharr 1990: Ch 4; 190-4). Many believe it is women workers' duty to serve tea, whatever their title. Office-based tea preparing and pouring is time-consuming and burdensome, a veritable symbol of status inequality and female service to men. When a group of women in a public bureaucracy mobilized against this task, not in their job definition, they achieved few long-term gains, their movement was isolated and contained, and much wrath was incurred among men.

Pornography, largely objectifying female images, is extensive, accessible in videos, comics, and street-level vending machines. Its pervasiveness legitimizes sexist attidues, according to women NGOs responding to the official CEDAW report. Moreover, sex tourism and trafficking in women, the latter illegal but from which officials turn away, affects foreign female workers and tourist locations outside the country (Ladin 1993).

Women's contraceptive choices are limited. The birth control pill is not legal, though condom use and abortion are widespread.

Future Trends

Although women in Japan live in one of the least promising contexts for balanced political representation, certain trends could predict change. First, women's widespread involvement in local organizations, including unpaid liaison work linking goverment and residents (Lebra 1984:282), provides them with knowledge and experience for transforming politics. Second, women gain visibility and experience in the upper house, even though is lacks much but the power to check the lower house. Third, disgust with corruption in politics could once again revive women's momentum toward involvement in politics, as well as political leaders to mobilize women. Finally, illegal immigration is on the rise in Japan, particularly of men since the late 1980s (Keiki 1993). White future policy might encourage more foreign labor, Japan might also enforce its equal employment opportunity laws and thereby look to its own labor force to deal with impending shortages.

Political culture limits the extent to which legalistic approaches will be effective and may slow change. The New National Action Programme for 2000, women's groups say, is based on an economic efficiency-first principle, to maximize profits and compensate for economic recession (Ladin, 1993, for women's NGOs on official CEDAW reports). When women share voices in future action programs, policy goals will better reflect all citizens.

*Doi Takako's optimistic remark of the late 1980s has been turned into a question.

Sources on Japan

NOTE: In accordance with Japanese practice, Japanese surnames are listed first without comma unless the author indicates otherwise.

Hitoshi Abe, Muneyuki Shindo, and Sadafumi Kawato, The Government and Politics of Japan (University of Tokyo Press, 1994)

Iwao, Sumiko, The Japanese Woman: Traditional Image and Changing Reality (Cambridge: Harvard University Press 1993)

Keiki Yamanaka, "New Immigration Policy in Japan and Unskilled Foreign Workers in Japan," Pacific Affairs 66,1(1993) 72-90.

Ladin, Sharon, IWRAW (International Women's Rights Action Watch) to CEDAW Country Reports (12 countries, including Japan), Hubert H. Humphrey Institute of Public Affairs, University of Minnesota, December, 1993.

Lebra, Takie Sugiyama, Japanese Women: Constraint and Fulfillment Honolulu: University of Hawaii Press, 1984)

Nuita Yoko, Yamaguchi Mitsuko, and Kubo Kimiko, "The U.N. Convention on Eliminating Discrimination Against Women and the Status of Women in Japan," inBarbara J.

Nelson and Najma Chowdhury, Women and Politics Worldwide (New Haven,CT: Yale University Press, 1994), 396-414.

Pharr, Susan J. Losing Face: Status Politics in Japan (Berkeley: University of California Press, 1990)

Pye, Lucian, Asian Power and Politics: the Cultural Dimensions of Authority (Cambridge: Harvard University Press, 1985), Ch 6.

Sawachi Hisae, "The Political Awakening of Women," Japan Quarterly (1989), 381-385.

Steinhoff, Patricia and Tanaka Kazuko, "Women Managers in Japan," International Studies of Management and Organization 23, 2 (1993), 28-48.

Stockwin, J. A. A., "Political Career of Doi Takako," Japan Forum 6, 1 (1994), 21-34.

Verba, Sidney, Norman H. Nie, and Kim Jae-on, Participation and Political Equality: A Seven-Nation Comparison (Cambridge: Cambridge University Press, 1978).

Successful Case

"Philippines: Women Occupy Democratic Space"

In terms of the conceptual model, the Philippines appears compatible with engendered politics. Indigenous traditions of gender egalitarianism prevail, and women's public labor is visible and valued. Low fertility rates are coupled with relatively widespread family planning (though not full reproductive choices). Occupational integration is evident in professional fields still highly segregated in industrial countries. A flourishing women's movement exists that connects with similarly flourishing gender research in university and congressional settings; these activities aid in developing a coherent gender policy agenda. Women's voter turnout typically surpasses men's, and women engage with the political process. In the transition to democracy, mostly female "Cory's Crusaders" mobilized around the support of former President Corazon Aquino. Although she did not bring **economic democracy** to her term, she was widely recognized as helping to bring procedural democracy into place. Women's strength in local and national representative offices is increasing, and policy levers exist throughout bureaucracy.

History and Culture

The Philippines achieved its independence from two colonial rulers, Spain and then the United States, in 1946 after foreign occupation during World War II. Besides colonial legacies, this archipelago of more than 7,000 islands also draws on Malay, indigenous, and Chinese cultures, as well as on Roman Catholic religion which influences the political process. Women struggled to achieve their suffrage in 1937, (the first female suffrage in Asia), obtaining almost a half million supportive votes (Aquino 1994: 595). With strong traditions of participation in economic and civic affairs, women now have considerable representation in politics and in government. It acquired the rare distinction of a 267-page Philippine Development Plan for Women 1989-92, which parallels the national planning document.

For most of its history, Filipino politics operated within a two- or multi-party framework. Rather than strong ideological policy agendas, parties were organized around personal relationships and patronage delivered to supporters. A lively and open press makes political conflict visible to voters in this society which places a premium on literacy and education. Elite representatives are privileged in national politics, including women from those classes. The sharpest political lines are drawn by class and landholdings rather than gender or ethnicity.

During the Marcos dictatorship, political cronies used the political process for enrichment. Coupled with the martyrdom of Benigno Aquino in 1983, "people power" emerged to destroy the dictatorship in 1986, with the help of the church and the military. Corazon Aquino, widowed in the assassination, became the newly elected President,

obtained support across class lines and with active women's participation.

Politics and Policy

Women gained a tenth of the seats of the bicameral legislature after the dictatorship. Many new, nonideological parties emerged in the campaigns; in 1992, two women ran for President, and one came in second place, while the other came in fourth (Imelda Marcos, wife of the former dictator, but former Manila Mayor and powerholder in her own right). Women gained 4 of 24 seats in the Senate (or 16.7%), and 10.6% of seats in the House of Representatives (or 21 of 199 seats). Women hold 2 of 24 cabinet seats (or 7.7%). Women form a significant pool of experienced political representatives at the local level. In 1992, 7 women became governors, 10 mayors (and 138 vice-mayors), and nearly 1500 councilors (Aguilar 1994). Women's voting turnout has surpassed men's in most elections since 1947.

Women participate in a wide variety of organizations and feminist movements, some of them cutting across class lines. Through lobbying and personal connections, women actively seek engagement with the political process. Women's organizations have sponsored political literacy and campaign training modules throughout the country, producing modules that have been translated into many dialects. Others participate in the still smoldering guerrilla movement, in a country where serious land reform has yet to take place. Women are active in professions and academia, including women's studies and women in development activities at the Institute for Philippine Culture.

Women's visibility as political actors spawns a gender policy agenda which is debated in Congress. The Congressional Research and Training Service, which produces studies of women in politics, documents the extensive male sponsorship of bills on women. Women representatives also introduce and co-sponsor legislation, though get pigeonholed into committee assignments considered traditional for women (even as gender-fairness spans all committee jurisdictions). A Congressional Caucus on Women's issues enhances coalition building prospects. While many bills are introduced, few get passed, true of nongender initiatives as well. Moreover, initiatives are introduced which counter women's policy achievements, such as religious efforts to end family planning. In the 1987 Congress, substantive laws passed against employment discrimination and the mail bride business. Even if unsuccessful in one session, new intiatives get visibilty and placement on the agenda, such as those to protect hospitality workers and to recruit qualified women to the civil service until they represent half of that workforce (Reyes 1991).

Though somewhat tainted with Marcos origins, the National Commission on the Role of Filipino Women, now called the National Commission for Women, has survived and thrived with the return of democratic process. On it sit energetic political appointees, linked to women's constituencies, working with executives who take gender-fair policy initiatives into the implementation process of government bureaucracies. Focal points in various departments form a "sisterhood sorority" network to reorient the civil service practices in conformity with policy. The Commission has sponsored gender training programs for bureaucrats. Former President Aquino signed an Executive Order enjoining all government units to implement the Philippine Development Plan for Women and authorizing the Commission to monitor their implementation (Rikken, summarized in Rao, et.al. 1991). Eighteen Sectoral Working Groups on Development Planning for Women exist, drawing together NGOs, government officials, and academics. Among the many sectors include agriculture, agrarian reform, industry, housing and others. Thus, gender transcends all types of policies, rather than getting segregated and reduced to a few and labeling them women's issues.

More recently, a women's umbrella organization successfully sought and obtained the signature of Fidel Ramos (current President) for a ten-point program on peace, the environment, agriculture, work (including penalties for sexual harassment), business and industry, health (including reproductive health), social services, education-culture-media (to eliminate stereotypes and promote "non-sexist and equitable representation"), violence against women, and equitable participation at 30%+.

Sources

Aguilar, Carmencita T. "Women in Democratization Process: Perspectives and Praxis," Paper Presented at the International Political Science Association Meetings, Berlin, August, 1994.

Aquino, Belinda A. "Philippine Feminism in Historical Perspective," in Women and Politics Worldwide, Barbara Nelson and Najma Chowdhury, eds. (Yale University Press, 1994), 590-607.

National Commission on the Role of Filipino Women, Philippine Development Plan for Women 1989-1992 (Manila: NCRFW 1989).

The Philippine Country Report on Women 1986-1995 (Fourth United Nations World Conference on Women, Beijing, 1995 [1994]).

Reyes, Socorro L. "Advancing the Women's Agenda in Congress: An Action Plan," and "Strenthening the Linkage Between Selected Women's Groups and Women in Government," (Manila: Congressional Research and Training Service, 1991).

Rikken, Remedios as cited in Aruna Rao, H. Feldstein, K.Staudt, and K. Cloud, Gender Training and Development Planning: Learning from Experience (New York and Bergen, Norway: Population Council and Chr. Michelsen Institute, 1991).

Santiago, Lilia Quindoza, "Rebirthing Babaye: The Women's Movement in the Philippines," in Amrita Basu, ed. The Challenge of Local Feminisms (Boulder: Westview, 1995), pp.110-128.

EUROPE

<u>Unsuccessful Case</u>

"Romania: A Totalitarian Transition to Democracy?"

In terms of the conceptual model, Romania has elements of cultural compatibility with engendered democracy. Female labor force participation was and is high, though both men's and women's labor reaps little value in an economy wrecked by several decades of Stalinist-like rule. Women's political representation was once among the highest in Eastern Europe, but the totalitarian system was a polar opposite of democracy. While all Eastern European countries experienced decline in female representation in their so-called "transitions to democracy" (for men?), Romania's drop was the steepest. Totalitarian rule left no room for independent civil organization, including women's organizations; new organizations are extremely limited and weak, given continued repression.

History and Culture

Romania has little history of democracy and its political culture reflects that legacy. After the second world war, Communist Party rule was established and in 1965, Nicolae Ceausescu established a particularly ruthless, if independent and nationalist, dictatorship. Economic policies forcibly uprooted peasant villages, extracted food for export leaving an undernourished populace, and rapidly industrialized (with virtually no regard for environmental consequences) the country. Control was maintained through police initimidation, paid informants, and a heavy security apparatus. No civil organization was permitted unless registered with the state. Even typewriters had to be registered, to prevent free communication. Human rights problems were rampant.

Ceausescu's rule had a gendered cast, and it may be uniquely labeled "reproductive totalitarianism." Like other Eastern European systems, women's labor force participation was promoted and supported with some (meagre) social support services. Unlike neighboring countries, however, women's reproductive rights were eliminated in 1968 due to Ceausescu's population growth plans. Pronatalist policies and penalties bore heavily on women's health. With extremely low living standards, bordering on deprivation with lack of heat, food, and housing, couples sought to limit births. At great risk to their political and physical health, women resisted state intrusion into their private lives, according to Nicolaescu. While fertility rates before the abortion ban were 55.7, jumping to 105.5 in the subsequent year, rates gradually declined back to 59.5 in 1983 (1994:119).

Politics and Policy

In 1989, a sudden almost spontaneous revolt ousted, tried, and executed Ceausescu. Unlike other Eastern European countries, the severity of Romanian repression inhibited opposition organization and civil society. The replacement regime, many of whose members were part of Ceausescu's regime, pursued popular policies: they annulled the abortion ban; they reduced food for export and markets nourished those hungry people with cash and work; they redirected limited energy to warm a chilled winter population. But, despite open elections, they also pursued some of the same repressive policies from the old regime.

Women in Romania once had the highest rates of representation on cabinets and in parliament, the former at 18%. (Mrs.) Elena Ceausescu, much feared and hated, was part of this female representation sham. Women's representation has fallen to 3% in the legislature, and zero representation on the cabinet. Women's issues go unarticulated in electoral campaigns and parliamentary debate.

Two women, important in the 1989 opposition and transition, continue to be active, but in the opposition. Blandiana is the president of an influential opposition movement Alianta Civica, which rallied other opposition parties to form a united block. Cornea, with Blandiana, helped designate a presidential candidate of the opposition.

Two women dissident writers, Gabriela Adamesteanu and Ileana Malancioiu are editors of prestigious opposition journals (Nicolaescu 1994). However, the legacies of past regime actions to divide workers (particularly the relatively regime-privileged miners, who assist in repression) from intellectuals continues to have its consequences for unifying opposition. Moreover, women and men both fight now for priority issues like consolidating this tenuous transition to democracy and improving grim living conditions.

Sources:

Robert Cullen, "Report from Romania: Down with the Tyrant," The New Yorker, April 2, 1990, pp. 94-112.

Kathleen Hunt, "Letter from Bucharest," The New Yorker, July 23, 1990, pp. 74-82.

Madalina Nicolaescu, "Post-Communist Transitions:Romanian Women's Responses to Changes in the System of Power," Journal of Women's History 5, 3 (1994) pp. 117-128.

Radio Free Europe Research (various issues on campaigns and elections, but not a word on women)

Christine Sadowski, "AutonomousGroups as Agents of Democratic Change in Communist and Post-Communist Eastern Europe,"in Larry Diamond, ed. Political Culture & Democracy in DevelopingCountries (Boulder:Westview 1994) pp. 155-188.

Successful Case

"Norway: Egalitarianism in the Mainstream"

Scandinavian countries, including Norway, have a long tradition of egalitarianism (including the lowest gender wage disparities, worldwide), homogeneity, and consultative rather than confrontational politics in corporatist political structures that rely on dialogue with designated interests. Such traditions are compatible with gender balance. Yet women's movements, at the turn of the century, and in the 1970s and thereafter, were crucial for making these cultural traditions "work" for women in their mobilizations for more women on party lists and expanded policy agendas to incorporate women's concerns. Norwegians are active civic participants, who increasingly value the difference women add to the whole political agenda. The Equal Status Law is comprehensive, providing levers for change and synergy with women's organizations, including an Ombuds office within the state. Norway (and Nordic countries) are widely recognized for their transformed politics that value human development, peace, global egalitarianism, and gender fairness.

History and Culture

The Kingdom of Norway boasts a flourishing democracy, in which more than 80% of the electorate turn out to vote in national elections. Like other Nordic countries, Norway's policy agenda changed nearly a half century ago to provide social support for families. Traditional women's organization members and women trade union members, in conjunction with men, pursued sex equality debates and developed a social democratic state.

In this corporatist state, officials interact with appointees in designated sectors to build consensus over public issues. Appointees are not as gender balanced as in national level electoral politics, but have grown to approximately a third.

Policy changes have been built upon social norms that value egalitarianism and accept public responsibilities for problems. In this and other Nordic countries, a strong sense of solidarity exists for fellow and sister citizens.

Politics and Policy

One of the earliest of countries to grant women suffrage in 1913, Norway is now famous as the world's most gender-balanced political system. Norway's multi-party system, and their women's sections within, produced the consistently most gender balanced cabinet, with around 40% women, until passed up by Finland. From 1986 to 1989, and from 1990 on, Norway's Labor Party Head, Gro Harlem Brundtland, has been Prime Minister. Her pathbreaking and courageous positions on the environment, population, and other issues have been an inspiration worldwide. Women's representation in local councils, however, is less than a third.

From the late 1960s onward, women sought political empowerment as a means to promote more gender-fair policy. This politics-first strategy departs from women's employment-first, or policy-first strategies utilized elsewhere. Most strikingly in the 1960s, women mobilized voters to support women using especially democratic procedures which allowed intense preferences to be expressed for female candidates through cumulative voting procedures. They increased their representation on local councils from 5% in 1963 to 12% in 1967. They developed voter education campaigns to teach women procedures and talk with them

about issues. While 179 local authorities lacked female voices in 1963, by 1971, only 20 of 444 had such gaps (Bystydzienski 1994). Of course, a gender-fair policy foundation had been built over time, interacting with increasingly gender-balanced process. This foundation interacted with women's experience in local office, where they demonstrated they could perform and thereby helped build a pool for national leadership.

Norway's institutions facilitate and ease the entry of underrepresented groups like women. This multiparty electoral system not only uses party lists, but permits voters to indicate preferences through cumulative voting. Also, the burdens of campaign financing are reduced through support from parties and public authorities to pay for work. Media focus on issues more than personalities during campaigns.

Women, in both parties and movements, used the slogan "women representing women" as a means to the ends they sought. Parties began instituting quotas for female representation in the mid-1970s, and up to now, left and central parties enforce these procedures. (Even without quotas, the Conservative and the Christian People's Parties have healthy levels (25%+) of women representatives.) Established male party elites worried that women's loyalty would be to their gender group, rather than to their parties. Over time, party loyalty has been maintained, but women within various parties bring perspectives that stretch their party agendas in ways that overlap toward gender-fairness.

Rather than a gender-neutral political culture, Norway's public celebrates and values the different competencies and vantage points women and men bring to the political process. These differences may be constructed stereotypes which obliterate individual variations among women or men, but they help to transform a political culture that once, like other countries, was a male monopoly into one with a broadened political agenda and with people-friendly domestic and international policies.

Some critics charge that the state has replaced individual men as women's guardians. No country is a female utopia. Women continue to press for a broadened political agenda that would address personal-political issues not fully addressed in the historic consensus which has evolved over gender. The women's movement sought to address large wage differences, job segregation, and violence against women through radical process and policy alternatives. Their engagement with the state produced some change, but molded in established ways.

Sources:

Bystydzienski, Jill, "Norway: Achieving World-Record

Women's Representation in Government," in Zimmerman and Rule, 1994, 55-64.

Gelb, Joyce, <u>Feminism and Politics: A Comparative Perspective</u> (Berkeley: University of California Press, 1989).

Hernes, Helga Maria, "The Welfare State Citizenship of Scandinavian Women," in <u>The Political Interests of Gender</u>, Kathleen B. Jones and Anna G. Jonasdottir, eds. (London: Sage 1988), 187-213. This is a slightly revised article from her <u>Welfare State and Woman Power</u> (Oslo: Norwegian University Press, 1987).

Matland, Richard E. "Putting Scandinavian Equality to the Test: An Experimental Evaluation of Gender Stereotyping of Political Candidates in a Sample of Norwegian Voters," <u>British Journal of Political Science</u> 24 (1994) 273-292.

Norway, Government of <u>The Norwegian Equal Status Act: With Comments</u> (Oslo: 1985).

Skjeie, Hege, "Ending the Male Political Hegemony: The Norwegian Experience," in <u>Gender and Party Politics</u>, Joni Lovenduski and Pippa Norris, eds. (London: Sage 1993), 231-262.

VanderRos, Janneke, "The State and Women: A Troubled Relationship in Norway," in Barbara Nelson and Najma Chowdhury, eds. <u>Women and Politics Worldwide</u> (Yale University Press, 1994),528-543.

LATIN AMERICA

<u>Unsuccessful Case</u>

"Mexico: Gender Oblivion in Official Male Political Space"

Mexico, for all its revolutionary rhetoric, is a nonegalitarian country which emphasizes high gender differentiation. In Hofstede's scheme, it is the second highest power distance country. Urban women participate in feminist groups, but these have usually operated independently of conventional politics, widely perceived as corrupt. Women's limited incursions into the male political world produces paltry policy gains. While women stand for office in increasing numbers,

this occurs without a gendered policy agenda. No government machinery provides policy levers to strengthen women's organizations in synergistic ways.

History and Culture

Mexico, land of complex Aztec and other indigenous kingdoms, achieved its independence from Spain in 1821. Under dictatorial leadership in the late nineteeth century, Mexico pursued a modernization strategy that resulted in widespread landlessness and inequality. The revolution of 1910 began years of mass struggle and inter-factional leadership feuds. It resulted in a 1917 constitution noteworthy for its rhetoric of justice, freedom, and equality. A formula for political stability was created with the Partido Revolucionario Institucional (PRI) in 1929, the single party which won all Presidential elections and all gubernatorial elections at the state and local levels until the 1980s. Men dominate virtually all executive positions, and nine of ten legislative positions, in an executive-dominant system. Since 1947 (local) and 1953 (national), women exercised the right to vote and hold office.

The PRI long drew on revolutionary rhetoric to legitimize its rule, even as it institutionalized a corporatist party structure to co-opt peasant, worker, and popular sectors. A patronage-style party machine and personal connections helped to contain major conflict, with exceptions in the 1968 student rebellion, sporadic peasant guerrilla movements in isolated regions, and the Chiapas rebellion initiated 1 January 1994 (the same day the North American Free Trade Agreement went into effect), which has captured the national democratic imagination. Widespread suspicions of corruption, coupled with economic crisis in the early 1980s, led to alienation and voter <u>abstentionism</u>, a codeword for great concern and watched carefully by the government and the PRI. The usual official response to abstentionism--reforms that inflate opportunities for fragmented opposition parties--gave way to official recognition to the Partido Accion Nacional (PAN) victories at state and local levels. Democratic activists split from the PRI, creating a party around the son of a popular, 1930s President. His Partido de la Revolucion Democratica (PRD) lost both the 1988 and 1994 Presidential elections.

Amid this political culture of revolutionary language and widespread cynicism is a gender culture that constructs polarized male and female temperament, work, and household responsibilities. Like elsewhere in Latin America, women are often viewed as more moral than men. Parties have their "feminine sectors," primarily used to mobilize women voters rather than to share decision making over policy and electoral agendas. Gender-fair policy agendas are virtually invisible during campaigns. Opposition parties court female constituencies, but their reward is to applaud women for dutifully meeting their civic responsibilities (Staudt and Aguilar 1992). During the 1994 election, PAN women's party loyalty allowed them to overlook their candidate's blatant sexist remarks.

Politics and Policy

Civic organizations, independent of parties, have been relatively rare until recently. However, neighborhood groups that organize around everyday life struggles and services for their communities are quite common. Women's participation therein, as leaders and members, is recognized and quite visible (Tunon Pablos 1992; Velez-Ibanez 1983). Besides these pragmatic interests around which women organize, feminist groups are also active in major urban areas. In their comprehensive attention to the politics of everyday life, they raise complicated strategic gender interests which are not easily processed and digested in establishment politics. Feminist groups are diverse, only sometimes involved in coalitions; their intellectual dissemination occured through fem, now Debate Feminista, radical journals which cover the gamut of women's concerns, and the La Jornada, which occasionally publishes an insert Doble Jornada (double day).

Widespread alienation and cynicism about official politics is heightened among women, but officials seem nonplussed about possible female abstentionism. (Gender-disaggregated turnout figures are not available.) Small parties of the fragmented left articulate gender issues. During 1994, also Presidential election time, only the Zapatista Army of National Liberation based in Chiapas had a coherent twelve-point gender agenda for indigenous women, ranging from communal kitchens to food processing technology (La Jornada 1 March 1994), and to female leadership and marital choices in previous communiques. Two of the nine candidates for President in 1994 were women, from small parties of the left. The PRD is the only large party with a 30% rule: a rule which requires not less than 30% men OR women in executive committees from local to national levels.

In many elections, women distance themselves from, rather than engage in the coarse and corrupt process. For feminist groups, ideological purity is maintained at the expense of the possibility of compromised power sharing. Although women are increasing nominated for legislative seats (18% in the 1994 elections), they rarely articulate women's issues.

Women's absence from positions of political representation is reflected in policies which maintain female subordination. Abortion is a crime, yet 78,000-140,000

women die yearly from unsafe, clandestine abortions. Rape is a serious problem in Mexico, viewed as low priority until (minimalist) legislation of the last five years increased prison terms for convicted rapists. Seemingly strong laws go unenforced with a weak judicial system. Feminists have pursued self-help strategies and street demonstrations to bring visibility to the problem. More recently, they collaborated with government agencies to establish several counseling centers in large urban areas. Men who batter women also represent a serious problem, the solutions for which may come in a long-term process of reducing machismo (hyper-masculinity) (Bartra 1994; Lamas et.al. 1995). Women have no formal advocates IN government, except for the Desarrollo Integral de la Familia, a semi-official social action agency headed by male political executives' wives (Rodriguez 1987). Lacking a civil service system, however, each election procedures a wholesale change in officials, from top to bottom of the hierarchy.

Once democratic transition occurs, more women may seek engagement with a cleaner political process. The 1994 elections, despite irregularities, were more credible than most previous elections. At the time when credibility is restored over an honest and transparent political process, substantive policies may emerge to engage participants.

Sources

Bartra, Eli, "The Struggle for Life, or Pulling Off the Mask of Infamy," in Women and Politics Worldwide, Barbara Nelson and Najma Chowhury, eds. (Yale University Press, 1994), 448-460.

La Jornada (continuous review)

Lamas, Marta, Alicia Martinez, Maria Luisa Tarres, and Esperanza Tunon, "Building Bridges: The Growth of Popular Feminism in Mexico," in Amrita Basu, ed. The Challenge of Local Feminisms
(Boulder:Westview, 1995), pp. 302-323.

Rodriguez, Victoria, "The Politics of Decentralization in Mexico: Divergent Outcomes of Policy Implementation," Unpublished PhD Dissertation, University of California at Berkeley, 1987.

Staudt, Kathleen and Carlota Aguilar, "Political Parties, Women Activists' Agendas, and Class: Elections on Mexico's Northern Frontier," Mexican Studies/Estudios Mexicanos 8(1992), 87-106.

Tunon Pablos, Esperanza, "Women's Struggles for Empowerment in Mexico: Accomplishments, Problems, and Challenges," in Women Transforming Politics:Worldwide Strategies for Empowerment, Jill Bystydzienski, ed. (Bloomington: Indiana University Press, 1992). 95-107.

Velez-Ibanez, Carlos, Rituals of Marginality: Politics, Process and Culture Change in Central Urban Mexico, 1969-74 (Berkeley: University of California Press, 1983).

Successful Case

"Costa Rica: Real Democracy?"

Egalitarian and democratic, nonmilitaristic haven in the usually military ridden Central American political scene, Costa Rica exhibits cultural compatibility with gender balance. Women's organizations are linked with women's studies in academia to produce a gendered policy agenda. Costa Rica's enthusiastic, democratic debate over a "real equality" comprehensive law, and the compromise finally forged, represents a model, gendered civic education campaign. Passage of the law produced policy levers in government to sustain momentum over this effort.

History and Culture

Costa Rica, which celebrated a century of democracy in 1989, is the only country in the Western Hemisphere without a standing army. It achieved independence from Spain in 1821 and developed a society in which literacy and health care are more widely available than most Latin American nations.

Costa Rica boasts a free, tolerant society with open and honest elections. Negotiation, the "Costa Rican way," is a widespread value that induces compromise. With an independent judiciary, the rule of law and the enforcement of honest elections have become realities. Term limits prevail, as victorious candidates cannot succeed themselves. In a two-party proportional representation system, incumbents do lose elections.

A Feminist League, created in 1923, initiated the struggle for female suffrage with other women's organizations of the time. The 1949 Constitution guaranteed this right, and women voted in the 1953 elections. Suffrage sparked a debate on women's largely domestic activities and a civil code that privileged husbands' authority over wives.

Politics and Policies

Women's voter turnout rates top 80%, a mere two point difference from men's. Their representation in the legislature held constant at 12%, and is now at 14%. Female cabinet representation is at 10%, above global norms. Costa Rica had a woman Vice President and a woman President of the National Legislature. Women are active in parties, but pressure rather than quotas affects the number of female candidacies and their positions on party lists.

Women's strategies emphasize equality through law and extensive participation in NGOs, some of which operate in self-help and in collaboration with other groups. CEDAW was ratified in 1984. Under President Oscar Arias, who cultivated women constituencies over women's important priorities of housing and peace, the 1986-1990 National Development Plan targeted women among other issues important to women. The Plan's Point 4 provided that:

"the policies and programs directed at women will search for ways to overcome the economic, legal, and political inequalities that present themselves and to develop action in cultural and educational fields to favor the changing of discriminatory patterns, under the premises of equalty of the sexes and shared responsibility in the home." (in Saint-Germain and Moran: 1991: 36) Principles like these indicate official support for action on women's strategic gender interests. Also, women make up two-fifths of judges, mainly in family and criminal courts.

To act on CEDAW ratification, a subministry center for women's development, the First Lady, and a working group proposed far-reaching legislation titled the Law of Real Equality for Women in 1988. Initially focused on balanced political power, it expanded to real equality in education, economics, and social protection, including laws to prevent sexual abuse and violence. Bold measures were proposed, dealing with 50-50% political balance, affirmative action in government, party funding to stimulate women's participation, stereotyped educational materials, and childcare among other topics. The proposal avoided discussion of full reproductive rights, not available to women.

Consistent with Costa Rican political culture, a spirited debate occurred within the wider public, with many groups aligning themselves for or against parts of or the whole document. Also consistent with political culture, negotiation and accommodation produced a compromise after two years which narrowed goals, left political representation up to parties, and instituted a Defender of Human Rights in the Department of Justice whose work, amid other topics, would continuously study the causes of women's inequality and solutions for its remedy. Few political representatives would go on record in opposition of women's equality. Other parts of the proposal were addressed through Presidential order and through the widespread public dialogue about women's equality.

Sources:

Curling,Lena "Costa Rica:Case Study," Expert Group Meeting on Equality in Political Participation and Decision Making, Vienna UN/DAW September 18-22, 198.

Gonzalez-Suarez, Mirta, "With Patience and Without Blood: The Political Struggles of Costa Rican Women," in Women and Politics Worldwide, Barbara Nelson and Najma Chowdhury, eds. (Yale University Press, 1994), 174-188.

Saint-Germain, Michaelle A. and Martha I. Morgan, "Equality: Costa Rican Women Demand 'The Real Thing'," Women & Politics 11, 3 (1991), 23-75.

WESTERN ASIA/NORTH AFRICA

<u>Unsuccessful Case</u>

"Morocco: Hands Off Male Control"

Morocco's religion and culture appear incompatible with balanced women's representation. Women's organizations are weak and limited, as are even practical women's groups. Civil organizations are weak generally in this "controlled partial democracy," where the king exerts considerable authority. Women's official voices are extremely weak, and their electoral turnout, unknown. Policy levers are limited to welfare measures rather than to empowerment.

History and Culture

The Kingdom of Morocco is a constitutional monarchy in which the King, reputedly a descendent of Muhammad, rules. French colonization from 1912 to 1956 left a legacy of strengthened centralization, reducing the autonomy of Arab and non-Arab Muslim Berber people. Yet an uneasy balance exists between the political center and kin-based rural authorities, with the co-existence strategy involving a

hands-off policy on male control over women.

The king appoints the Prime Minister and cabinet members, without the advice of Parliament. In this multi-party system, pro-government and opposition forces compete for office, but the king has constitutional authority to dissolve Parliament and govern by decree.

Political culture has historically made politics men's affairs. Prior to Islam, women had few, if any rights. Islamic codes give male kin extensive control over women's lives. The Malikite [elsewhere, Maleki) version of Islamic law, predominant in the Maghreb [elsewhere, Maghrib] region, gives husbands rights to break marital bonds at will and to marry multiple wives. Men consent to women's marriages, not women, at no legal minimum age. Maleki laws institutionalize unequal inheritance based on gender.

Despite common religious heritage in the Maghrib, Tunisia and Algeria have changed family laws. Tunisia's changes are most far reaching: brides must attend marriage ceremonies and give their verbal consent; husbands and wives are entitled to file for divorce, in courts; polygyny is outlawed, punishable with prison and fines. Morocco, instead, has codified Maleki family law. Compulsory marriage is possible; male divorce continues, but repudiation must be witnessed by two; polygyny is legal.

Politics and Policies

In 1959, women were granted suffrage and the right to hold office. Fourteen women ran as candidates, among 17,174 in the first local elections of 1960, but no women won. In 1976 and thereafter, some women were victorious at the local level, but face obstacles due to prevailing public beliefs about politics as men's affairs. No woman has ever been elected to Parliament. Parties nominate women, primarily the opposition parties.

Political affairs at the national level are elite affairs. Several princesses have held positions of authority in government and foreign affairs.

Morocco has high rates of illiteracy overall, with consistently higher rates for women. After independence, literacy campaigns and universal education were promoted, but are enforced more in urban than rural areas. Several program initiatives exist. In one, the Ministry of Handicrafts and Social Affairs offers education through centers. In another, the Ministry of Youth and Sports coordinates programs for girls, promotes awareness of family planning, and works with women's centers. Even though women's literacy has increased, males received almost three-fourths of educational funding, based on a 1982 study.

Women's fertility is considerably higher than neighboring

Muslim countries, at 4.8 children per women (a figure down from the 7.2 of 25 years ago). A minority of women receive prenatal care, and half of women in the childbearing years are estimated to be undernourished.

Sources:

Afifi, Aicha and Rajae Msefer, "Women in Morocco: Gender Issues and Politics," in Women and Politics Worldwide, Barbara Nelson and Najma Chowhury, eds. (Yale University Press, 1994), 462-477.

Charrad, "State and Gender in the Maghrib," Middle East Report, 163 (1990), 19-24.

Kandiyoti, Deniz, "Women, Islam and the State," Middle East Report, 173 (1991), 9-14.

Mernissi, Fatima, Beyond the Veil (London: Al-Saqi Books 1985).

Successful Case

"Turkey: Contradictory Pressures in Pluralism"

Religious and cultural compatibility with gender balance is limited, but Turkey unlike many of its neighbors in the region, established an early break with sacred law in preference for secular law. Kemalist nationalist, secular principles, whether self-serving or paternalistically progressive, created a foundation unique in this part of the world. Yet women's representation has declined from its high point of 5% in the 1930s to just 2%, including however a female prime minister. Two conditions set Turkey apart from its regional neighbors: higher levels of appointive women and flourishing women's organizations.

History and Culture

Turkey, independent in 1923, was central to the Ottoman Empire. Mustafa Kemal Ataturk was nationalist leader and first President in a one-party system until 1946. Under his regime, secularism was adopted as a constitutional principle. During multi-party politics thereafter, the military intervened three times, beginning in 1960, again in 1971, and finally in 1983, for one to three year periods.

Tension between religiosity and secularism has long existed in the area, from the Ottoman Empire onwards. In the nine-teenth century, rulers responded to outside pressures in com-

merce. In the area of personal status and family law, however, Muslim clergy exercised authority. Muslim law, an improvement for women over customary laws in most circumstances, was ignored even then in the interests of stable relations between rulers and kin-based authority groups.

Religiosity more recently expresses itself with fundamentalism. Through constitutional mandate in 1982, religious education is taught in primary and secondary schools, linked to a state ideology emphasizing the Turkish-Islam synthesis. Public opinion has polarized over Islamic dress. Although a lively women's movement exists, politicizing issues such as harassment, virginity tests for civil service, and battering, women fundamentalists also promote views through magazines and organizations.

Politics and Policies

Women received political rights through a constitutional amendment in 1930, and in several years gained electoral seats in local offices. In 1934, women voted in national elections. Women's groups were active early in the century, mobilizing around reforms Ataturk promoted, but state action pre-empted broader, civil-society initiated reforms on gender. New women's groups rose again in the 1970s and 1980s, active in politics and academia. Turkey's rate of academic women, at 32%, is higher than countries like the U.S.; its women's studies programs flourish. Turkey's female prime minister plays a pioneering role, though her priorities rest with party agendas and political survival.

Women's representation in parliament, despite the proportional system, is very low, at 2%. Their representation in local councils is less than 1%. Turkey's female cabinet representation is 5%, above the developing world norm and that of neighboring countries (many of which are stuck at O). After 1985, a woman was appointed governor, and 3 women, deputy district governors. With the military in the background, politics often seems like risky business to many, including women. The Social Democratic Populist Party introduced a 25% quota for women candidates and party structures in 1989.

Gender policies constrast with most neighboring countries in the region. Once strongly pronatalist, state policy toward family planning and limited reproductive choice changed under military rule, without female consultation, however. With state secularism, polygyny has been outlawed, and spouses have equal divorce rights and child custody rights. During the 1980s, women's groups have pressed for new equality laws. The right to work, without husbands' permission, now exists. Rape is equally punished, whether victims are prostitutes or not. Women also organized around

Turkey's signature of CEDAW, with petition campaigns. The growing female labor force is strengthened more with extensive male out-migration, leaving women by default to fill jobs.

In 1990, cabinet woman and Kemalist feminist Imren Aykut successfully introduced legislation to create a Ministry of Women, later absorbed with another ministry. Women's groups raised questions about the ways in which the unit would interact with organizations and researchers in academia. These voices from civil society helped forge an acceptable compromise. Simultaneously, the same government sponsored a report on the Turkish family structure, emphasizing fatherly and motherly sacred and revered roles. A Family Research Institute was established in 1989. The contradictory forces of a more plural society infuse the state with these mixed signals.

Sources:

Abadan-Unat, Newmin and Oya Tokgoz, "Turkish Women as Agents of Social Change in a Pluralist Democracy," in Women and Politics Worldwide, Barbara Nelson and Najma Chowdhury, eds. (Yale University Press, 1994),705-720.

Kandiyoti, Deniz, "Introduction" and "End of Empire: Islam, Nationalism and Women in Turkey," in her Women, Islam & the State (Philadelphia: Temple University Press, 1991), 1-47.

Kardam, Nuket, "International Norms, The Turkish State, and Women," in Color, Class, and Country, Gay Young, ed. (London: Zed, 1994).
Turkey, Government of, "The Status of Women in Turkey: The Turkish National Report tothe Fourth World Conference on Women, 1995," (State Ministry for Women's Affairs and Social Services, 1994).

The ten cases demonstrate the importance of understanding history, culture, and politics and the meaning they bring to cross-national indicators of women's representation. In the interests of providing global representation through successful and unsuccessful cases from each region, the analyses make painfully obvious how a best case in one region might be worse than the worst case in another. Turkey and Ghana represent the weakest of "best" cases.

The cases provide insight on how global formulas might work differently, in different institutional contexts. Nevertheless, without imposing institutional formulas, the path model illustrates the key areas in which to plot countries in their moves toward engendering democracy. From this path model, conclusions and recommendations are drawn in the final section, IV, which follows. Successful countries are marked below; the rest are stuck at the left.

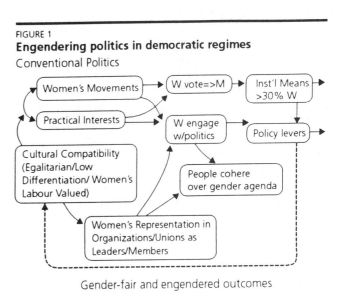

FIGURE 1
Engendering politics in democratic regimes
Conventional Politics

Gender-fair and engendered outcomes

Conclusions and Recommendations

To summarize basic findings, near male monopolies prevail in politics for all but a few countries. Where women have the voting franchise (in most countries of the world), they presumably represent half of eligible voters, yet only a tenth of national representatives, 7 percent of cabinet members, and four percent of chief executives. In 47 countries for which we have data on local female representation, women's proportional representation is higher than at national levels in a half to two-thirds of cases.

While local representation and cabinet representation are on an ever-so-slow rise, national representation is on the decline. Ironically, this decline occurred in the "transition to democracy" in eastern and central Europe and the former USSR where seemingly progressive measures like quotas and appointments had inflated female representation in ways unconnected to independent women's organizations. **The lesson here is to avoid too heavy a reliance on state apparatus, apart from people's own civil organizations.**

Low female representation has been explained in three categories. First, political or governmental support for human development priorities are low, and women's voice is not figured into human development in some wealthy countries.

Second, some cultures are incompatible with engendered politics in several ways. Gender differentiation is pronounced, in educational achievement and economic value. Women's human capital is not easily translated into what are considered skills and characteristics demanded of political leaders. Cultural values are conveyed which program prejudices among the electorate and those eligible for leadership. Women face conflicts between household/mothering responsibilities and active political lives. Egalitarianism is limited in class and hierarchical terms. Women's movements, which paradoxically arise out of gender differentiation (by choice or segregation), cannot or choose not to engage with public decision makers to broaden and gender the policy agenda and thereby transform politics.

Third, institutional barriers deter women from seeking public leadership. Those barriers allow prejudice, wealth inequalities, and exclusive men's networks to perpetuate the male monopolization of politics. Measures to increase representation are often unenforced.

Yet efforts to increase female representation have been successful in a variety of countries. These measures include:

*__sizeable__ objectives and/or quotas for female candidacies and seats, at minimum, beyond the global norms toward skewed representation (15%+) and ultimately balance.
*__enforcement__ of these objectives and quotas.
*significant, critical mass (i.e. more than a token one or two) numbers of female appointees amid the considerable latitude for appointment that already exists in 44 nations.

*family-friendly meeting times and spaces for political party work.

*subsidies, civic fund-raising, and/or public funding for campaigns which address the gendered economic disparities that exist in most countries.

*more women standing as candidates (FFM 1990).

*efforts to circulate and expand the pool recruited into politics, from legal term limits to voluntary networking.

*revaluation of the backgrounds and skills useful for leadership (expanding from law and military to service and helping professions).

*women's organizations which pursue several fronts, from autonomous self-help to supporting women's candidacies and maintaining connections with victors.

*coalitions with progressive men.

*state-based bureaus which are connected with and accountable to independent women's organizations.

These measures are most effective in countries which have especially democratic political institutions which facilitate diversity in representation and ideology. Institutional reforms[8] are in order for severe underrepresentation. Especially favorable institutions include:

*multi-party, proportional representation electoral systems with party lists.

*party lists which expand voters' abilities to make their own preferences.

*sizeable multi-member districts.

*secular, singular legal systems.

Democratic institutions flourish in culturally compatible environments, particularly those that value egalitarianism. Institutions can foster policies to increase egalitarianism through:

*equitable income distribution,
 *"people friendly markets" (UNDP HDR 1993)

*human development priorities, and

*supportive contexts to foster civil organizations. Rigid registration requirements deter free organization among citizens.

From success cases, we also derive lessons to increase representation, among them:

*the importance of flourishing women's organizations to press political parties, to renew energy and vision to officials (even female officials), and to hold representatives and executives accountable for their work.

*the need to make gender gaps and gender turnout rates visible to the electorate and candidates, so that strategies develop to address those differences.

*research to inform a gendered policy agenda, whether in the representative body, academic institutions, or both.

*the reliance on supportive men in coalitions for gender-fair change (Philippines, Costa Rica).

*the urgency to look beyond national to local legislatures (Ghana, with appointive seats for women; Norway's 1970s mobilization at local levels that preceded national increases in female representation).

*the urgency to assure critical mass numbers on national and local boards and commissions (Norway's Equal Status Act).

*the healthiness of spreading gender policy issues to a wider electorate through political literacy campaigns (Philippines), civic education (Norway), and debates over proposed legislation (Costa Rica).

*spreading women's responsibilities beyond social affairs, such as Norway. (Related are regional appointments, such as Turkey's experience with governor and deputy governorships.)

*the interactive effects of legislation and policy levers with women's organizations and change coalitions (Costa Rica, Norway, Philippines).

*the usefulness of organizational mobilization around CEDAW ratification AND enforcement (Japan), which appears to be minimally enforced and therefore, less meaningful, in most countries.

From unsuccessful countries, we derive lessons about the dangers of state cooptation of once-independent women's organizations (Kenya), of desperate poverty (Morocco), of consolidating democracy so that people's organizations can turn to other policy issues (Mexico, Romania), of legal pluralism (Kenya, Morocco), of religious intolerance based on local interpretation rather than principles of the faith itself (Morocco), of criminalizing women's everyday reproductive lives (Romania before 1990), of women's avoidance of seemingly corrupted politics (Japan, Mexico), of state-driven control over organization and registration (Romania), but yet of wealth which does not solve female underrepresentation (Japan).

From the global and case study analyses, we also appreciate the fragmented and incomplete data on gender and politics. Mainstream political science ignored the topic until just recently, (and it usually falls upon the few women in the field to publish research for the public record).

*Conceptions of democracy and human development must recognize gender balance and include this in criteria for judging "good governance."

*Regular gender-disaggregated data should be collected and reported on voter turnout and representation at <u>all</u> levels and in <u>all</u> branches of government, including boards and commissions which are especially important in corporatist regimes.

*International and regional Centers of Women and Politics should be established to collect AND disseminate data.

*Studies of good governance and politics should be accountable for including analyses of gender.

*Multilateral assistance, such as UNDP election assistance, should always mainstream gender concerns.
*Assistance criteria based on democracy, part of some bilateral and multilateral donor practices, cannot be complete without using conceptions and measures which incorporate gender and accountability to women.

*"Engendered Democracy" was a term first used in Alvarez, 1990.

NOTES

1. The criteria used to identify and define democracies generally draw on the following characteristics:
-regular open and honest elections, which require political stability;
-choices available to citizens in selecting those to represent them (usually within or between parties);
-free speech and press;
-equal citizenship for adults;
-rule of singular, **secular** law (not legal pluralism) and enforced respect for human rights;
-independent civil associations (Nongovernmental Organizations, NGOs).
For the five successful cases in Section III, these characteristics prevail.

Curiously, such characteristics could be present amid total male monopoly and control of the political process and government. Half or more of the population could, under conventional definitions like the above, be officially "silenced," with their interests. See Conclusion which calls for expanded definitions of democracy.

2. An especially glaring example is the four-volume series by Larry Diamond on <u>Democracy in Developing Countries</u> that covers 29 nations with no more than a phrase on women, if that, in chapters (Boulder: Lynne Rienner, 1989+). See also Staudt and Weaver, 1996, forthcoming.

3. Dough is slang in the U.S. for money.

4. Further theoretical refinements of the gender gap, using survey research in the U.S., attributes the difference to those women who support feminist goals versus men (Conover 1994), thus lending support to those who view gender difference as socially rather than biologically constructed.

5. The countries which prohibit female voting are Kuwait, with its male-only parliament, and Bahrein, which no longer has representative institutions. The IPU, which conducts periodic surveys in countries with representative bodies, also doubts that women have electoral rights in the United Arab Emirates (IPU 1992:5).

6. Two countries where women were eligible to represent and were elected before the franchise was obtained are excluded.

7. National political cultures interpret turnout quite differently. In the U.S., low voter turnout may produce some hand-wringing and concern, but is often attributed (incorrectly, in many cases) to overall voter satisfaction or voter fatigue with frequent elections for national, state, city, county, special district, judicial, bond, and referenda elections.

In great contrast, low turnout in Mexico, labeled "abstentionism," is cause for alarm for the the dissatisfaction it conveys; high absentionism frequently stimulates political reform to engage larger numbers of the electorate in establishment politics. Why did no one worry over probably historic female abstentionism?

8. While constitutional change, even overhaul, ("Five Republics" v. a two-century-plus constitutional document in western democracies) is common in some countries, it is problematic in others.
At U.S. local levels, "at-large councils" (more favorable to female representation) gave way to SM district-based elections, at city, county, and school-board levels after court challenges alleging minority discrimination. While minority representation has gained (in still-segregated urban areas), women did not. Women as a group "cut across" geographic

spaces into which ethnic and racial groups are concentrated.

Still, women's representation has been rising, for other reasons (fund-raising, flooding candidacies, experienced female pools, rising gender consciousness, rising female labor force participation). CAWP's 1994 Fact Sheet and <u>News and Notes</u> report:

*21% women state legislators (up from 4% in 1969) and

*20% women majors and council members in cities over 10,000 (up from 4% in 1975).

When a Clinton nominee for a civil rights appointment in the U.S. Department of Justice was discovered to have advocated cumulative and/or preferential voting (as practiced in some European democracies) in published work, she was publicly castigated for such suggested "tampering" and asked to withdraw. Conservatives in the opposition labeled her and other liberal women "quota queens." In the U.S. 1990s, such labels are extremely damaging politically, given severe backlash to affirmative action policies of the last two decades.

BIBLIOGRAPHY
(The bibliography for cases is listed after each case.)

Abdullah, Hussaina, "Wifeism and Activism: The Nigerian Women's Movement," in Basu, pp. 209-225.

Adams, Carolyn Teich and Kathryn Teich Winston, <u>Mothers at Work: Public Policies in the United States, Sweden, and China</u> (New York: Longman 1980).

<u>Africa Report</u> (special issue on women, September/October 1993), including G. J. Kelso, "The Fight for Equal Rights," and Anne Shepard, "Standing Up to Sexism."

<u>Africa Demos</u> 3,3 (1994), plus all previous issues) (Map) ((African Governance Program, The Carter Center, Atlanta, GA)

Alvarez, Sonia E. "Contradictions of a Women's Space in a Male-Dominant State: The Political Role of the Commissions on the Status of Women in Postauthoritarian Brazil," in Staudt 1990 pp. 37-78.

Arat, Yesim, <u>The Patriarchal Paradox: Women Politicians in Turkey</u> (London: Associated University Presses, 1989).

Asian Studies Review 17, 3 (1994) special issue on women and politics.

Bashevkin, Sylvia, ed. Women and Politics in Western Europe (London: Frank Cass, 1985).

Basu, Amrita, ed. The Challenge of LocalFeminisms (Boulder: Westview 1995).

Bystydzienski, Jill M., "Norway: Achieving World-Record Women's Representation in Government," in Rule and Zimmerman, pp. 55-64.

Bystydzienski, Jill, Women Transforming Politics: Worldwide Strategies for Empowerment (Bloomington: Indiana University Press, 1992).

CAWP (Center for the American Woman and Politics), The Impact of Women in Public Office: Findings at a Glance; Women Make a Difference (New Brunswick, NJ: CAWP, Rutgers University, 1991, 1990). Also quarterly newsletters (over recent years).

Centre for Social Development and Humanitarian Affairs

Charlton, Sue Ellen, Jana Everett, and Kathleen Staudt, eds. Women, the State, and Development (Albany: State University of New York Press, 1989) (contains regional studies chapters).

Chou, Bih-Er and Janet Clark, "Electoral Systems and Women's Representation in Taiwan: The Impact of the Reserved-Seat System," in Rule and Zimmerman, pp. 161-170.

Clark, Janet, "Getting There: Women in Political Office," in Githens, pp. 99-110.

Conover, Pamela, "Feminists and the Gender Gap," in Githens, et.al, pp. 51-60.

Costain, Anne N. "Women's Claims as a Special Interest," in Mueller, 1988, pp. 150-182.

D'Souza, Neela and Ramani Natarajan, "Women in India: The Reality," in Women in the World: 1975-1985 The Women's Decade, Lynne B. Iglitzin and Ruth Ross, eds. (Santa Barbara, CA: ABC-Clio, 1986, second edition).

Dominelli, Lena and Gudrun Jonsdottir, "Feminist Political Organization in Iceland: Some Reflections on the Experience of Kwenna Frambothid," FeministReview 30, 1988, pp. 36-60.

Einhorn, Barbara, Cinderella Goes to Market: Citizenship, Gender and Women's Movements inEast and Central Europe (London: Verso 1993).

Everett, Jana, "Women and Political Leadership," in Joyce Lebra, et.al. eds. Women and Work in India (New Delhi: Promilla and Co. 1984).

Flexnor, Eleanor Century of Struggle, (NY: Atheneum 1974)

Freedom Review January-February 1994 (Map of Freedom)

Freeman, Jo, The Politics of Women's Liberation (NY: David McKay Publishers 1975)

Frohmann, Alicia and Teresa Valdes, "Democracy in the Country and in the Home: The Women's Movement in Chile," in Basu, pp. 276-301.

FFM, (Fund for the Feminist Majority), The Feminization of Power in Government (Arlington, VA: FFM 1990).

Geisler, Gisela, "Troubled Sisterhood: Women and Politics in Southern Africa," African Affairs 94, 377 (1995), pp. 545-578.

Gelb, Joyce, Feminism and Politics: A Comparative Perspective (Berkeley: University of California Press 1989).

Githens, Marianne, Pippa Norris, and Joni Lovenduski, Different Roles, Different Voices: Women and Politics in the United States and Europe (New York: Harper Collins 1994).

Hofstede, Geert, Culture's Consequences (Newbury Park, CA:Sage Publications, 1984).
Inter-Parliamentary Union (IPU), "Distribution of Seats between Men and Women in National Parliaments," #18 (Geneva, 1991).

IPU list of % Women in National Parliaments, 1994.

IPU, Women and Political Power #19 (1992).

IPSA, (International Political Science Association), Conference Abstracts (Berlin 1994).

International Women's Rights Action Watch, various publications and newsletters, University of Minnesota 1989+

Jaquette, Jane, The Women's Movement in Latin America: Feminism and the Transition to Democracy (Boston: Allen Unwyn 1989, Boulder: Westview 1994, second edition).

Jaquette, Jane and Sharon Wolchik, Women and Political Transitions in South America and Eastern and Central Europe: The Prospects for Democracy Conference, University of California, Berkeley, December 3&4, 1992.

Jeffrey, Robin, "Governments and Culture: How Women Made Kerala Literate," Pacific Affairs 60, 3 (1987)447-472.

Jenson, Jane and Mariette Sineau, "The Same or Different? An Unending Dilemma for French Women," in Nelson & Chowdhury, pp. 243-260.

Jones, Mark, "Increasing Women's Representation Via Gender Quotas: The Argentine Ley de Cupos," Women & Politics, forthcoming, 1996.

Karlsson, Gunnel, "From Support Group to Conflict of Interest or Should Women Follow Men?" Viewpoint Sweden 14 (NY:Swedish Information Service 1994).

Kanter, Rosabeth, Men and Women of the Corporation (New York: Basic Books, 1977, 1993, second ed.).

Katzenstein, Mary Fainsod, "Comparing the Feminist Movements of the United States and Western Europe: An Overview," in Katzenstein and Mueller, pp3-20.

Katzenstein, Mary Fainsod and Carol McClurg Mueller, eds. The Women's Movements of the United States and Western Europe (Philadelphia: Temple University Press, 1987).

Kelber, Mim Women and National Governments (New York Greenwood 1994).

Kelly, Rita Mae and Mary Boutilier, The Making of Political Women: A Study of Socialization and Role Conflict (Chicago: Nelson-Hall, 1978).

Kemp, Amanda, Nozizwe Madlala, Asha Moodley, and Elaine Salo, "The Dawn of a New Day: Redefining South African Feminism," in Basu, pp. 131-162.

Khalil, As'ad Abu, "Toward the Study of Women and Politics

in the Arab World: The Debate and the Reality," Feminist Studies 13, 1 (1993)3-22.

Kraditor, Aileen The Ideas of the Women's Suffrage Movement (NY: Norton 1965)

Klein, Ethel, "The Diffusion of Consciousness in the United States and Western Europe," in Githens, et.al pp. 176-184.

Kriger, Norma, "Popular Struggles in Zimbabwe's War of National Liberation," in Cultural Struggle & Development in Southern Africa ed. Preben Kaarsholm (1991).

Lamas, Marta, Alicia Martinez, Maria Luisa Tarres, and Esperanza Tunon, "Building Bridges: The Growth of Popular Feminism in Mexico," in Basu, pp. 324-350.

Leijenaar, Monique, "Positive Action and Quota Policies in Europe: Empower Women in Politics," Paper Prepared for the American Political Science Association Annual Meetings, New York, September 1-4, 1994.

Leijenaar, Monique and Kees Niemoller, "Political Participation of Women: The Netherlands," in Nelson & Chowdhury, pp. 496-511.

Lemke, Christiane, "Women and Politics: The New Federal Republic of Germany," in Nelson & Chowdhury, pp. 261-284.

Lloyd, Raymond, "Women Heads of State and Government Ministers Throughout the World," for UN/DAW (1991).

Lovenduski, Joni, "The Rules of the Political Game: Feminism and Politics in Great Britain," in Nelson & Chowdhury, pp. 298-310.

Lovenduski, J. and P. Norris, eds. Gender and Party Politics (London, Sage 1993).

Mueller, Carol M. The Politics of the Gender Gap: The Social Construction of Political Influence (Newbury Park: Sage Publications, 1988).

McNelly, Theodore, ""Woman Power" in Japan's 1989 Upper House Election," in Rule and Zimmerman, pp. 149-160.

Molyneaux, Maxine, "Mobilization Without Emancipation?

Women's Interests, the State and Revolution in Nicaragua," Feminist Studies 11, 2 (1985) - THE classic work on "practical" and "strategic" interests, which others like Caroline Moser have adapted for WID/GAD analysis.

Momtaz, Khawar and Farida Shaheed, Women in Pakistan: Two Steps Forward, One Step Back? (London:Zed 1987).

Mortier, Remi, "Women's Political Participation" (3 reports), UNDP/HDR (1994).

Nelson, Barbara and Najma Chowdhury, eds. Women and Politics Worldwide (New Haven, CT: Yale University Press, 1994).

Norderval, Ingunn, "Party and Legislative Participation Among Scandinavian Women," in Bashevkin, 71-88.

Norris, Pippa, "Women's Legislative Participation in Western Europe," in Bashevkin, pp. 90-101.

Nuss, Shirley, "Women in Political Life: Variations at the Global Level," Women & Politics, 5,2/3 (1985), pp. 65-78.

Parpart, Jane and Kathleen Staudt, eds. Women and the State in Africa (Boulder: Lynne Rienner Publishers 1988).

Rao, Aruna Women's Studies Internationally (New York: Feminist Press 1991).

Ruggie, Mary, "Workers' Movements and Women's Interests: The Impact of Labor-State Relations in Britain and Sweden," in Katzenstein and Mueller, pp. 247-266.

Rule, Wilma, "Electoral Systems, Contextual Factors and Women's Opportunity for Election to Parliament in Twenty-Three Democracies," Western Political Quarterly 40, 3 (1987), pp. 477-498.

Rule, Wilma, "Parliaments of, by, and for the People: Except for Women?" in Rule and Zimmerman 1994, pp. 15-30.

Rule, Wilma and Joseph F. Zimmerman, eds. Electoral Systems in Comparative Perspective: Their Impact on Women and Minorities (Westport,CT: Greenwood Press, 1994).

Sainsbury, Diane, "Gender and Comparative Analysis: Welfare States, State Theories, and Social Policies," in Githens, et.al pp. 126-135.

Skard, Torild, w/ Helga Hernes, "Progress for Women: Increased Female Representation in Political Elites in Norway," in Access to Power: Cross National Studies of Women and Elites, Cynthia Fuchs Epstein and Rose Laub Coser, eds. (London:George Allen & Unwin 1981)76-89.

Soares, Vera, Ana Alice Alcantara Costa, Cristina Maria Buarque, Denise Dourado Dora, and Wania Sant'anna, "Brazilian Feminism and Women's Movements: A Two-WayStreet," inBasu, pp. 302-323.

Staudt, Kathleen, Women in High-Level Political Decision Making: A Global Analysis," Monograph prepared for Expert Group Meeting on Equality in Political Participation and Decision Making. UN/DAW, Vienna, September 18-22,1989. (Country Papers Prepared by Nationals for this Meeting as well.)

Staudt, Kathleen, "Gender Politics in Bureaucracy: Theoretical Issues in Comparative Perspective," in her ed. Women, International Development and Politics: The Bureaucratic Mire (Philadelphia: Temple University Press, 1990), pp. 3-36.

Staudt, Kathleen and William Weaver, Feminisms and Political Science: Integration or Transformation? (NY: Twayne/MacMillan, 1996, forthcoming).

Swarup, Hem Lata et.al, "Women's Political Engagement in India: Some Critical Issues," in Nelson & Chowdhury, pp. 361-379.

Sylvester, Christine "Simultaneous Revolutions:The Zimbabwean Case," Journal of Southern African Studies 16, 3 (1990).

Taagepera, Rein, "Beating the Law of Minority Attrition," in Rule and Zimmerman, pp. 235-246.

Thomas, Sue, How Women Legislate (New York: Oxford University Press 1994).

United Nations, The World's Women 1970-1990: Trends and Statistics (New York: UN 1991)

UNDP, Human Development Report (NY: UNDP 1993, 1994).

U.N./DAW, "Women in Government," (1992).

UN/DAW 1994 list on women in cabinets.

U.N. Women of the World (New York: UN 199).

Walker, Nancy J. "What We Know About Women Voters in Britain, France, and West Germany," in Githens, pp. 61-69.

Watson, Peggy, "The Rise of Masculinism in Eastern Europe," New Left Review (1993), 71-82.

Wolchik, Sharon, "Women and the State in Eastern Europe and the Soviet Union," in Charlton, et.al. pp. 44-65.

Women & Politics (quarterly scholarly journal) 1980-94

Trends in Female Employment in Developing Countries : Emerging Issues

Jayati Ghosh

Introduction

It is probably true to argue that work defines the conditions of existence even more for women than for men, because the responsibility for social reproduction which largely devolves upon women in most societies ensures that the vast majority of women are inevitably involved in some kind of productive/reproductive activity. Despite this, in mainstream discussion, the importance of women's work generally receives marginal treatment simply because so much of the work regularly performed is "invisible" in terms of market criteria or even in terms of socially dominant perceptions of what constitutes "work". This obviously matters, because it leads to the social underestimation of women's productive contribution. Even more importantly, as a result, inadequate attention is typically devoted to the *conditions* of women's work and their implications for the general material conditions and well-being of women.

This is particularly true in developing countries, where patterns of market integration and the relatively high proportion of goods and services that are not marketed have implied that female contributions to productive activity extend well beyond those which are socially recognised, and that the conditions under which many of these contributions are made entail significant pressure on women in a variety of ways. In this paper, an attempt will be made to consider some of the issues arising from trends in female employment patterns, with special consideration of those questions which have recently emerged and which may help to identify potential problem areas. The implications of state macro-policies and explicit women-oriented interventions will also be briefly considered.

The next section contains a very summary look at some of the main conceptual issues that have been identified in the literature with respect to women's employment. The third section takes up the matter of female labour force participation : its measurement, the social and economic conditions which influence it, the trends in various countries over the past decade, and their implications. In the fourth section, the question of the nature of women's jobs is addressed, with particular emphasis on patterns of occupational segmentation and on male-female wage disparities; and also the questions of open and disguised unemployment of women in developing countries. The fifth section deals with the effects of government macro-economic policies on women's employment. The final section contains a short discussion of possible alternative policies and other forms of intervention that have been more successful in improving the conditions of women's employment.

A fundamental premise of this paper is that since most women are actually employed in some kind of productive/reproductive work, whether or not this is recognised and quantified by statistics, the issues relating to female employment are qualitatively different from those of male employment. Thus, the unemployment-poverty link which has been noted for men in developing countries is not so direct and evident for women : many women are fully employed and still remain poor in absolute terms, and adding to their workload will not necessarily improve their material conditions. Nor is the pressing policy concern that of increasing the volume of explicit female employment, since simply adding on recognised "jobs" may in fact lead to a double burden upon women whose household obligations still have to be fulfilled. Instead, concern should be focussed upon the quality, the recognition and the remuneration of women's work in developing countries, as well as the conditions facilitating it, such as alternative arrangements for household work and childcare. All of these are critically affected by broader economic policies as well as by government interventions at micro and meso levels, in ways that will be elaborated below. And it is these together which determine whether or not increased labour market activity by women is associated with genuine improvements in their economic circumstances.

Conceptual Issues

The relative invisibility of much of women's work has been the focus of a substantial amount of discussion. Since many of the activities associated with household maintenance, provisioning and reproduction - which are typically performed by women or female children - are not subject to explicit market relations, there is an inherent tendency to ignore the actual productive contribution of these activities. Similarly, social norms, values and perceptions also operate to render most household-based activity "invisible". Indeed, "much of women's work is hidden because of denial or lack of recognition". [Lynch and Falmy, 1984, p 4]

This invisibility gets directly transferred to data inadequacies, making officially generated data in most countries (and particularly in developing countries) very rough and imprecise indicators of the actual productive contribution of women. Nuss et al [1989] have identified six major ways in which data limitations affect our knowledge of women's work. (1) Typically, the available data do not distinguish between factors that are especially important for women, such as : seasonal work versus usual or current work; full time versus part time work; paid versus unpaid activities; etc. (2) There is substantial undercounting of female work activity, especially the activities of unpaid family workers. (3) There tend to be arbitrary variations across countries with respect to the inclusion of subsistence activities in "economic activity". (4) In general, data on the informal sector are very imprecise, and this tends to be a significant if not primary source of female employment in developing countries. (5) The whole issue of household work remains one untouched by data. There are numerous problems in determining the ways in which household work should be incorporated into both national accounts data and statistics on economic activity, [Goldschmidt-Clermont 1989] and these have meant that in general the issue is formally ignored. (6) There are also problems relating to the attitudes and values of respondents, and such social and cultural considerations may determine the extent of women's work that is actually reported.

The impact of social structures is reflected not merely in the data, but in the actual determination of explicit labour market participation by women. Thus, in many developing countries social norms determine the choice between participation in production and involvement in reproduction, and consequently inhibit the freedom of women to participate in the job market or engage in other forms of overt self-employment. The limitations on such freedom can take many forms. While the explicit social rules of some societies limit women's access to many areas of public life, the implicit pressures of other supposedly more emancipated societies may operate no less forcefully to direct women into certain prescribed occupational

channels. It is also evident that, since the activities of reproduction and child nurture put so many and varied demands upon women's labour and time, combining these activities with other forms of productive work is only possible when other members of society (whether within the household or outside it) share the burden at least partially. The issue of social responsibility for such activities is therefore critical. Certainly, involving women in other forms of work without ensuring for the sharing of tasks and responsibilities associated with child-rearing and household work puts tremendous pressure on both mothers and children.

In addition to the socio-cultural factors, there are important political and economic forces which condition the ability of women to enter the labour market with a modicum of independence, equality and security. The combination of these factors can de decomposed (following and expanding upon Standing [1989]) into the various types of control by women which determine their labour force participation and its implications for their material well-being. At least ten types of control which affect working women can be identified :

(1)   Control over self, over one' own labour power. Bonded or indentured labour, which can still be found in several parts of the developing world, is the most extreme form of such lack of control on the part of the women worker. But aside from this, women are especially vulnerable in being subject to other, possibly less extreme forms of such control. Often this lack of freedom is particularly evident within the family. Compulsory involvement in certain types of work naturally constrains the ability of women to engage in other (possibly more lucrative) activities.

(2)   Control over labour time. Many employed women have little choice about whether their hours of work suit their own requirements, and this is especially the case for less skilled women in informal sector employment and in export processing zones where they may be forced to work for very long hours given conditions of excess labour supply. This is typically more significant for women workers than for men given the competing claims of housework and childcare upon women's time.

(3)   Control over the type of work contract. Many more women than men are employed in contracts such as piece-rate or flexible payments, which put

much greater pressure upon workers. This is particularly the case in informal sector activities, including agriculture, services and informal manufacturing, but it is also frequently found even in formal sector enterprises in which certain activities are subcontracted out or allocated in terms of piece rate, often to women workers.

(4) Control over the means of production, such as land, tools and work spaces. Women, even self-employed women, tend to have little or no control in this respect. The issue of land rights is particularly important in agricultural economies, where most of the women are still employed in developing countries. Many women across the world participate actively (and may even dominate) in household cultivation, yet typically have no legal rights over the land which they farm, or only usufructuary rights at best. Even in non-agricultural activities, it is often found that self-employed women do not have ownership rights over their tools and instruments.

(5) Control over raw material. Lack of access to such inputs may imply that workers are exploited by middlemen, and it has been found that self-employed women are more susceptible in this regard.

(6) Control over output. Similar to the access to inputs, this can determine the price at which women workers may be forced to sell their products, and whether they need to rely on middlemen. In fact, the problem of access to marketing channels has often been found to be the chief difficulty for self-employed women engaged in producing goods.

(7) Control over the proceeds of output and over income derived from work. It has been suggested that crude earnings data can be far more misleading indicators of net disposable income for some categories (such as women, and also children) than for others. How much income is actually retained by the women worker herself or disposed of according to her wishes, is critical for deciding whether policy interventions should focus upon gross income or on other factors.

(8) Control over labour reproduction and skills. This operates at different levels. Many poor women have so little control over their working lives that their working capacity is debilitated by the different types of activity they are forced to be involved in. Also, many women workers in developing countries are trapped in activities in which there is little or no possibility of developing skills. This reinforces the already large skill gap between men and women, which results from differential patterns of education and training.

(9) Control over the work activities normally assigned to women. In almost all societies, and particularly in developing countries, there remain essential but usually unpaid activities (such as housework and childcare) which are seen as the responsibility of the women of the household. Several community-based activities outside the household also fall into this category. This social allocation tends to operate regardless of other work that women may perform. For working women in lower income groups, it is particularly difficult to find outside labour to substitute for household-based tasks, which therefore tend to devolve upon young girls and aged women within the household or to put further pressure on the workload of the women workers themselves. In fact, as Elson (1987) has pointed out, it is wrong to assume that unpaid tasks by women would continue regardless of the way resources and incomes are allocated. "Gender neutral" economic policies may thus imply possible breaking points within the household or the collapse of women's capacity. Social provision for at least a significant part of such services and tasks, or changes in the gender-wise division of labour with respect to household tasks, therefore become important considerations when women are otherwise employed.

(10) Control over resources and incomes within the household. This is different from (7) above because it raises the possibility of implicit markets within households. This has been emphasised by Palmer [1993] who has found the existence of separate gender-determined accounting units within households to be widespread across Africa, in agriculture and other informal sector activities. In all societies, the question of the final disposition of total household incomes between its members tends to be critical, and gender bias usually operates quite strongly in this regard.

In addition to these factors, it is clear that other broad economic tendencies and patterns can also play important roles. Thus, job market segregation by gender, both explicit and implicit, can affect not only the aggregate extent of labour market participation by women, but also the degree of mobility within structures. This point is further elaborated in Section IV.

Trends in Female Labour Force Participation

Data on the labour force participation of women are notoriously inaccurate, for reasons which have already mentioned above. Not only are the problems of undercounting and invisibility rife, but there are often substantial variations in data across countries which may not reflect actual differences but simply distinct methods of estimation. Further, even statistics over time for the same country may alter dramatically, as a result of changed definitions of what constitutes "economically active" or because of more probing questions put to women, or simply due to greater sensitivity on the part of the investigators. In India, for example, the increase in female labour force participation rates evident in the 1991 Census (like the 1961 Census before it) was certainly related to the changed nature of the questions posed and a slightly different training given to enumerators. Such a shift is even more marked for Bangladesh, where a change in definition was associated with an increase in female activity rates between 1983 and 1989 by 35 percentage points - an eightfold increase.

It is therefore clear that the available data (which are in any case patchy and incomplete for many countries) cannot be used rigorously for cross-country comparisons or even for assessing trends over time, except in the most broad and suggestive way. With these caveats in mind, it is possible to draw some rough inferences from the data presented in Table 1 on the activity (labour force participation) rates over the 1980s in selected developing countries. These activity rates present employed men and women, as well as those who are unemployed but available for work, as proportions of the total male and female populations. Obviously, such rates are critically affected by the definition of employment, the demographic structure (given the usual estimate of working age population as falling between 15 and 60 years), as well as the prevalence of such undesirable features as a high incidence of child labour in some countries. The fact that the data also relate to varying age groups makes them hard to use for purposes of

comparison. But it is evident that in most of the countries listed in the Table, female activity rates have been reasonably high and moderately increasing. There are some countries (such as Egypt, Morocco and Nigeria in Africa; Argentina, Costa Rica, Ecuador, Guatemala and Mexico in Latin America; Iran, Pakistan and India in Asia) in which the female participation rates have been low and significantly below male rates. But in these countries as well, the data suggest that female participation has been increasing even if only slightly. (Mexico and Iran are exceptions to this.) In other countries where there has been a very large increase in the female participation rate in the course of a few years (such as Bangladesh and Bolivia) the likelihood is that a substantial part of the difference can be explained by altered definitions and estimation procedures. But there are certain other countries, primarily in Asia (Hong Kong, South Korea, Philippines and Thailand) but also in Africa (Burundi being the most obvious) where female activity rates have been very high, and also increasing over the 1980s.

A slightly different approach to the issue of women's involvement in economic activity is to look at the female share of total employment. Table 2 presents these data for selected developing countries, disaggregated by sector. (The services sector, which often accounts for the bulk of female employment, is not included directly since it is composed of many different subsectors and can be implicitly gauged from the other indicators.) What is interesting in this Table is the extent to which the female share of employment has been growing over the 1980s. In the African countries mentioned, while these ratios are typically lower than for other continents, women workers have been increasing as a proportion of total workers. Such increases have been significant in Botswana and Malawi.

Similar, if less marked, increases in the proportion of women workers to total workers are evident in Latin America. The Bolivian case is of interest because the female share of total manufacturing employment and total employment have been roughly stationary even though aggregate employment in manufacturing and in the economy as a whole declined substantially over this period. (The index of total manufacturing employment fell by 14 percent between 1983 and 1991.) This suggests that the type of marginalisation feared by some writers, (see Elson [1987]) of women being displaced from employment in greater numbers than men during periods of economic recession, certainly was not evident in Bolivia nor in several other countries of Latin America during the 1980s. In fact in Asia, the share of women workers to the total has been high and increasing in many countries, so much so that in certain countries such as Indonesia, South Korea, the Philippines and Thailand, women account for nearly half the manufacturing workforce and also a significant share of total employment. In Sri Lanka, women account for slightly more than half of total agricultural employment, indicating their prominence in plantation labour, and also around half of manufacturing employment. In general the evidence suggests that women have become increasingly important in terms of share of total employment, and that this has been most obvious in the newly industrialising countries.

Thus, there appears to be not very much basis for the fear expressed by Boserup [1970] and echoed by some later writers, that women would be pushed out of productive work over the processes of industrialisation and development. On the contrary, there may be an opposite tendency in operation, that of the feminisation of work as the female share of production worker employment and the female labour participation rates are high and rising in many developing countries. This is borne out by a more systematic study of trends in male and female activity rates in the 1980s by Standing [1989]. In a consideration of more than forty developing countries, Standing found that more than two-thirds of the countries studied showed rising female labour force participation rates over the 1980s, and that two-thirds of these cases involved simultaneous <u>declines</u> or no changes in male participation rates. While the data presented here and in that study are still inconclusive, they point to the possibility that, far from marginalising women workers, certain types of development strategy - and in particular economic liberalisation and export-oriented industrialisation - tend to favour increases in female employment. Indeed, as Table 3 indicates, over the decade of the 1980s, the growth rate of female empployment was substantially higher than that of male employment throughout the regions of the developing world. As evident from the earlier discussion, this was so not only for rapidly growing industrialisers but also for countries in the grip of structural adjustment-induced recession.

Clearly, the earlier perception of implicit preference of employers for men in job "queues" must be revised in the light of the apparently growing inclination to hire women. The reasons for this will be examined in more detail in Section VI below. But if this is the case, then it is clear that the basic policy issues relate not simply to the availability of employment for women, but the quality and remuneration of the work that they do perform. It may be that women are marginalised not by joblessness, but by types of work

and working conditions that condemn them to low-wage low productivity occupations which involve greater pressure and more drudgery. It is this possibility, and its ramifications, that are considered in the following section.

The Nature of Women's Jobs

Occupational segmentation

There are numerous theories which attempt to explain occupational segmentation of male and female workers, which account for both differences in occupational pattern and structure of pay. These explanations can broadly be divided into supply-side and demand-side explanations. Naturally, which model is accepted has critical policy implications, since the choice of policy intervention to remove gender gaps will depend upon the explanation for them. Supply-side models, including the human capital model, are essentially based on the argument that the quality of labour supplied by men and women to the labour market is different, both because of physical differences, and because of social determination of the ability/willingness of male versus female workers to perform particular tasks. Demand-side models vary quite widely. At one extreme is Gary Becker's rather far-fetched "personal prejudice" model, in which employers with disutility from hiring women will do so only if the female wage is low enough to compensate them, thus implying that female wages will be less than the marginal product of such labour, there will be a gender gap in earnings and even possibly segregated workplaces. There are other, less subjective explanations. In one argument, implicit job "queues" give primacy of place to men because women tend to have a lower level of some productive characteristics which may be desired. Conversely it has been argued [Cohen, 1985] that in certain jobs - typically those with short learning curves and seniority-based pay scales, employers may prefer to hire women because they actually favour high worker turnover. This can be achieved by hiring women and forcing them to quit at particular life-cycle points such as marriage and childbirth. Marriage bars are still frequently found in developing countries. Thus, in South Korea, employment contracts of private firms typically specify that the woman must retire in the event of marriage [Jose, 1987].

In an empirical study of gender-based employment preferences in developing countries, Anker and Hein [1985] found that statistical discrimination in pay between men and women was usually associated with relatively high birth rates; legislation granting adequate maternity leave and any other protective legislation; the perception of the greater absenteeism of women associated with childcare responsibilities (although it was found that in actual fact female absentee rates were no higher than those of males for other reasons); cultural restrictions against the social mixing of males and females in the workplace; and strongly held cultural norms about which jobs are suitable for women - typically in occupations corresponding closely to household-related tasks. These factors which may contribute to employers' negative attitudes towards female workers can be particularly important in developing countries where there is considerable excess demand for jobs in the modern sector. Yet, as evident in the earlier section, there are also strong and growing forces which favour female employment in particular sectors (export processing activities for example) and particular types of work.

The issue of occupational segmentation is closely related to the gender gap in wage earnings, and attempts to disentangle the two are both conceptually and empirically difficult. It is the combination of both forces - the concentration of women at the lower skill, lower pay end of the job spectrum, and the fact that they tend to receive less pay even for broadly similar work, which have ensured that, despite the rising rate of female labour force participation across most countries, the ratio of female to male earnings has not risen substantially and in several countries has actually fallen over the 1980s.

There are several established ways of measuring occupational segmentation in the literature. In general, a gender-dominated occupation is defined by first calculating the female proportion of total employment and then selecting some percentage points spread around that figure, the range usually being between 5 and 20 points. Alternatively, the gender-based activity rate for the whole population across sectors can be taken as the benchmark for assessing gender domination in particular industries and subsectors. Comparable worth studies, which have thus far mainly referred to developed countries, use the 70 per cent rule - thus female dominated occupations are those in which 70 per cent or more employees are female. The most systematic measure is probably the Duncan Index or Index of Dissimilarity. This refers to the minimum proportion of persons of either sex who would have to change their occupation to one in which their sex is under-represented , in order for the occupational distribution of the two groups to be identical. Obviously, this index varies with the number of occupational classifications.

Barbezat [1993] in a cross-country study of occupational segregation has found secondary evidence of recent declines in the Duncan Index in some countries of Latin America and Asia, following a long period in which the index remained unchanged. This would suggest a decline in occupational segregation, but the data need to be interpreted with care. Firstly, the index shows very wide variation across developing countries, ranging from only 9.7 per cent in China to 62.3 per cent in Qatar. Secondly, despite the reductions in dissimilarity, considerable sex segregation in work still exists in virtually all countries. The level of occupational segregation is particularly high in Latin America and the Caribbean, with Duncan Indices of 50 per cent or more in several countries. The recent and relatively small declines in the value of the index must therefore be seen in this context. Thirdly, the index is susceptible to being influenced by gender patterns in one very large occupation - agriculture. Thus, while the Duncan values for East and Southeast Asia are noticeably lower than those for other developing countries, some of the explanation for these low measures of dissimilarity stem from women's higher participation in agriculture in these countries, with the exception of Singapore, Hong Kong and even the Philippines. But it is certainly true that the declines in the Duncan Index in this region are also associated with the feminisation of certain types of previously male occupations as a result of greater export orientation.

It is widely accepted that occupational sex segregation is associated with lower pay, lower occupational prestige, less opportunities for skill formation and in general reduced opportunities for women. However, published statistics deal at such a level of aggregation that the full extent of differentiation by gender is not revealed, since even within subsectors women are typically concentrated at the lower end of the job spectrum. Thus the data presented in Table 4 underestimate the extent of occupational segregation in the selected countries, although very broad indications can be found there. Some very general idea of the quality and degree of skill involved in women's work can be had from this table. It is evident that women are heavily clustered in the categories of production workers in both agriculture and non-agriculture and (in some countries) sales and service workers. The relative importance of production work is greater for women than for men in all the developing countries for which comparable data are available. They are much less evident in the professional and administrative categories. In some instances, such as Egypt, Ecuador and Bangladesh, the proportion of women in such occupations seems to have declined over the 1980s. However, in a number of other countries the proportion of women workers in professional and administrative occupations has actually increased, and these tend to be the more successful (in terms of GDP growth rates) of the newly industrialising countries. Thus, while Costa Rica, Chile and Venezuela have shown marginal increases in the proportion of women in such occupations, much more significant increases are to be found in Southeast Asia, in Singapore and South Korea, and to a lesser extent even in Malaysia. Obviously, rapid economic growth over a sustained period plays a role in allowing women to shift to more qualified and paying professions. This is particularly so in countries where labour markets relying primarily on men have experienced tightness and problems of labour supply resulting from rapid expansion of production facilities and output. This can even lead to changes in employment norms and practices : in South Korea, over the past decade, 24 of the 30 jobs formerly legally barred to women there have been opened to them. There is similar evidence from other high-growth countries in the region, as noted by Standing [1992] who found a strong positive correlation between the proportion of manual production jobs taken by women and the feminisation of higher level white collar jobs in Malaysia and the Philippines.. However, it is worth noting the point made by Elson [1991] in a comparative study of labour in the textile and electronic industries in industrial and developing countries. She observed a tendency for female labour to be replaced by male labour whenever changes in production techniques involved relative declines in the use of unskilled versus skilled labour. Such reversals have also been noted in other industries in developing countries.

The broad statistical data on occupational segmentation has to be examined in the light of evidence of micro-studies from particular countries, all of which point to similar conclusions. That is, there is a strong tendency to prefer women for particular types of production work - those that involve repetition, painstaking attention to detail, relatively low levels of skill formation and possible "burnout" in the work activity which actually means that employers would prefer high labour turnover in order to maintain productivity. Certain types of assembly line work (espeically in the newer electronic sectors) fit this very well, as do specific jobs in sectors such as textiles and clothing. And women workers are well known to possess other socially determined characteristics which suit employers : greater susceptibility to work discipline, less inclination to unionise and to go on strike, more flexibility in terms of the willingness to accept not only part-time contracts such as time-rate and piece-rate which put more pressure on the workers, etc. And, most important of all, both the "reservation" and "aspiration" wages are typically lower for

women than for men, implying that they may be much cheaper sources of labour for employers in jobs for which physical characteristics are less relevant. For these reasons, it may be the case that as technological change and other structural changes in the economy proceed in particular ways, job opportunities for women open up much faster than for men and indeed may result in female employment expansion even as male employment shrinks. Such an argument appears to be reinforced by the experience of female employment generation in the fast-growing Asian economies [Horton, ed., 1995; Mitter and Rowbotham, eds., 1995].

Modern technologies have been associated with changes in the pattern of skill requirements for labour that are especially significant in this context. In the first place, there is declining reliance on traditional guild or craft skills, which were earlier associated with apprenticeships, sustained on-the-job training and even hereditary systems of skill formation. This decline has actually reduced male control over a range of occupations and opened up possibilities of work for "non-traditional" workers in these activities. Secondly, there is a strong tendency (resulting primarily from new technology but also from other economic forces such as employer preference) towards skill polarisation. This leads to the co-existence of a relatively small elite of very technically skilled, specialist workers with high status and high level institutional qualifications, with a large mass of semi-skilled workers who require only minimalist short-term training and can be easily drawn from the population at large. This type of skill structure, which is already established in industrial countries, is emerging in a range of developing countries driven by the twin forces of technological change and global economic integration. Within national labour markets this means that implicit contracts between employer and worker are much less necessary or relevant, that the degree of mobility and worker turnover increase, and that greater reliance is placed by employers on flexible "external" contracts in which the freedom to hire and fire is greater. As a result, enterprises (both public and private) in developing countries have increasingly resorted to workers on causal or temporary contracts, part-time workers and sub-contracting, as means of reducing fixed labour costs. Not only does this mean that the labour market in general is more insecure for most workers, but it also means that more of them are involved in "static" jobs in which there is little chance of upward mobility or skill formation through employment. The processes of deregulation of labour markets, macro-economic structural adjustment and economic liberalisation generally, which are discussed in Section V below, are closely related to these tendencies.

Gender-based differences in pay

As mentioned earlier, the issue of occupational segregation is closely related to the gender gap in earnings, and interestingly also seems to be associated with rapid increases in female employment. Thus, the developing countries with the largest differences in male and female earnings in the aggregate are typically those where the growth in female employment in recent years has been the fastest. This is evident from Table 5, which gives the male-female earnings ratios for several developing countries. It should be noted that these data are raw unadjusted ratios of average earnings of females relative to males. They are umbrella figures which cover a wide range of factors which affect the average pay by sex, ranging from the type of activity and the specific sectors where male and female workers are concentrated, to different levels of skill and training between sexes, as well as different rates of pay for similar work. Since this ratio does not control for the myriad of factors that influence the wage gap, it does not indicate the independent contribution of each of these to the earnings gap. However, this can provide a useful picture of time patterns if the composition of the workforce does not change dramatically, and illuminate cross-country differences for broadly similar labour force structures.

South Korea emerges as one of the countries with the largest gender gap in earnings (although, exceptionally, the gap seems to have narrowed over the 1980s), and other "Asian tigers" such as Singapore and Hong Kong also show very wide differences. The gap is also very large in Chile, where women receive on average less than half the pay of male workers, and in other newly-industrialising countries of Latin America. The limited time series data available (not reproduced in the table) suggest that in many countries the gender gap in pay has actually increased over the 1980s, the period of increasing employment opportunities for women. This tends to confirm the process described in the earlier paragraphs, of women workers being preferred by employers precisely because of the characteristics which make them more susceptible to becoming lower-wage, lower-skilled workers operating under more insecure working conditions.

This association of low-wage low-skill jobs with women workers can extend into shifts in the pattern of occupational segmentation. Thus Banerjee [1991] has described how, in the electrical industry in eastern India, women did the armature winding for electrical fans, but as

soon as the wage rates for that job went up, it was taken out of their hands. Similar reversals have also been noted in large-scale Indian industries such as pharmaceuticals and toiletries, where previously female-dominated activities have been taken over by men. Conversely, many previously male jobs are redesignated as "women's work" especially when they require flexible labour in relatively subordinate and inferior positions. This has been frequently observed in Southeast Asia as well as some countries of Latin America.

Women working in the urban informal sector

Gunderson [1994] has observed that there are certain typical features of developing economies which militate against the implementation of "comparable worth" policies of the type which are being seriously considered in developed countries. These include : (1) Lower levels of industrial development, wages, capital-labour ratios and unionisation (2) Smaller formal urban sectors and much larger informal urban sectors and rural traditional sectors (3) Informal urban sectors with characteristics like non-fixed work sites, small enterprises sometimes situated even within the household, self-employment, wide spread of piece-rate work, informal work arrangements and non-fixed hours of work.

These phenomena makes female workers in the urban informal sector particularly vulnerable to pressures emanating from the conditions in the labour market. Although it is not generally known, women constitute in aggregate the majority of rural-urban migrants in developing countries [Standing 1987], and many of them are teenage girls or young women who enter low-level, low-paid and insecure forms of employment. Thus, in a number of Asian countries impoverished rural families have been known to send their daughters to the cities to earn their living, and send back remittances of incomes received, not just in productive manufacturing jobs but also in services including domestic service, prostitution and related activities. Thailand is the most infamous and well-documented case [see Phongpaichit 1982] but similar processes have also been observed in other countries, including India. Such activities represent the extreme case of female employment in the urban informal sector, but in general women tend to be disadvantaged within the informal sector, and often remain unpaid for at least a part of their work. Many more women tend to occupy jobs in the small-scale informal sector than in the formal sector, particularly in Asia. In Africa, too, it has been found that in small-scale businesses in African cities and towns, women are overwhelmingly concentrated in petty commerce, and are very rarely noted in manufacturing employment with long-term contracts.

The phenomenon of sub-contracting has become increasingly significant as it involves women working at home in a complex production and distribution chain in which large companies benefit indirectly from the cheap labour supplied by such unorganised women for all the labour-intensive activities in the production process. Beneria and Roldan [1987] have provided an example of such a sub-contracting chain, known as "maquila", in Mexico City, which is represented in the diagram below. The ability to fragment the production process and isolate and sub-contract out the most labour-intensive activities contributes to the "flexibility " of production for the employer, but such forms of outwork can and have pushed many women into positions of dependent and impoverished insecurity. Similar subcontracting patterns have been observed for India [see Shah and Gandhi 1992] and throughout southeast Asia.

Diagram 1 : Typical Subcontracting Chain, Mexico City

Productive Unit	Character	Workers and Wages
A. Producer of electrical appliances	Multinational; draws on regular list of 300 subcontractors to send out 70% of its production	3000 workers, mostly male, with regular work and high wages with benefits
B. Producer of radio/T.V. antennae for A.	Mexican enterprise; one of various units linked with A; subcontracts 5% of its production.	350 workers, male and female; lower wages and fewer benefits than A.
C. Producer of electronic coils for firm B.	"Sweatshop" operating illegally in basement of owner's house	6 young female workers (age 15-17) providing homework for D; bare minimum wage without fringe benefits
D. Homeworkers producing electronic coils for C.	Homeworkers duplicating some tasks of C.	Women working individually at home; average wage equal to one-third of minimum wage

Source : Beneria [1986, page 8] quoted in Standing [1987, page 52].

This example and similar evidence from other developing countries suggest that policies to improve the conditions of working women should also be concerned with legislation and regulations designed to control labour contracting and subcontracting more effectively. Otherwise a large and specially disadvantaged section of workers - primarily women working through their home - would remain outside the pale of any action or policy to improve working conditions in general.

Women working in agriculture

The largest informal sector activity - agriculture - is also the largest single employer of women in developing countries. Most often women work as part of family labour on plots owned/leased by male members of the household, although they are also significant among agricultural wage labour. (In some states of southern India, for example, women constitute the majority of wage labourers in agriculture.) For women working as part of household labour, the issue of land rights is crucial. In large parts of the developing world, women do not have legal control over the land they farm, even when they are operating in female-headed households, and this colours their ability to benefit from particular policies designed to help agriculturalists as well as from new technologies. Thus, in Africa, women typically have only usufructuary rights, and in parts of Asia, even these rights must be mediated through men. However, Palmer [1991] has pointed out that there is probably more spread of women's own-account farming than is generally perceived, particularly in Africa.

There is evidence of fairly strong patterns of gender division of labour in agricultural activities throughout developing countries. These typically tend to allocate the most laborious, manual and labour-intensive cultivation tasks to women. New technologies thus have complicated effects on the employment potential of women in agriculture. On the one hand, mechanisation and agricultural modernisation tend to displace or reduce women's participation both in the actual process of cultivation and in the post-harvest processing. However, biotechnological innovations such as the introduction of HYV seeds and chemical fertilisers, especially in Asia, have been observed to lead in the first phase both to increases in total unskilled labour demand and to a sharper rise in the demand for female labour than for male labour [Nayak-Mukherjee, 1991]. This is because of the resulting increase in incremental tasks traditionally associated with women, such as transplanting and weeding, the application of fertilisers, and more harvesting and basic processing of the produce. But in the second phase, with the growing use of specially bio-engineered fertilisers and pesticides, many of these tasks also get displaced, and the greater peaking of agricultural labour demand means that all workers (male and female) find more employment for shorter periods, along with longer slack periods. In general it is the case that over the longer term, agricultural modernisation and new technologies displace landless female (and male) workers. Falling employment elasticities of agricultural output in the more mature Green Revolution areas of South Asia , Mexico and elsewhere suggest that high agricultural growth need not be sufficient to generate sufficient employment for the rural population - male and female - who are still forced to seek work in agriculture.

Often - as in parts of Africa as well as in Asia - there is a socially determined division between women's and men's crops. The determination of which crop is to be farmed by men or women is usually through two features : the degree of market access involved (cash crops are more likely to be male) and the production technique involved (the more "modern" and mechanised techniques are likely to require men). Thus the pattern is often one of women predominantly producing food for subsistence and/or working as unpaid family labour on men's cash crops field, although of course the picture is more complex and geographically diverse. The commercialisation of agriculture thus has the effect of reducing the importance of women vis-a-vis men in terms of controlling the cultivation process. In Burkina Faso and central Nigeria, export and industrial crops have usually become men's crops. In Gambia, IFAD [1992, p48] noted that there is "considerable evidence that when a new technique makes a new crop more profitable, men will move in to take over", and similar patterns have been observed in Brazil and parts of India. However, this need not always be the case; apparently in Jamaica and Papua New Guinea, rural women have been able to move into new technology-based export farming on their own account. [IFAD 1992] These examples are still more than exception than the rule, but they do suggest that the negative implications of technological change on women's own-account activities in agriculture may have more to do with the inadequacy of extension, credit and support systems which should enable women to access and make use of available innovations. This conclusion is confirmed by the positive results shown by non-governmental voluntary groups' efforts in these directions, such as the Grameen Bank in Bangladesh and Mahila Samakhya in Karnataka state of India.

In terms of the impact of new technology and relative prices of agricultural inputs and outputs, a distinction obviously must be made between "surplus" and "distress" sellers of agricultural produce : the latter, who ar typically net food buyers, are households which may be materially worsened by the phenomena of commercialisation and rising prices of agricultural output. In sub-Saharan Africa, female-headed households, who comprise a significant (25-35 per cent) and growing proportion of all rural households, tend to be over-represented among net food-buying households. [Gladwin, 1993.] In Asia too, especially in areas where male migration has involved substantial increases in female-headed cultivating households, this pattern has been noticed. This may have been one of the factors contributing to the growing immiserisation of some groups of rural women, and to the "feminisation of poverty" noted by Buvinic [1993] and others. Thus, between 1970 and 1988, the number of rural women below the poverty line in 114 developing countries grew by 47 per cent while the number of absolutely poor rural men increased by 30 per cent. In 1988, according to one study, females constituted 60 per cent of all rural poor people in the developing world. [Jazairy, Alamgir and Panuccio, 1992]

Conditions in the agricultural sector are critical for female employment, and affect not only women working within agriculture, but also those women who are forced by rural poverty to migrate elsewhere in search of employment. The position of such female workers in the urban informal sector has already been discussed, but international female migration is also of great significance. In Asia, where such migration is the highest, domestic workers make up the bulk of the flow of female migrants. Depressed conditions in agriculture are usually the primary cause of such moves, and women migrants are encouraged to leave first because they are considered to be less important to maintaining the peasant family holding. In the Philippines, which has the highest outflow of migrants in Asia totalling 600,000 workers annually, women migrants (usually heading for domestic service) outnumber men 12 to 1. [Lim, 1993] Rural women are also found to head for employment in export processing zones, with consequences described below.

Women working in export-processing zones

In terms of the sectoral distribution of their employment in manufacturing industries, women workers have tended to be concentrated in two areas in developing countries : home-based or sweatshop-based production as part of a sub-contracting chain, in the manner described above, and the "inner core" of large-scale enterprises in export-oriented industries and export processing zones. For developing countries, such export processing and other special economic zones are the single most important avenue of foreign direct investment in terms of jobs created. The World Investment Report [1994] calculates that there are nearly 200 EPZs spread across approximately 60 developing countries, providing around 4 million direct jobs. These are mainly in traditional labour-intensive manufacturing (textiles, clothing, electrical and electronic appliances) but there is also some increase at the margin of jobs in newer areas such as data processing.

The preference of employers for female workers in export-processing zones is by now well-known : Joekes [1993] estimates that on average women constitute around 70 per cent of the workforce in any given enterprise in an EPZ. A study by Standing [1992] found in general and strong positive relation between export-orientation and preference for female employment in Malaysia and the Philippines.. The most notorious example is that of the electronics industries based in EPZs in southeast Asia, which have relied largely on young, single women workers, many drawn from distant villages and expected to work for very low wages and very long work weeks (with 50-60 hours per week being common) for two or three years, before being replaced by fresh recruits. Further, in EPZs the typical bans on union activity and the non-enforcement of minimum safety and other labour standards (which are seen as necessary to ensure export competitiveness) put women workers in very vulnerable positions as far as incomes and working conditions are concerned. According to Standing [1987], some studies (eg in Java Indonesia) have suggested that the wages paid to young women in such EPZs are insufficient to meet even their basic needs.

Like many of the other avenues for female employment, such work in EPZs involves a general lack of opportunity for training and upward occupational mobility. Indeed, it has been noted that as products and processes move up the skill and technological ladders, women tend to replaced by male workers. Thus in the Mexican maquiladoras, the proportion of women workers fell from 77 per cent of the workforce in 1982 to 60 per cent in 1990. Resisting such a tendency (of women being displaced from work as wages and working conditions improve) is part of the general need to ensure the training and skill-upgradation of women workers throughout the economy.

Standard concepts of unemployment are likely to have little relevance in developing countries where a large, often dominant, proportion of economic activity takes place in the rural and informal sectors. As noted above, these are typically characterised by irregular or seasonal employment, and social security systems are limited or non-existent. Further, the high proportion of self-employment suggests that there is considerable scope for underemployment to reach substantive levels without being recorded in the statistics. The problem of accurate data is particularly relevant for women, because of the fact that, especially in traditional developing societies, female household members typically bear most of the responsibility for household tasks as well as activities associated with child rearing. Thus the open and declared unemployment of women may actually go along with simultaneous performance of these unpaid tasks.

The data on open unemployment for women are thus very sensitive to social conditions. Also, as in the case of men, these tend to underestimate substantially the existence of disguised unemployment or surplus labour. Nonetheless, the data on open unemployment presented in Table 6 do indicate a surprising trend. Despite the trend across developing countries towards the feminisation of employment over the past decade, female unemployment rates also have been usually higher than those of their male counterparts. Thus, while the growth in joblessness has characterised virtually every region of the world, women have had to bear a much larger burden of unemployment. Historically, female open unemployment rates in sub-Saharan Africa as well as in Latin America and the Caribbean have been substantially higher than male rates, and this trend has persisted into the 1990s. However, the pattern is not uniform across countries. Standing [1989] in a study of more than 40 developing countries over the 1980s, found that in 60 per cent of them, female unemployment rates had risen more slowly than those for males, while they had risen faster in only 33 per cent of the countries.

The failure of adjustment policies to bring about significant employment creation has meant that unemployment rates have remained at very high levels and have even increased. This has come about also because of a significant increase in female labour force participation rates. This is not necessarily a positive feature, since the explicit economic activity of women seeking work may simply be a response to declines in real household income due to recession and economic policies of structural adjustment - a survival strategy in the face of potential impoverishment. Thus, participation rates and unemployment rates are both observed to be noticeably higher for poorer women than for better off women. The "discouraged worker" effect noted in the developed countries, whereby women simply withdraw from the labour market because of the absence of opportunities during economic recession, applies largely only to middle class women in developing countries. Women from lower income groups typically have no option but to continue to seek work, no matter how limited the options.

Here too, the issues of quality of work and wages received are crucial. In Latin America, urban underemployment seems to be an exclusively female phenomenon. Francke [1992] points to the close relationship between the growth of female employment and the expansion of female underemployment in Peru : as more women are employed, more of them work for lower pay. In Asia, particularly in rural areas, underemployment is a more general phenomenon, and indeed, women are actually <u>less</u> likely to be underemployed given their involvement in household-based economic activities.

The Impact of Macro-economic Policies

There is no doubt that over the past decade, the forces that have been most critical to the economic condition of women, including women workers, in developing countries are the macro-economic policies being pursued across the world. The period since 1980, and even more since 1990, has been remarkable for the uniformity of macro-economic strategy that has characterised not only the developing world, but many of the OECD countries and the formerly socialist countries of Eastern Europe. In some countries, this strategy began as part of a package of measures proposed/imposed by the multilateral lending agencies the IMF and the World Bank, on developing countries in general and debtor countries in particular. But the subsequent universality of this strategy suggests that there are broader forces at work, in particular the domination of international finance capital and the globalisation of the elites in developing countries (not the mass of workers), which influence the adoption of this strategy in country after country. The connotation of the term "economic reform" now invariably is to move towards greater market-orientation and deregulation, rather than state action to improve conditions for poorer and more disadvantaged groups, including women. Yet it may be argued that this strategy, which is likely to have adverse effects on the material conditions of women in a variety of ways, is neither necessary nor desirable, and that other macro-economic alternatives are possible which are more sensitive to the needs of women as workers.

As background, certain concepts which are often used interchangeably in the literature should be clarified : stabilisation, structural adjustment and economic liberalisation. Essentially, "<u>stabilisation</u>" refers to the short-term attempt to stabilise or steady the economy in the face of sudden shocks or macro-economic imbalances, especially those reflected in the balance of payments or expressed in inflationary tendencies. Such measures are typically deflationary, but there are numerous ways to achieve this, depending on what the longer-term aim of "<u>structural adjustment</u>" is. The latter refers to medium-term or long-term changes in the productive structure, in accordance with overall goals. The way the term is currently used usually denotes the desire to make the economy more "flexible" and internationally competitive, but this is not the only possible aim of structural adjustment. It could as well be directed towards the more efficient and equitable provision of basic needs for the entire population, or an attempt to improve labour productivity throughout all sectors in the economy without involving slack in the form of unemployment. Indeed, these aims, are not always mutually compatible, and it could even be the case that striving for enhanced external competitiveness on the basis of existing resource and income distributions actually reduces the economy's ability to provide basic needs and to improve aggregate productivity. The concentration on international competitiveness alone is part of an approach which puts primacy on the unfettered functioning of markets as the best means of achieving growth and efficiency. This constitutes the essence of "<u>economic liberalisation</u>", which therefore determines that the stabilisation-cum-structural adjustment strategy takes on particular contours.

The main elements of this standard package are as follows :

(1) Reduction in the government fiscal deficit, in a context of simultaneous lowering of direct tax rates. This typically involves often large declines in public capital formation and in expenditure on social infrastructure and poverty alleviation schemes by the state.

(2) Control over domestic credit expansion and liberalising interest rates, which typically causes them to rise in developing countries and leads to industrial recession, at least for a time.

(3) Devaluation of the currency followed by moves to some sort of floating or market determination of the value of the exchange rate

(4) Liberalisation of external trade, with a move from quota controls to tariffs and a gradual reduction of tariff barriers, as well as the removal of restrictions on exports particularly of agricultural goods.

(5) Easing of conditions for foreign capital inflow and incentive packages designed to attract more such inflow.

(6) Domestic deregulation and freeing of controls including those on prices of essential commodities and services.

(7) Cuts in covert and overt subsidies by the state, both as part of the budgetary cuts and to bring domestic relative prices into line with international prices.

(8) 'Reform" of public sector enterprises, typically implying rising output prices, closure of loss-making enterprises, disinvestment and full privatisation.

(9) Liberalisation of financial markets, strengthening stock markets vis-a-vis banking intermediaries, and increasing the scope for financial innovation.

(10) Labour market reform and deregulation, directed towards increasing the insecurity of work contracts and doing away with protective legislation for workers that is supposed to make labour market structures "rigid" and "inflexible".

The implications for the material conditions of women of such a package can be usefully assessed in terms of the following variables : access to basic needs, such as food clothing and shelter, and to the provisioning of common property resources; access to education and skill formation which would allow women to move out of low-skill low-productivity jobs; implications for total household incomes of labouring households in different sectors and the gender-based distribution within households; access to the requirements for reproduction and nurture of the young, including not only health care and other social services but also child care; access to productive employment outside the home and recognition of household work; control over the allocation of resources, both socially and within households.

In general, each of these is negatively affected not only by the reduction in government expenditure that comes as part of the stabilisation exercise, but also by the general withdrawal of the state from various aspects of the provisioning of goods and services and greater reliance on the market mechanism. Thus, declines in public productive

and infrastructural investment affect not only growth prospects for the future but also production conditions and work situations in agriculture and the unorganised sector as well as in organised manufacturing and services. As we have seen, the move from formal to informal employment and public to private sectors typically favours the feminisation of employment at the margin, but almost always in much more insecure and poorly paid conditions with minimum regard for labour standards. [Standing, 1989; Beneria and Feldman, 1992, etc.] Women are literally pushed into the labour force, usually on highly disadvantaged terms, due to the pressure to maintain minimum levels of household income as the particular structural adjustment policies lead to falls in real wages, unemployment, and reduced availability of and cuts in subsidies on basic goods and services. The combination of reduced income and greater costs on necessary items is in addition to the burden of household and other unpaid work which results from cut-backs in public expenditure programmes. [Baden, 1994, Joekes, 1991.]

Public expenditure cuts thus affect women in their roles as producers, mothers, household managers and community organisers, and almost inevitably the implications are negative in terms of reduced incomes and standard of living, and greater burden of unpaid work. It is true, as Elson [1993t] has pointed out, that it may be difficult to separate the effects of structural adjustment policies per se from those of economic recessions which are also associated with declines in formal sector employment and real wages. The points, however, are twofold : firstly, in most developing countries across the 1980s and 1990, recessions typically were induced by the stabilisation policies followed, which themselves were designed to deal with earlier imbalances; secondly, the <u>type</u> of stabilsation-cum-structural adjustment path is crucial in generating recessions and adversely affecting the economic conditions of women. There are other possible paths, different from the standard package and elaborated in the section below, which provide far greater protection to the material circumstances of disadvantaged groups, the provision of basic needs and the maintenance of some growth in the economy.

The general trend that has been observed in all the developing countries where structural adjustment has been accompanied by more or less prolonged recessions (Latin America and the Caribbean, Africa) has been that of increasing female labour force participation, primarily in the informal sector which has also grown in relative terms. In a study of women's work in Lima, Peru, Francke [1992] found that female labour force participation behaves counter-cyclically in a recession but does not closely follow GDP; rather it tends to be negatively correlated with wages with a one-year lag. This implies that women's first strategy is to adjust consumption levels - if this is unsustainable, or the cuts required are too great, then they enter the labour force. Moser [1992] with reference to a low-income community in Guayaquil, Ecuador, found that women are working longer hours in paid work than a decade previously in order to maintain the same income, and are also entering the labour market earlier in relation to the age of their children. In Bombay, India, Shah and Gandhi [1992] found substantial increases in stress of women workers resulting from the greater pressures on energy and time use resulting from such increased labour market involvement on adverse terms and greater demand of unpaid household work. A summary of case studies by the Commonwealth Secretariat [1991] comes to similar conclusions for a range of countries. Thus, under adjustment, female open unemployment tends to rise and is typically more than that for males; women's involvement in informal sector work increases, with a deterioration of the position of women (in terms of real wages and working conditions) in that sector; there is an increase in women's unpaid family labour in agriculture; the small scale of women's independent operations in agriculture and in the informal sector typically limits their ability to take advantages of any new incentives that may have emerged in these sector. On the other hand, it is also true that women tend to be the main "beneficiaries" of the expansion of employment in export processing areas, although, as noted earlier, such employment is often on very adverse conditions and may occur in a context of declining aggregate household incomes. There is also no evidence that women suffer more than men from retrenchment in the organised sector.

The implications of stabilisation measures which result in cuts in public expenditure of the type described above tend to be adverse for women, but they can still be reversed through sufficient public pressure. But the likely effects of economic liberalisation measures which move towards greater market orientation are more long-term and much more difficult to reverse because they typically set in motion major changes in the economy, in society and in ideology. Such liberalisation has usually involved greater freedom of action for large capital - both national and international, both industrial and financial - rather than a genuine liberation of the capabilities of working women and men. The main thrust of these measures is not only the greater commoditisation of all aspects of everyday life and

work, but also a reduction of the subsidisation of activities not valued by the market, and a preoccupation with enhancing profitability for exporters and foreign investors through the deregulation and manipulation of labour. Two aspects of this require further elaboration : the inequalising nature of market processes and the nature of labour market deregulation.

The domination of market processes undervalues everything which is not directly calculable in those terms, household work being a prime example. At the same time, such work itself becomes both more time-consuming and more arduous when common property resources become privatised because of the way commercialisation operates. The reduction of subsidies to basic amenities such as energy sources, sanitation and water supply, and to basic services such as health, not only reduces household income, but also puts an especial burden on women, who typically bear the responsibility for provisioning these within the household. Reduction of food subsidies and of the scope and extent of any public distribution system for necessities puts pressure on the food security of households, a circumstance from which women are generally the greater losers [Sen, 1990]. Thus, as mentioned above, many women may be forced to enter the labour market through sheer necessity of economic survival of the household, at the same time that governments and other social institutions abdicate the associated responsibilities of providing childcare and easing the load of housework. The recent experience of East European countries shows how quickly institutions and facilities which allow women into the labour market with some degree of ease and equality can be eroded as market processes gain sway. Elson [1994] further argues that the basic inadequacy of structural adjustment programmes from the women's perspective is that they emphasise price changes and market forces as the preferred instruments of resource allocation, but fail to consider explicitly the process of reallocation. Thus they implicitly rely upon a supply of extra unpaid labour, pushing the burden of adjustment from the paid to the unpaid segment of the economy, and ignore the fact that it is women who will have to supply that labour.

Labour market deregulation has affected the position of women in various ways.. It is interesting that countries that have not ratified the ILO's Equal Remuneration Convention No. 100, which promotes the principle of "equal pay for equal work" include a disproportionate number of those pursuing export-led industrialisation strategies, especially economies in which there are large export processing zones. Thus, the non-ratifiers include

Hong Kong, South Korea, Malaysia, Singapore, Sri Lanka and Thailand. Other countries such as India have different legal minimum wages for men and women in certain industries, on the false presumption that women do less arduous work than men. Other than that, there are numerous loopholes in existing laws, and the greater informalisation of labour tends to undermine whatever protective effects regulation on equal wages might have. Greater labour market flexibility involves both explicit and implicit deregulation. Thus there have been in some countries actual alteration of existing protective legislation such as reasonable maternity leave and benefits, compensation for work-related illnesses and accidents, and other labour standards; while more generally the implementation of such laws and norms has been increasingly ignored in practice, as part of the drive towards greater competitiveness through labour market flexibility.

Alternative Policies for Women Workers

It may be obvious from the previous section that the critical policy issue relates not simply to how to help women workers cope with the ongoing changes in macro-economic policy in the developing world, but more significantly to lobby for the design of macro-economic policies that are sensitive to the needs of working women and which do not put the burden of adjustment on already disadvantaged groups in general. Thus, it would be mistaken to view macro-economic policies as given by some "higher" authority and then discuss the impact on women, or to relegate women to the grey zone of "weaker sections" eligible for safety nets from the charitable coffers of the state. As Mao Tse Tung said, (based on the Chinese ideogram) "women hold up half the sky" - and in many developing countries in particular they hold up much more than half in terms of total productive and reproductive contributions to economy and society. Thus any desirable and sustainable economic interventions by the state, at macro, meso and micro levels, must be both "gender-sensitive" and focussed upon liberating the capabilities of the mass of women and men.

Clearly, the design of macro-economic policies will be highly dependent upon the specific circumstances of each country, and universal prescriptions are neither possible nor desirable. But some general indications are in order, especially if the broad strategy is one that has to be counterposed to the specific type of structural adjustment package that is now in such general use.

To begin with, no structural adjustment package (gender-sensitive or otherwise) can be economically successful if it does not involve substantial outlays by the government on physical and social infrastructure. Physical infrastructure, including transport and communications networks, supply of energy and buildings for necessary services, water and sanitation facilities etc, are crucial not only for the current well-being of the people but also for future growth prospects. And it is equally important to emphasise social infrastructural spending, on health, education, provision of public goods and services. The mistake is to see these as "soft" sectors which governments may try to protect solely out of a magnanimous concern for welfare : experience across the globe has led to the awareness that investment in health, education and skill formation of the people in general rather than a selected group (whether determined by gender or other considerations) is absolutely crucial for future growth and a sound economy. The increases in aggregate social productivity that some from such physical and social investment have a bearing on both the potential for growth and the material conditions of women (and men) workers. And it is similarly critical that such investments are undertaken by governments without undue obsession with cost-recovery and profitability in purely market-determined terms, for the social rates of return from such activities are likely to be substantially higher than private returns. Thus, leaving these activities "to the market" is a recipe for disaster.

Secondly, such investments have been found to be much more effective the more decentralised the control over resource allocation and type of investment. This is important not only in the broad democratic sense, but because it allows women much greater say in the social allocation of resources and typically encourages much greater efficiency of use. The specific form of decentralisation must vary according to social context, but it remains an important general principle.

Thirdly, the push towards industrialisation must not allow a neglect of minimum labour standards. The usual argument that such standards are "luxuries" for developing countries and can be ignored until certain levels of development are reached, is specious because of the important role such standards play in improving economy-wide productivity and laying the foundations for stable, social welfare-improving economic growth. As evident from the earlier discussion, such standards are particularly relevant for women workers, whose marginal employment increases in developing countries have been largely in the informal and export-oriented sectors, in which labour standards and minimum protection for workers are typically absent.

In addition, there are certain micro-level interventions which have been found to be effective in improving the conditions faced by women workers. The informal sector, where conditiond faced by working women are typically the worst, should be the main focus of such interventions. One of the most important areas of such interventions is in the field of provision of credit to women. Those attempts that have focussed upon targeting women for access to credit through revolving funds or other (typically non-subsidised) forms, have been very successful in generating more self-employment among women or increasing the viability of existing economic activities including in agriculture. The success of the Grameen bank in Bangladesh, and other similar ventures such as the Mahila Samakhya in Karnataka, India, etc., indicate that the simple access to credit can become a catalyst for all sorts of change in both rural and urban informal sectors. Other non-governmental interventions in Bangladesh, such as the Ganoshasthya Kendra and Banchte Shekha, have indicated the scope for innovations in the occupational diversification of women, although the basic problem of economic viability of different occupations may remain. [Afsar, 1990.]

Usually it is a combination of measures - some legal, some economic, some social - which work together to increase occupational diversification and material welfare of women. A study of Sri Lanka [Rodrigo and Deraniyagala, 1990] concluded that certain welfare measures such as in education policy interacted with a well-distributed network of transport and communications and some conducive socio-cultural changes operating on the supply side of the market to promote mobility (sectoral and occupational) of Sri Lankan women into the non-household sector of the economy to a degree unmatched in much of the rest of the developing world. While the government strove to be a benevolent employer to its own 150,000 female workers, labour legislation in the form of Minimum Wage protection, maternity benefits, Factory Ordinances, retirement benefits,etc. (some of which actually dated from colonial times) made a significant contribution towards improving terms and conditions of employment for females in the formal private sector. As a result, there is clear evidence that women's occupational spread in Sri Lanka became more diversified over the 1980s, although there have been some reversals in the recent past as a result of the recent focus on export-processing employment.

References

Afsar, Rita [1990] "Employment and occupational diversification of women in Bangladesh", ILO-ARTEP Working Paper, New Delhi

Ahmed, Iftikhar [1994] "Technology and feminisation of work", Economic and Political Weekly Review of Women Studies, April 30.

Anker, R and C Hein [1985] "Why third-world urban employers usually prefer men", International Labour review, Vol 124 No 1.

Anker, R and C Hein (eds) [1986] Sex Inequalities in Urban Employment in the Third World, London: Macmillan.

Baden, Sally [1993] "The impact of recession and structural adjustment on women's work in developing and developed countries", ILO Geneva Working Paper 19, IDP-Women.

Banerjee, Nirmala (ed) [1991] Indian Women in a Changing Industrial Scenario, New Delhi : Sage Publications.

Barbezat, Debra [1993] "Occupational segmentation by sex in the world", ILO IDP Women Working Paper, no 13, Geneva.

Beneria, Lourdes and M Roldan [1987] The crossroads of Class and Gender : Industrial Homewrok, Subcontracting and Household Dynamics in Mexico City, Chicago : Univ of Chicago Press.

Beneria, Lourdes and Shelley Feldman (eds) [1992] Unequal Burden, Economic Crises, Persistent poverty and Women's Work, Boulder : Westview Press.

Boserup, Ester [1970] Women's Role in Economic Development, New York : St. Martin's Press.

Buvinic, M [1993] "The feminisation of poverty ? Research and policy needs", Paper presented to a Syposium on Poverty, Geneva : IILS.

Commonwealth Secretariat [1991] "Women and structural adjustment : Selected case-studies commissioned for a Commonwealth group of experts", in Commonwealth Economic Papers, No 22, London.

Cornia, GA, R Jolly and F Stewart [1987] Adjustment with a Human Face, a study for UNICEF, Oxford: OUP.

Duncan, OD and B Duncan [1955] "A methodological analysis of segregation indexes", American Sociological review, No 20.

Elson, Diane [1992] "Male bias in structural adjustment", in H Afshar and C Dennis (eds) Women and Adjustment Policies in the Third World, London : Macmillan.

Elson, Diane [1993] "Structural adjustment with gender awareness : "Vulnerable groups", gender-based distortions" and "male bias", Gender Analysis and Development Economics Working   Paper No 2, Univ of Manchester.

Elson, Diane [1994] "Structural adjustment with gender awareness ?", in Indian Journal of Gender Studies, Vol 1 No 2.

Francke, M [1992] "Women and the labour market in Lima, Peru : Weathering economic crisis", International Centre for Research on Women.

Garson, J-P. [1992] "International migration : facts, figures, policies", OECD Observer, No 176, Paris.

Ghosh, Jayati [1994] "Gender concerns in macro-economic policy", Economic and Political Weekly Review of Women Studies, April 30.

Gladwin, C [1993] "Women and structural ajustment in a global economy", in R Gallin, A Ferguson and J Harper (eds) The Women and International development Annual, Vol 3, San Francisco : Westview Press.

Goldschmidt-Clermont, Luisella [1982] Unpaid Work in the Household, Geneva : ILO.

Gunderson, Morley [1993] Comparable Worth and Gender Discrimination : International aspects,   Geneva : ILO.

Horton, Susan, ed [1995] Women and Industrialization in Asia, London : Routledge.

IFAD [1992] The Report on Rural Women Living in Poverty, Rome.

ILO Yearbook of Labour Statistics, various issues, Geneva.

ILO [1988] Equality in Employment and Occupation, Geneva.

ILO [1993] Workers with Family Responsibilities, Geneva.

ILO [1993] Women Workers' Rights : International labour standards and women workers, Geneva :
   ILO.

ILO [1993] World Labour Report, Geneva.

International Institute for Labour Studies [1994] "Women workers in a changing global environment :   Framework for discussion", International Forum on Equality for Women in the World of Work,   Geneva : ILO.

Jaziry, I., M Almagir and T Panuccio [1992] The State of World Poverty : An Inquiry into its Causes and Consequences, New York : NYU Press.

Joekes, Susan [1991] "Women and structural adjustment " Operational implications for the JCGP memebr agencies", mimeo.

Joekes, Susan [1993] "The influence of international trade expansion on women's work",, BRIDGE Paper, Brighton : IDS.

Jose, AV [1987] "Employment and wages of women workers in Asian countries : An assessment",   ILO-ARTEP Working Paper, New Delhi.

Kirkpatrick, C and B Evers [1992] "The impact of trade liberalisation on industrial sector and labour market performance in developing countries", ILO-ARTEP Working Paper, New Delhi.

Lim, LYC [1990] "Women's work in export factories : the politics of a cause", In I. Tinker (ed) Persistent Inequalities, OUP.

Lim, Lean Lin [1994] "Women at work in Asia and the Pacific : Recent trends and future challenges", paper for international forum on Equality for Women in the World fo Work, Geneva : IILS.

Lynch, PD and H Fahmy [1984] "Craftswomen in Kerdassa, Egypt", ILO Working Paper on Women,   Work and Development, Geneva.

Mitter, Swasthi and Sheila Rowbotham, eds [1995] Women Encounter Technology : Changing patterns of employment in the Third World, London : Routledge

Moser, C. [1989] "The impact of recession and adjustment policies at the micro-level : Low income women and their households in Guayaquil, Equador", UNICEF The Invisible Adjustment : Poor Women and the Economic Crisis, New York : UNICEF

Nayak-Mukerjee, V. [1991] "Women in the economy : A selected annotated bibliography of Asia and the Pacific", Asian and Pacific development Centre, Kuala Lumpur.

Nuss, Shirley, et al [1989] Women in the World of Work : Statistical analysis and projections to the year 2000, Geneva: ILO.

Ouedraogo, Allice [1994] "Women's employment in Africa: prospects and challenges", paper for international Forum on Equality for Women in the World of Work, Geneva : IILS.

Palmer, Ingrid [1991] Gender and Population in the Adjustment of African Economies : Planning for change, Geneva : ILO.

Phongpaichit, Pasuk [1987] From Peasant Girls to Bangkok Masseuse, Geneva : ILO.

Rodrigo, Chandra and Sonali Deraniyagala [1990] "Employment and occupational diversification of Women: Sri Lanka case study", ILO-ARTEP Working Paper, New Delhi

Sen, Amartya [1990] "Gender and co-operative conflicts", in I. Tinker (ed) Persistent Inequalities, Women and World Development, New York : Oxford University Press.

Shah, Nandita and Nandita Gandhi [1992] Shadow Workers : Women in home-based production, Bombay.

Shah, Nandita, Nandita Gandhi, Sujata Gothoskar and Amrita Chhachhi [1994] "Structural adjustment, feminisation of labour force and organisational strategies", Economic and Political Weekly Review of Women Studies, April 30.

Standing, Guy [1987] "Vulnerable groups in urban labour processes", WEP Labour Market Analysis Working Paper No 13, Geneva : ILO.

Standing, Guy [1989] "Global feminisation through flexible labour", World Development, Vol 19 No 12.

Standing, Guy [1992] "Cumulative disadvantage ? Women industrial workers in Malaysia and the Philippines", ILO WEP Working Paper, Geneva.

Standing, Guy and Victor Tokman (eds) [1991] Towards social adjustment : Labour market issues in structural adjustment, Geneva : ILO.

UNCTAD [1994] World Investment report: Transnational corporations and employment, Geneva.

The Analytical and Political visibility of the work of Social Reproduction

Antonella Picchio

Introduction[1]

The present invisibility of the work of social reproduction in national accounts arises from a blank spot in the current analysis of the economic system. This spot obscures the major part of the process of social reproduction of the population, and of the labouring population in particular. The visibility of domestic work requires the visibility of the whole process of social reproduction within the basic structure of the economic system. Economic theories from the start had a reductive approach to "subsistence" and progressively the whole issue has been removed or marginalized, with major effects on gender, class and development analysis. Economic policies related to gender and development particularly need a macro framework which brings out the role of the social reproduction of people, and which discloses the gender and class conflicts inherent in the capitalist relationship between the production of commodities for profit and social reproduction of people.

This paper is composed of seven sections: the first deals with the dilemma between integrating domestic work into the picture of the economic system and taking account of the differences between the work of producing commodities and the work of reproducing people; the second introduces a perspective of livelihood economies in which the sector and the process of reproduction find a more systematic analytical location; the third introduces a classical surplus approach to visualize the conflicts inherent in the capitalist production-reproduction relationship; the surplus approach is then used in the fourth section to locate domestic work in a macro analysis of the economic system; in the fifth, the present structuring of global labour markets is presented as the context in which reproduction and work - paid and unpaid - have to be

analyzed; in the sixth, gender policies of the World Bank are assessed on the basis of their capacity for challenging main stream theories and production-reproduction relationships; finally, the case for a strategic policy of reversing the direction of the production-reproduction relationship is argued on the basis of a human development in which production and markets are made resposibile and accountable institutions of human well-being.

A theoretical embarassement and a political dilemma

Domestic work is the core of the social reproduction of people. Not only does it require physical and emotional energy, but, most important, it carries a responsibility for the survival, well-being and happiness of other people. It is unequally distributed by gender, as women are historically the ones made responsible for the dependent sections of the population (children, the old and the sick) and for adult males as well. It can be supplemented by waged work at home, waged work in public and private services and voluntary social work, but unpaid family work still has the final responsibility for harmonizing other work and/or absorbing its inadequacies.

Domestic work is not strictly demarcated by place (the home), or by functions, or by the fact of being unpaid. It is characterized by the form of command which derives from personal family relationships. As in the case of waged work, the lack of autonomous means of subsistence is the material basis of command, though the cultural and psychological forms of involvement are too complex to be reduced merely to economic dependence.

The problem of visibility is not merely statistical but also theoretical and political. Domestic work constitutes a theoretical embarassement. Either it is considered natural or it is left to be controlled within the family. Thus the family functions as an institutional enclave within which the general principles which regulate social relationships are somehow suspended. In political thought this has been noticed with regard to the question of consent (Pateman, 1988).

Economic thought has not taken sufficient cognizance of the contradictions related to domestic work. Becker (1981) has made an attempt at using the tools of economic theory to analyse the household. The exercise is wholly based on a simple extension of focus with no change of analytical perspective. The result is the usual economic reductionism squared. The way "household economics" has been

---

[1]   I thank Joan Hall for editing my English and for teaching me the pleasure of playing with words

approached, treating the family as a firm, the work of reproduction as waged work and the contingent process of daily choices as an idealized maximisation of utility, leads to misleading formalizations.[2]

While no integration of women's reproductive work into economic theory is possible on the basis of hiding the differences between the work of producing commodities and that of reproducing people, these differences must be recognized within a macro perspective where the links between different processes, markets, agents, activities, social subjects and personal and social relationships are made visible.

The point is not to see reproduction of people as a process of commodity production, to treat caring like waged work and rationalize times and places in order to make production of commodities less costly and reproduction more efficient. It is, rather, to use women's experience in social reproductive networks and to introduce radical changes in the real system and its analysis.

Human reproduction is not definable as a merely natural process. Even giving birth and breast feeding are embedded in social and historical contexts (Maher,1984; Duden, 1994). Religious and juridical norms are designed to control women's fertility and - for this very reason - their sexuality. Objectives, tools and degrees of control differ in time and space. For instance, policies may alternatively aim at the expansion or the reduction of the population. Different institutions (for example states and churches) can disagree over means and objectives, although they usually do not disagree on the need to control women's fertility. The management of the daily process of the reproduction of people, on which this paper focuses, is even more explicitly social and historical.

The degree of visibility of domestic work varies according to contexts and subjects. For instance, it is clearly visible to those who perform it but fades from view in the biased blindness of those who receive it; it is visible at home and invisible in national accounts; recognizable in personal experiences and hidden in theories.

Domestic work cannot just be added to other types of work simply broadening the definition of work. The problem is not breadth but depth. Domestic work is hidden because it sustains other types of work, formal and informal, waged and unwaged. The difficulties of measurement are partly related to

the problem of placing this work and the whole process of the reproduction of people within the analytical framework of the basic economic processes, and within the scheme of the social relationships that link different kinds of work, social subjects and economic processes.

Statistical measurements are conventional and depend upon analytical perspectives. It is hard to measure housework in time units because it usually involves the overlapping of different tasks and because it includes the emotions and anxieties of caring. Note that emotions are part of the process, as people need love as well as commodities (as firms well know when they advertise their products). The way out is to experiment with pragmatic ways of defining and measuring complex tasks, as is done in time budgets. But to measure the work of reproduction in monetary value is also difficult. Relative prices are used to compare: commodities, services for the market, incomes and wealth. Heterogeneous aggregates are made comparable through prices. Prices depend on sets of values. But in economic theories the determination, distribution and measure of value represents the core of the analysis. Value deals, in an abstract way, with the crucial questions of what wealth is and how it is produced and distributed. In a system in which social labour and products are allocated via the market, the question of value is the question of how relative prices reflect the basic processes of production, distribution and exchange and last, but by no means least, of social reproduction.

The statistical accounting of domestic work must actually be seen as a phase in a bargaining process regarding the division of labour and resources between genders, generations and classes. The interests involved lead to potentially deep conflicts: at stake are an enormous amount of physical and emotional energy and the material and psychological security of individuals, i.e. the quality of their lives. Also at stake is the cost of waged labour in local and in global markets. Thus statistics involve not only the measurement of the quantity of domestic work, but also the visibility of a bargaining process regarding the division of responsibilities for life conditions. This goes beyond the traditional private sphere of family politics. In recent decades the women's (feminist) movement has been raising the political issue of the process of reproduction (sexuality, fertility, self-identity, unpaid work) making explicit its inherent gender conflicts at international level (Dalla Costa and James, 1973; Federici, 1976). With regard to unpaid work, since the U.N. Women Conference in Nairobi, numerous NGOs, under the leadership of the organization "Counting Women's Work", have waged, in the preparation and negotiations of the U.N. Women's Conferences and in the

---

2   The point is not only to include altruism in utility preferences, but to recognize the fact that men and women , altruistic or selfish, cannot avoid relating to others in a proc Tess of continuos adaptation and reaction which dynamically shapes individual preferences, choices, and criteria of rationality.

other major conferences on enviroment, rights and social conditions (Rio, Vienna and Copenhagen) a vigorous battle on the issue of providing official statistics on the time and value of unpaid domestic work.

Starting from the visibility of unpaid women's work, the whole process of social reproduction of the population can find a more direct and powerful focus. Reproduction is generally seen by economists as a relevant question only in the analysis of subsistence economies and of poverty. It is usually reduced to the question of subsistence agriculture or to the basic needs of the poor sections of the world's population. The central role of the process of social reproduction within the core of any economic system is ignored in the North as well as in the South, just as its inherent gender and class conflicts are also ignored.

Economic analysis focuses basically on production, distribution and exchange. Social reproduction of people is seen either as a natural process with no cost, or as a final by-product of other processes which in itself does not require any specific analysis, or as a process located in a separate sphere. None of this is true. This only means that the basic problem for any social system, i.e. the relationship between the process of production of goods and services and the subsistence of people, is bound to come into the analytical picture only in an episodic and fragmented way.

This concealment of a fundamental process is not possible in the case of women, as it has systematic repercussions on their social conditions. The fact that women always maintain a visible link with their role in the process of social reproduction is usually interpreted as a specific problem of women rather than a general one; it appears as a handicap in equality, rigidity in competition, backwardness in modernization. As a matter of fact, women internalize a conflict between production and reproduction which is not adequately worked out in the social arena. Both in the family and at the paid workplace women bear the costs of a basic contradiction in the system. These costs are high whether they resist or patiently adapt.

In order to understand the social position of women it is necessary to consider the family. Nonetheless this broadening of scope is by no means sufficient. Womens rights and interests do not necessarily coincide with family interests because women are not reducible to their reproductive functions. Moreover, the family cannot be separated from other institutions such as markets and states, as they all interact in the economy.

Here lies a dilemma which women have to face. On the one hand, the recognition of the economic role of reproducing people is a step towards clarity and an explanation of many of the difficulties women encounter in reconciling their lives and work; on the other hand what is made visible is also reductive, because women as individuals tend to be identified with their role of reproducers and locked in it. The dilemma is a political one: if women -and men - lack the power to use visibility of the conditions of life as a lever to change economic and social systems, women fear that a recognition of the economic productivity of domestic work will lead to more social control and a more rigid crystallization of their historical roles. At the same time they cannot afford to hide their burden. Women individually find their tactical ways of dealing with this dilemma. But in the aggregate female population the costs of the hidden contradiction emerge in their widespread poverty and in the violence they encounter within the family and in society, showing the need for a collective strategy. In this, counting unpaid work has become a step forward.

Modern livelihood economies

In order to understand the structure of economic systems it is important to focus on the modes of subsistence, in both in the developed and developing countries.

The modes of subsistence may be defined by the modes of production of subsistence goods and services, by the social relationships which filter access to the means of subsistence, and by the network of market, state and family which shapes the process of social reproduction (Picchio, 1992). In capitalist economies, access to the means of subsistence is filtered by property and wages: those who have no property and/or no wages have no way to subsist other than by personal dependence, public assistance or by crime.

At present, at the global level, both production and reproduction are being restructured with the result of increasing tensions. We are passing through a new phase of poverty amid plenty in the North and of new enclosures in the South. The problem is that the analytical focus is only on productive and exchange processes.Reproduction is made invisible in social and political analysis but it surfaces, with all its conflicts in the experience of women and men who suffer the disruption of the subsistence economy in the South, the effects of social dumping in the North, and of radical restructuring of both production and of reproduction in the former Socialist countries.

In order to draw an analytical picture in which the process of social reproduction of the population - in its quantitative and qualitative aspects - is taken into proper account, one can start from two directions. The first departs from women's historical experience with regard to the conditions of life and sustainability of individual and social enviroments; the other, from main stream economic theories. On the one hand women's art of life is pragmatic, diversified, local, dynamic, interweaving personal and social relationships, open to needs and desires, rationally making choices on the basis of both calculations and emotions. Hence the results are necessarily indeterminate. On the other hand, economic theory in its main stream version is an idealization of static and ahistorical reality. In its monotounos use of the same technique of rational calculus and disregard of the impact of social relationships, it looks for determinacy. This means that the two directions cannot meet without critical changes in theories.

The tension involved in the relation between production and reproduction is deeply rooted, and it can no longer be brushed aside as a problem peculiar to women. Although women are constantly forced to juggle their roles in the processes of production for the market and care of people, each time weighin up to relative priorities and responsibilities it is not only they who must deal with the divisions of individual and collective responsibilities with regard to the conditions of life in the broadest sense.

With the visibility of unpaid domestic work the whole process of social reproduction gains in clarity, not only in traditional subsistence economies but also in the most advanced industrial-service economies of the North. Subsistence sectors, social norms and institutions differ in time and space; what does not change is their importance for the understanding of the structural dynamics of economic systems. In the process of social reproduction of the population and its different sections , economics, politics and ethics are necessarily linked. This combination ought to shape economic theories in their foundations to give proper visibility to the conflicts inherent in the modes of production of wealth, the distribution of income and the organization of exchange with regard to their effects on people's well being. Observation and practical experience of the conflitc over social reproduction can bring out the inadequacy of policies apparently centred exclusively on the conditions of production and exchange but, in reality, attacking directly the rising expectations of the labouring population and counting on a mass of unpaid reproductive labour to make these attacks sustainable.

The experience of life, both individual and collective, is so dramatic and complex that many cultural languages have been used to express its practical difficulties (Nussbaum, 1990). The philosophical enquiry to necessities, wants, desires was strong and fruitful in the Enlightenmen when the foundations of political economy were being laid. The basic questions of

the new scientific discourse were not only money, international trade and, later, production and distribution, but also justice, conflict, power relationships, population, insatiable needs, tastes, etc. The problem in fact was to locate man in society in a world which had lost God as the father figure providing order and care to a human race visualized at the center of the universe (Bryson, 1945).

The social reproduction of people is a material and moral process. It requires goods, commodities, services, work, love It is embedded in social conventions and institutional frameworks which are formed to regulate the division of social responsibilities towards the standards of living of society as a whole and of its sections.

A deeper analysis of the process of social reproduction allows one to grasp also the functioning of markets. Production processes and markets are socially embedded not merely because they move within historical social contexts, but also because they connect human activities and relationships on the basis of social rules.The fluidity of markets needs trust, conventions, etc. Exchanges occur not between commodities but between individuals and/or groups of people with different aims, expectations, power, trust, sympathy. The market is defined by the exchange agents and their relationships as well as by the nature of the commodity exchanged. Relative values of commodities reflect the social setting of the agents who assess them and the conditions of life play a crucial part in the setting. In the case of labour, the social evaluation is even clearer because the commmodity itself is human: it partecipates in setting its own price, in defining what is exchanged and, most of all, resists being reduced to a mere commodity.

In this context the social question appears as a complex mosaic of rights, material conditions, desires, collective and individual responsibilities. Its pattern changes in time through a long process of sedimentation of norms, customs, habits and power balances.[3]

Economic theories and paradigms

In order to grasp the social nature of the work of reproduction of people it is important to grasp the historical link between the processes of reproduction and production. In

---

[3]   For example, the demand for control over one's body is a question of personal integrity, in other words of civil rights and security of access to the means of subsistence in the broad sense of the full development of personal capabilities.

the capitalist system a separation has developed between these two as a separation of places, institutions, social organizations, norms and cultures, distinguishing waged work from the unpaid work of reproduction. This progressive separation favoured the concealment of the link between the different types of work and processes. In order to restore that link in economic analysis we must look at the course of history in reverse, moving from the present neoclassical objectivization of markets to the original moral economy in which subsistence was the explicit goal of productive systems, and the relation between rich and poor was regulated through a more visible command. The idea of this backward look, of course, is not to advocate a return to past social systems that were intolerable for exploitation, repression and paternalism. What such a perspective can do is help us to identify the stages whereby the process of bargaining over the material, cultural, and moral conditions of life carried on by the whole labouring population has been progressively obscured from view.

In approaching economic theories we must look first of all at the current confusion between abstraction and idealization of human behaviour Because of this confusion between the two different cognitive processes, some features of the social system are seen by economic theory as ahistorical and absolute. In this way, as in the case of neoclassical theory, some important, persistent and general aspects of historical experience are bound to be considered marginal and accidental solely because they do not fit with the idealized picture. This is what happens with the process of social reproduction of labour, where some fundamental human characteristics (such as the need to be fed and lodged adequately and to relate to other people) which should be reflected directly in the general framework, are treated as rigidities and frictions, and relegated to the marginal and accidental aspects of the analysis or else confronted only at policy level.[4]

Some reflections of the complexity of the process of social reproduction surface now and then, for example, in: the analysis of consumption, poverty, efficiency wages and the treatment of standards of living.

Consumption, is seen by neoclassical economics as a final process activated by individual choices generally made on the basis of the idealized criteria of utility maximization whereby any interdependence of utility functions is considered a curiosum. In this context the household becomes a crucial economic unit for empirical surveys, but it is not used to challenge the methodological individualism of the general

theory of allocation. It is usually left to anthropologists to speculate on consumption as a means of communicating social status, rank, habits, tastes (Douglas and Isherwood, 1979), as it is left to historians to question the actual distinction between necessities and luxuries (Braudel, 1970, chap.3).

Studies on poverty represent the bulk of the studies on standards of living. It is in fact at the bottom of the social ranking that the "exogeneity" and complexity of subsistence becomes most dramatically evident (Sen, 1983, 1987; Atkinson, 1989). Only at this level has the process of reproduction been taken explicitly into account in the form of basic needs (absolute poverty) and unequal distribution of income (relative poverty).

Poverty is usually separated from the general insecurity of historical standards of living inherent in the normal functioning of the labour market, and from the the theory of wages. Only at poverty level do needs and distribution of income come to the forefront. At this point poverty is dealt with, at best, more in terms of solidarity with the weak sections of the population rather than in terms of the general insecurity. Instead of questioning the normal functioning of the waged labour market as the main filter of access to the means of subsistence, the issues of class-and-gender power relationships and equity are handled in neoclassical theory as marginal aspects which do not challenge the general theory of the distribution of income

A critical debate on poverty (Desai, 1986; Sen, 1983; Townsend, 1979) focuses on the possibility of drawing an empirical and theoretical concept of relative deprivation of those "whose resources do not allow them to fulfil the elaborate social demands and customs which have been placed upon citizens of that society" (Townsend, 1993, p.36).

A new approach to standards of living has been proposed by Amartya Sen (1985, 1985b, 1987). Sen escapes the reductionist interpretation which presents them merely as a bundle of commodities and stresses the human factor. He presents standards of living in terms of capabilities and functions which are defined historically and socially embedded in a context within which the individual interacts with other individuals to fulfil his/her practical well-being and respond to personal and collective esponsibilities. In this context, individual and collective welfare necessarily require more complex criteria of choice.

Reflections of the process of social reproduction appear also in economic analysis when wages higher than marginal productivity, are seen as an element of higher efficiency. The case for "efficiency wages" is argued in terms of the consent of some strong sections of the labour force which must to be gained and maintained in order to guarantee higher

---

[4]   The split between theory and policy is a characteristic of the neoclassical approach . In this respect, supply-and-demand theorists like Senior can be seen as forerunners.

productivity within the firm (Akerlof and Yellen, 1986). Thus in this case there is a partial recognition that social norms and the material and moral conditions of the social reproduction of labour are important factors in wage determination . Once again, though, this aknowledgement is not deployed to challenge the traditional theory of wages and employment. In fact efficiency wages, being higher than marginal "technical" productivity, continue to be seen as a cause of unemployment in an ideally automatically clearing labour market.

At the macro level standards of living are directly related to the distribution of income and, consequently, to the dynamics of the labour market.Thus the way in which the question of the standards of living is seen depends very much on the way in which we analyse the labour market and the distribution of income. In this sense, the analysis of standards of living is directly affected by the paradigmatic split on the theory of value and distribution which runs through the history of economic thought (Dobb, 1973; Garegnani, 1984; Sraffa, 1960).

Although both paradigms (classical and neoclassical) tend to overlook the role of the process of reproduction, reducing it to a simple question of a bundle of commodities, they differ greatly in terms of the theory of wages and on the historical determination of the economic aggregates. This methodological aspect has major implications for the analysis of the reproduction of labour as an historicla social process.

This is not the place to speculate on the classical surplus approach, but it may be useful to recall some of its analytical characteristics as they have relevant implications for the analysis of the link between production and reproduction (Picchio, 1992). 1) Profit is defined as a residuum given by the difference between production and the incomes (wages and transfers) of the labouring classes. 2) wages, as norm, are the reflexion of conventional standards of living, historically given in time and space; they relate not to the individual but to his family as a unit of reproduction of the "race". 3) Wages are determined separately from other prices; hence, the analytical framework is partly founded on the specificity of labour as a human commodity. 4) prices are costs of production, directly reflecting the physical process of production; generally (apart from all the complications of the trasformation of values into prices) changes in distribution between classes do not affect relative prices. 5) The productive sector of subsistence goods and services plays a central role in the structure of the system.

The most important aspect of the surplus approach is the central role in the analytical core of surplus as residuum between the value of production and the value of subsistence of the labouring population. The rate of profit, which is the key objective in a system based on the production of commodities, is defined as the ratio between surplus (production minus subsistence) and advanced capital. The relationship can be expressed in the Ricardian formulation in which all capital is transformed into variable capital as:

$$(1) \qquad r = \frac{P-wL}{wL}$$

where r is the rate of profit, P production, w wage and L labour units.

If we include public transfers (T) in the subsistence of the labouring population the relation becomes:

$$(2) \qquad r = \frac{P-(wL+T)}{wL}$$

In 1 and 2 the trade-off between profit and the costs of social reproduction is made clearly visible.

Classical analysis expresses the main structural relationships in terms of aggregates and representative behaviour. The main structural processes (production, distribution and exchange) are explained differently. In particular: production is a physical process which relates output to input; distribution is an institutional process reflecting the social norms and power relationships which historically shape the rules for distribution of the product; and exchange rates of producible commodities (by definition not generally and persistently scarce) reflect the normal conditions of production once the distribution between wages and profit has been specified on the basis of social relationships; effective demand depends on the historical dimension of markets, the rate of growth, and income distribution.

Different markets (labour, commodities and money) are analysed differently. The competitive mechanisms of adjustment between supply and demand are analysed separately from changes in the structural relationships as market fluidity, guaranteed by producibility and mobility of commodities, is seen as a different process from the structural dynamics of the system. The former is regulated by competition, the latter by technical innovation, the opening of new markets and, last but not least, the "insatiable needs" of the population. Distribution between classes is located at a different analytical level than distribution within classes. One is reflected in the structure of normal prices, the other in the adjustments of market prices to normal prices. Normal prices are not defined by the mechanisms of adjustment activated by allocation but by the structural forces of the system, i.e. not by scarcity but by production processes and social power relationships. A general model of systematic interrelationships between different processes and different markets is not considered plausible (Garegnani, 1984) .[5]

In this framework, the labour market can be disciplined through insecurity and poverty, but it cannot be sterilized of its complex human factor. The analytical perspective based on the surplus approach leaves a space open, precisely at the core of the analysis, for the visibility of a deep potential conflict between production of commodities for profit and the social reproduction of the labouring population. The conflict is not only over the quantities which define the surplus and the rate of profit, but over the very objectives of the two processes.

Production of commodities and the process of the accumulation of profit can be partly consistent with increasing standards of living of the labouring population. This "harmony", nevertheless, does not hold for ever and for all the sections of the labouring population, and this fact can lead to serious contradictions and to recurrent crisis of social reproduction.

In order to create a more advanced and stable ground for human development it is necessary to see the deep tensions between production of commodities and social reproduction of people. Human sustainable development is both a question of revealing hidden costs and of setting new priorities and of legitimising new political subjects. In order to accomplish the shift of priorities, it is necessary to focus on the structure of existing economic systems locating subsistence in the analytical framework as a process which involves not only quantities of commodities but also social relationships and conflicts.

A classical macro approach to reproductive work

After we have located the process of reproduction of labour within the basic processes we can locate domestic work among the main national aggregates.

The production of commodities embodies not only paid work of production but also unpaid work of reproduction even if one of them is hidden from theory. To add domestic work into the national aggregates does not mean to increase production. It means to reveal the hidden <u>quantum</u> of labour embodied in production which is hidden. In this way we are revealing a hidden cost, not a hidden product. The dimension of the work hidden, calculated by Goldsmith Clermont as near to that of paid labour, reveals the entity of the analytical problem.

It is interesting to speculate on some of the analytical implications of this way of proceeding.

First of all we can define a simple relationship whereby product P is a function of waged labour (L_w) and domestic labour (Ld)

$$(3) \ P = f(Lw + Ld)$$

The product is distributed between labour (waged and domestic labour) and profit (R), hence:

$$(4) \ P = LwW + R + L_d0$$

From relation (4) we could say that the share of P going to domestic labor is zero because its wage is zero. Or we could say that part of the product goes to domestic workers for subsistence but is transferred from W, considered as a family wage. Nevertheless, although it is true that waged labour is vertically integrated with family labour, the rule of distribution within the family is not specified. The problem is obviously crucial for women, but we might dimiss it analytically if we could consider L_d a given quantity, depending, for instance, exclusively on habits and customs, not affecting or affected by other variables. These two arguments - the family wage and the separate sphere - have been effectively used to dismiss the whole question of the value of domestic work.

As we have seen, the point of making domestic work visible is not to separate it from other variables but to clarify its relationship with them. In this context we should specify the relationship between domestic work and the other variables: product, the quantity of waged labour, wages and profit (Lw, P, W, R).

Domestic labour affects the quality and the quantity of waged labour (Lw). The impact on quality is depending not on professional training but on the more complex primary reproductive processes involved in health, self-identification and socialization which are crucial for building consent and cooperation at the work place. It is a kind of human capital which is not produced by training in schools but by education in the family: on the basis of nurturing capabilities (Ruddick,

---

[5]   It is important to draw attention on the fact that in neoclassical theory an objective price determination is seen as exogenous to power relationships: i.e. unions have no power in setting wages (Keynes, 1930, p.110); while in the classical surplus approach power relationships are exogenous to the determination of relative prices i.e. real normal wages are set separately from relative prices (Sraffa, 1960).

1990). Domestic work also affects the hours of waged work in the sense of freeing waged labour from the responsibilities of caring for dependent persons. It is very flexible work which adapts continuosly to changing circumstances; it is regulated by conventions, but, as women are active subjects, it is also open to a bargaining process within the family and society. With regard to wages (W), the role of family work is very important as there is a certain degree of substitution between domestic work and wage commodities, and standards of living do not depend exclusively on commodities but also on non market goods and services. Moreover, through domestic work the family partly absorbs the conflicts which originate at the work place transforming them into private conflicts.

If the quality and the quantity of labor depend on family work, P , which is a function of labor, also depends on it. Wages and profit are inversely related within a given product; but as, historically, profit is more likely to impose wages as a residuum domestic work bears the final responsibility and burden of the quality of life given the wage bundle. This residual role accounts for the harshness of domestic work, since reproduction is caught between a given wage and necessities and wants. This is a joint problem of class and gender power relationships as the inverse relationship between wages and profit becomes a direct relationship between the amount of unpaid housework and profit.

The gap between women's work load, the high social productivity of their work, and the poverty of resources distributed to women and to the social reproduction of the labouring population in general, shows how social and non-objective is the link between work and the distribution of income. The roots of widespread women's poverty lie precisely in their unpaid work in reproduction.

The visibility of domestic work as a political demand aims not only at making the relationship between reproductive work and the social product explicit, but also at opening a debate on the rules of distribution, on the modes of production and on the quality of the production-reproduction relationship.

In policy terms the visibility of the large mass of unpaid reproductive work and the stress on its social character opens different possibilities. First of all the magnitude and the quality of the problem explodes the myth of equality both in terms of more paid work for women than in terms of more unpaid work for men, although both perspectives can be positive for the quality of women and men's lives. Making the double load visible and better shared does not relieve the burden it simply adjusts it and it does not increase wages or reduce the total amount of work. Also the use of the sector of social reproduction for a major expansion of the market

economy must be carefully examined taking into proper account the issues of the unequal distribution of incomes and the growing insecurity of wages which are high in current tertiary sector. Social deprivation could even increase by a restructuring of reproduction as a market for profit. Moreover while organizing the process of social reproduction through non profit organizations may tap new resources, it does not balance the growing irresponsibility towards the standards of living of the working population of the leading multinationals and financial speculators which, at present, on the whole, are undermining the conditions of life all over the world. [6]

A global labour market

At the global level a profound restructuring of the traditional forms of access to subsistence is now in progress. Property rights are being introduced in new areas with the result that, especially in the South, traditional means of subsistence - land, water, woods, etc - are made less and less accessible. Moreover, the traditional ways of producing subsistence goods and services are being crowded out by export-led production of commodities for profit, with the final result, at present, of a net outflow of resources and growing poverty and increasing corruption.

In the western countries, welfare programs are shrinking just when insecurity increases in the labour market. Public expenditure shrinks in response to the financial pressure of growing public debts also fuelled by speculation in an increasingly volatile global financial market. National states are expected to guarantee the risks of international financial agents at the cost of explosive internal social risks. The result is the dismantling of the postwar safety nets which had made growing standards of living and a decrease of inequality possible in the period between the fifties and the mid seventies.

The ways in which social recession takes place differ according to local history and institutional frameworks. At the world and national level, the effects are unevenly distributed among the various sections of the population according to the existing relative power relationships. In particular, women's poverty has become striking.

---

[6]   The policy issues to be drawn from the inclusion of unpaid work within economic aggregates is too complex and new to be worke out here. Moreover the impact of the Bejiging IV Women's Conference on gender and development policies is not yet forseeable.

In Europe, for instance, the positive trend characterizing all the basic indicators of the post-war labour market has been slowing down and even reversing. Unemployment, inequality and poverty, which had decreased in the early postwar decades, are again rising (Room, 1990; Atkinson, 1990; Townsend, 1991). After the havoc of the war, in a general mood of distrust in the capacity of the free market to maximize social welfare, and with the competition of the socialist states, western states took on new responsibilities towards employment and standards of living of the population. Rather than in terms of relief to the poor, the new policies were argued on the grounds of maintaining a basic standard of income and supply of public services, in the recognition that the free market would not guarantee full employment and adequate standards of living. This universal approach was meant to prevent poverty and destitution and, more ambitiously, wars (Beveridge, 1944). Full employment was assumed both as the objective and as the key to what today we could call "sustainable human development".

Policies differed in the various European countries, but, on the whole, the period between the late forties and the early seventies can now be recognized as a "golden age" with regard to the rates of increase of living standards and of social security of the labouring classes. Nevertheless their levels were still inadequate for large sections of the population and an enormous amount of housework was still on women's shoulders, under the umbrella of a family wage. The progressive policies explicitly recognized domestic work as a foundation of the wealth of nations and aimed to rationalize and maintain the capitalist relationship between production and reproduction (Beveridge, 1943).

Starting with the first oil shock (1973) - presented as a "natural" event - followed by the increase of interest rates, the positive trends of the main social indicators began to slow down and deteriorate. The effects of the oil crisis were global and it was soon clear that they had more to do with international trade and the instability of financial markets than with the scarcity of natural resources.

High interest rates fuelled a state fiscal crisis which transformed overspending into a financial trap. Major reforms were necessary. A rethinking of the whole structure of public expenditure and of the accountability of state administrations was demanded together with new norms for the global financial market. The crisis was tackled by simply regressing to pre-war economic dogmas, in theories and in policies, and by leaving state administrations even less accountable in terms of the results of public expenditure and financial markets increasingly deregulated.

Priorities changed and the problems of the labour market

and the responsibilities of the state towards social security lost political and theoretical simpathy. Policy main concerns have become international trade and budget deficits; anti-inflationary policies are systematically juxtaposed to full employment, and the revolution of rising expectations induced by the positive trends of previous decades is harshly repressed.

The "social question", at best, is argued in terms of solidarity with the poor rather than in terms of citizens' rights. International competition is once again seen merely in terms of relative low costs of labour. The whole question of the complex network of market-state-family responsibilities and of a socially embedded labour contract has been reduced to a schematic and unrealistic market-state dichotomy.

Budget constraints shape social perspectives and policies. The scarcity of (producible) resources and moralizing about people's laziness and excessive expectations are the main arguments used in designing the regressive reforms of the eighties. The well-being of the labouring population is once more seen merely as a cost for the productive system, and responsibility for it is increasingly shifted onto the family. Social conflicts are relegated to private affairs or left to criminal law when they come out in the streets.

The reversion of northern economic policies has had dramatic effects on the developing countries. The free market policies developed in the North are imposed on social systems in the South where the waged labour market not only has to be disciplined but has yet to be fully established. In the South, "primitive accumulation" is still going on: this means that with the current development policies traditional forms of access to the means of subsistence are being eroded while new ones are not yet open. The centuries-long process needed in Europe to transform the labouring population into the labouring poor and finally into the waged labour force, is being forced on the South by the impositions of the global labour market. The problem is that while production is globalized, reproduction of the labouring population remains local. Hence it is easy to hide the growing tensions between production and reproduction, although their effects become dramatically visible in the mass starvation of some areas of the South, particularly Africa.

In this context of deprivation the opposition between the labour market and the financial market is striking. The global financial market, which is going through a process of accelerated fluidity with the inherent risks of great instability, rules national economic policies. The risks are no longer controllable by any central bank, and fears of financial crisis lead to domestic policies involving high social and human costs.

International institutions such as the I.M.F. and the World Bank subordinate the social question to the efficiency of the markets. Their experts seem to be convinced that the structural adjustmentent policies will lead to growth. They admit that there is a desert to be crossed and that in the process not all sections of the population have the same chances of survival, but in the end, on the other side, the garden of free markets and of capital accumulation will bear fruits and flowers for most. It seems that they do not realize that a desertification process is taking place, leading to dramatic impoverishment.

With regard to the complexity of the social question, economists are at the moment very inadequate and non-accountable advisors. The adjustments introduce reforms in order to establish efficient markets of "factors of production" and products. In this context, social issues are interpreted as frictions that delay the adjustment process. Failures are attributed to time lags and rigidities rather than to the inadequacy and reductivism of the analytical perspective.

The economists of the World Bank seem to be ready to recognize failures, but they also seem determined not to question economic theories. At the end of the day it is individuals, and mainly women, who are expected to adapt their behaviour, cope with necessities tame their desires and conform their choices to idealized models of market efficiency. These models are idealized to the point of being monotonously used for very different contexts. Some parameters change but the assumed functional relationships and the assumed interrelationships between different markets and social subjects remain unchanged. The models are idealized but by no means neutral. The effect have been a major redistribution of income from the poor to the rich segments of the population, and of resources from the South to the North (Townsend, 1993).

The policies implemented are: a) stabilization, seen as reduction in balance of payments deficits; b) promotion of the private sector, i.e. deregulation, contracting out of public services, sale of state enterprises and the creation of economic, institutional and political environments congenial to savings, investment and entrepreneurship; c) market liberalization and price reforms, based on more foreign and domestic competition and exchange rate liberalization; d) rationalization of public sector institutions (World Bank, 1994a, pp.12-13).

On the basis of these policies SAPs are defined as follows:

Adjustment is necessarily concerned with how economic change and resource reallocation come about, and on whom the costs and benefits fall and why. It is about factor mobility and productivity resulting from shifts and incentives from what are seen as economically less productive activities to economically more productive activities, as well as from non-tradable to tradable goods. It is concerned with the meaning and measurement of efficiency in resource allocation and use, especially the functioning of factor markets. It is about prices and the role of prices in defining economic opportunities, and the strength and limitations of prices as economic signals. It is also about the role of the state in the economy, the relationship (or balance) between the public and private sectors, and public expenditure priorities and policies (World Bank, 1994a p. 13).

The scope of the World Bank's structural interventions is well presented but, the problem is that the neoclassical theory of prices, on which the World Bank experts rely, embodies a theory of distribution which basically does not recognize the specificity of labour as a factor of production and the social conflicts inherent in the profit-subsistence trade off.

Women, work and social traps

In the implementation of structural adjustment policies the World Bank's experts have started to acknowledge the specificity of households, subsistence and domestic work.

A well known paradox - already mentioned by Pigou and others - surfaces once again:

Cooking, according to economists, is "active labour" when cooked food is sold, and "economically inactive labor" when it is not. Housework is "productive" when performed by a paid domestic servant and "non-productive" when no payment is involved. Those who care for children and orphanages are "occupied"; mothers who care for their children at home are "unoccupied" (Horn, 1992, p.2, quoted in World Bank, 1994a, p. 3).

In a document presented at a women's meeting in Oslo for the preparation of the Beijing conference, the World Bank experts seem to be aware of the analytical implications inherent in the inclusion of domestic work in economic analysis:

The resulting invisibility of work (both "economic" and "non-economic") undertaken predominantly by women, has important repercussions for the theory and practice of economics. It suggests that women's work is (in an economic sense) irrelevant, and can be (in effect is) discounted, or that men's labour time (though not women's) will shift and that this will occur without impact or cost for the allocation of labor and resources within the household. However, it can also suggest that women are able to (and will) shift to the same incentives in the same way as men do. Whatever the interpretation the underlying issue is that women's labor time is not given a monetary (economic) value, it is easy simply to assume that shifts in labor time allocation are possible for both men and women and that they have neglegible costs for all concerned (World Bank, 1994, p.3).

On the basis of the work of feminist economists Diane Elson and Nancy Folbre, the document of the World Bank "Paradigm Postponed: Gender and Economic Adjustment in Sub-Saharan Africa" presented in Oslo, points to the crucial issues and acknowledges the different phases of the debate on women in development.

The problem is no longer merely to "engender" economic activities and the effects of adjustment, but to focus the analysis directly on the subsistence sector and the work of reproduction. Nevertheless, this is not enough: the foundations of economic theory itself have to be seen from a women's perspective giving a proper location to reproduction in the general analytical framework and bringing out its inherent conflicts.

One result of the debate has been that at least the inadequacy of Becker's household economics has been recognized. His idealization of the allocation of time and energy (love included) within the household is seen as being not only unrealistic but also misleading:

In view of the significance of the gender division of labor in shaping economic constraints and opportunities, it is necessary to examine the social and institutional context, which at the micro economic level is provided by the household, within which the allocation of labor operates.... How a household is defined, whether in economic or statistical terms, is problematic especially in SSA. In conventional neo-classical economic analysis, simplifying assumptions are made about the nature and functioning of households as economic actors and as the medium for transmission of welfare. ...there are still many shortcomings in its - mostly implicit - assumptions. These are that a household functions as a socio-economic unity, that there is a perfect substitutability of factors of production in the household division of labor, that the household is seen as a unified entity of consumption and production, that the household has a joint utility function, that the household head serves as a proxy for the collective utility maximization of the household (the benevolent dictator), and the relations within households are characterized by pooling and sharing of their income and resources (Evans, 1989, reported in World Bank, 1994a, p.7).

The point is that the neoclassical theory of optimal allocation of resources not only fails when it is extended to the family, but is also inadequate when it analyzes the basic

structure of markets. As we have seen, its inadequacy is rooted precisely in its failure to locate the process of social reproduction of labour in the right place, i.e. at the core of the theory of prices and distribution. Moreover, the analytical problems related to the complexity of the relationship between production and reproduction concern not only the analysis of the work of women in developing countries - which the World Bank is ready to admit - but also analysis of economic systems, in the North as well as in the South.

If the production system is based on the production of commodities for profit, and the ruling social istitutions are geared to the interests and the management of the major multinationals and financial gamblers, the well-being of people is bound to be seen merely as a cost of production. The language of scarcity and budget constraints wipes out the language of individual and collective rights. Health, for instance, becomes just an entry figure in public expenditure - the easiest to cut - and not a fundamental right to well-being recognized by the states.

The process of social deregulation currently taking place is also fed by institutional changes. Multinationals can easily escape forms of social insurance introduced historically by state mediation between labor and capital. At the national level, even if the state political representatives were willing to maintain social standards, they find themselves more and more powerless, constrained by the impositions of the global financial market and by the increasing tendency to avoid social responsibilities on the part of the multinational corporations. The whole international institutional context is changing (Collingworth, Goold and Harvey, 1994).

This means that women are being left with ever fewer resources to cope daily with the responsibility of the survival and well-being of the population. The isolation of women goes hand in hand with an increase in their work load. It is becoming more difficult to discipline the rising expectations of the younger generations. The older generations feel frustrated and insecure at their marginalization as they are exposed to a high risk of poverty and lack of care. The deterioration of the enviroment makes the protection of health more troublesome and money- and time-consuming, while the public health services deteriorate. Growing flexibility and insecurity in the labour market make adult males more demanding on the family.

Practical and strategic gender policies

Since Nairobi, Women in Development (WID) sections have been established in some International Organizations including the World Bank. The focus has progressively moved. It started with gendering "neutral" aggregates in order to disclose inequalities in economic activities. In this context policies aimed at training women to equality and at removing barriers to their entrance into traditionally male activities Moser, 1993) Then efforts turned to making hidden activities visible, such as work in the agricultural subsistence economy and in social communities. This made it easier to expose the double and triple load of women (Beneria, 1992). Finally poverty, enviroment and social issues have been tackled (Braidotti, Charkiewicz, and Wierenga, 1994; Fisher, 1993; Harcourt, 1994; Mies and Shiva, 1993; . It is now time to link these different policies within a macro analytical framework which, starting from the work and the needs of reproduction, brings out the links between poverty and the structural insecurity of labour markets; i.e: to challenge the normality of the economic system not merely its accidents.

The existence of a widespread international women's movement moving directly on reproduction and livelihood, and the practice of women's networks, have led to a fruitful development of fora where grass roots, NGOs, academics and officials of international organization, come together. The preparation of the Bejing Conference has accelerated this sharing of different experiences. At present the international women's networks might offer a political space for formulating economic policies capable not merely of criticizing the present male-biased ones but also of formulating new ones, in which a general picture of the social system interlocks with local livelihhood experiences.

In this context the visibility of the work of social reproduction in national accounts could become an important step towards new perspectives on the production and distribution of resources. Once the amount of women's work is made visible, productivity and growth will also have to be redefined, for example, giving. due attention, to the numerous productive and commercial enterprises women undertake for survival and well-being of themselves and their families.

Within this context of a collective search for new perspectives, the analytical macro approach suggested in previous sections of this paper could be used to visualize more directly some basic aspects of the social systems, and this may have important implications for economic policies. The main results of this approach are: a direct, normal focus on the modes of reproduction; the visibility of a profound potential tension between production of commodities and reproduction of people; the emergence of a social subject that operates, organises and struggles directly with the objective of defending and improving livelihood.

If the process of social reproduction is made visible and

interventions on the productive and exchange processes are assessed on the basis of their effects on well-being, it is easier to trace responsibilities and implement social accountability, preventing major damage in the social enviroment and releasing tensions. In this context it should become more difficult to externalize social costs originating in market activities and to use women as the final buffer for social dumping.

Hiding social costs is a trick, not a solution. It can no doubt affect the distribution of resources and hence make some sections of the population better off, but in the end social dumping will emerge as destruction of the system's potential capacity. Increasing costs of social control, armed conflicts, collective self-destructive behaviour, personal frustrations, all added to the massive destruction of natural resources, in the long run must undermine the sustainability of the present production-reproduction relationship.

I shall give two examples in which the link between production and reproduction is seen as essential for development policies: a) the case of subsistence agriculture in Sub-Saharan African countries; b) the interaction between social productivity and competitive small firms in the industrial districts of Emilia-Romagna (a region of northern Italy).

In the first case the structural adjustments policies led to an excessive impoverishment of the subsistence sector, with disastrous effects on health, education, women's access to resources and increased risks of mass starvation (Elson, 1993). This demonstrated that there are downward limits within which production for profit can extract resources and work from the subsistence sector. Elson has called attention to the rigidity of the subsistence economy, seeing it as a structural productive problem and not as a mere friction in the fluidity of allocation of resources. Women's work is not an infinitely elastic resource and subsistence cannot be sacrificed to favor export-led production (ibid). Production and reproduction are linked in a circular flow which structures the system. Cash crops are profitable for the exporters but can be fatal for local and national development. If new crops and new market agents undermine the process of reproduction, what appears as a plus in the international trade balance is in fact a minus in the productive capacity

Women resist changes and defend subsistence crops not because they resist modernization but because they are wise and rational. In the end even the experts of the World Bank had to recognize this, and also acknowledge the fact that if some land and credit are given to women they manage to activate a virtuous cycle of subsistence and accumulation of surpluses that makes it possible to pay the debts and contribute to local economies (World Bank, 1994b).

A policy which explicitly aims at balancing production and reproduction could ultimately produce greater net effects than SAPs. Market activities can benefit from subsistence enterprises. The problem of activating innovative activities lies more in the support of people's drive to better the conditions of livelihood - giving them some initial resources - than in sacrificing subsistence for cash crops to be exported, often to pay for state burocracies, aggressive armies, and debt servicing.

The second example regards the "industrial districts" of Emilia, an Italian region run by a progressive administration since the end of the war. It is a case in which small firms are highly competitive in the international market, benefiting from a social enviroment where the network of relationships between market, state and civil society presents a high degree of synergy. High standards of living originating from high wages and a social policy of efficient public services, feed back in high productivity within the firm and thus create the basis for workers' greater consent and commitment to the firms objectives (Brusco, 1995, pp.1-17).

The firms compete in the international market, not in the old Fordist model of mass production at low price, but in the market of quality products, highly diversified to satisfy consumer' choice and sold at high prices (textiles, tiles, shoes, etc.). The quality of the product and the flexibility of production is guaranteed by workers' participation, which may be defined as:
the accountability of workers in facing all the problems of the productive process, coping with unforeseen difficulties, noticing initial signs of malfunctioning of machines and looking for solutions to the problems, making suggestions on how to modify designs in order to avoid defects in the product (Brusco, 1995, p.1, translated).

It is recognized by progressive administrators, economists and even employers that the quality of the social enviroment outside the firm is an important component of productivity within the firm. It is the mixture of high living standards, social commitment, leisure, and social services which allows for higher integration of workers' intelligence and responsibility in the productive process (ibid.).

It is interesting to note that in the same geographical area the social services cover all the demand for nursery education for children aged 3-6 and are internationally known for their high standards. Moreover, the women are known for their autonomy, and activism in political parties and unions. Female activity rates are among the highest in Italy and women's entrepreneurship is also widespread.

The example is given to show that a policy of investment in the social structure and support of living standards can

create an enviroment which is market-friendly, though not necessarily friendly to destructive market practices. Social control is based on the implementation of democratic ways of coping with conflicts. The success story supports the idea that an unbalanced growth of production based on social dumping is inefficient, as well as unethical and politically risky.

The Emilian case is obviously just a progressive example of positive synergy between different institutions - local administration, unions, employers associations, political parties women's groups, etc. It provides for a relatively higher quality of civic life, showing in practice that there can be more progressive mediations between production for the market and social reproduction of people.

Potential tensions within society can be coped with in less destructive ways, but it shows also that the double load of women remains. Responsibilities remain unequally distributed between genders; this fact is shown directly in time budget surveys and indirectly by the different behaviour of men and women in the waged labour market. Men's activity rates, hours of work and flexibility continue to be almost totally unresponsive to family conditions (the number of children and wife's work situation); women, on the contrary, reflect their family cycle directly in their work time. Women as an aggregate are ready to offer very diversified time schedules (including night shifts and holidays), though individually they offer rigid time schedules.The difficulties that women face in composing their lives, combining production and reproduction, are persistently reflected by gender differentials in activity rates, productive sectors, qualifications, wages and careers.

Both examples have been argued purely in terms of market efficiency to show that a policy focusing on the link between production and reproduction can lead to good market results. All the effort required to make this common sense clear arises from the inadequacy of theories and policies for visualizing the necessary link. The integration of reproduction into the capitalist system is a fact of life. It is the integration of social reproduction into theories which is difficult. As a consequence of the analytical blindness, policies deal with reproduction only with a patching-up approach. It could be said that theories do not see reproduction because they cannot visualize the social conflicts between production and reproduction regularly encountered at policy level. In this respect, we could say that both theories and policies are blinded because they are gender and class biased.

In both the examples cited, in the African subsistence case and in the opulent and emancipatory Emilian context, women maintain full responsibility for the "survival, well-being and happiness" of dependent family members and of adult males. Some of them may gain from higher standards of living but on the whole they still have a double work load and absorb the tensions of the dialectical relationship between production of commodities and reproduction of people. This tension cannot be relieved until it is tackled directly in practices, theories and policies.

In both cases, the market system integrates women into its objectives and takes on responsibilities for the quality of life only within the limits of the maximization of profits. Progressive perspectives in this respect allow for higher margins of mediation in class and gender conflict but they do not solve them.

In the one example reproduction is concerned with survival and in the other with well-being; happiness is out of sight in both. To get even a glimpse of it the perspective is not merely to integrate reproduction and women into the market, but to integrate the market into the moral economy of a good life. It is not only a question of integration but of inverting priorities, putting livelihood first. In market integration profit remains the leading motive, if priorities could change desire could become the driving force.

Desire is one of the basic forces of the economy of life and has shaped human experience and the processes of civilization. This is well expressed by the art critic, N. Frye:

> Civilization is not merely an imitation of nature, but the process of making a total human form out of nature, and it is impelled by the force that we have just called desire. The desire for food and shelter is not content with roots and caves: it produces the human forms of nature that we call farming and architecture. Desire is not a simple response to needs, for an animal may need food without planting a garden to get it, nor is it a simple response to want, or desire for something in particular. It is neither limited to nor satisfied by objects, but it is the energy that leads human society to develop its own form. (Frye, 1957, pp. 105-6)

Strategic gender policies aim at the fulfilment of desire and not only integration into the market. Inverting priorities means integrating market and state with women's reproductive responsibilities. The inversion does not take place in stages - first subsistence, then well-being and finally happiness. People's struggles for livelihood must be seen in their richness and complexity, even in emergency. Human lives are not frictions to the economic system but a precious dynamic force. In this regard women's experience in resistance, innovation and enterprise is crucial, together with

their ability to link survival, well-being and the hope of happiness. People in fact need beauty, pleasure, hope and relationships as much as food, even in wars and in refugee camps.

Women's struggles for a good life, the feminist movement, and the international networks working on gender and development, have the merit of questioning the quality of the relationship between production and reproduction[1]. This is the basis of their practices, policies and analytical perspectives. Women play a leading role in a human development perspective: not merely for their reproductive function, but for their political experience in facing the conflict inherent in the present perverse relationship between profit-oriented production and the social reproduction. Women are shifting the balance of power through the visibility of their unpaid work, the authority of their responsibility and accountability, and the politics of need and desire.

---

[1]   The international networks I am referring to are : DAWN (Development Alternatives with Women for a New Era), WEDO (Women Enviroment Development Organization), WIDE (Women in Development Europe).

BIBLIOGRAPHY

Akerloff, R.C., and Yellen, A.R., eds., 1986, Efficiency Models of the Labour Market, Cambridge, Cambridge University Press.

Bateson, M. C., 1989, Composing a Life, New York, The Atlantic Montly Press.

Becker, G., 1981, A Treatise on the Family, , Cambridge, Harvard Univerity Press.

Beneria, L., 1992, "Accounting for Women's Work: the Progress of two Decades, in World Development, vol 20, n. 11, pp. 1547-58.

Beneria, L., and FELDMAN, S.,eds., 1992, Unequal Burden, Boulder, Westview Press.

Beveridge, W.H., 1944, Full Employment in a free Society, London, Allen and Unwin.

--- 1943, The Pillars of Security, London, Allen and Unwin.

Braidotti, R., CHARKIEWICZ, E., WIERINGA, S., eds., 1994, Women, the Enviromrent, and Sustainsable Development, London, Zed Books.

Braudel, F., 1974, Capitalism and Material Life, 1400-1800, Glasgow, Fontana.

Brusco, S., 1995,"Competitività, partecipazione e condizione operaia", in, P. Bartolozzi e F. garibaldo. Roma, Ediesse.

Bryson . G., 1945, Man and Society: The Scottish Enquiry of the Eighteenth Century, Princeton, Princeton University Press.

Collingsworth, T., Goold, F.W., Harvey, P., 1994, "Time for a Global New Deal", in Foreign Affairs, vol 73, n.1, pp. 8-13.

Dalla Costa, M., and James, S., 1972, The Power of Women and the Subversion of the Community, Bristol, Falling Wall Press.

Desai, M., 1986, "Drawing a Line: On Defining the Poverty Treshold", in P. Golding, ed Excluding the Poor, London, Child Poverty Action Group[.

Dobb, M., 1973, Theories of Value and Distribution since Adam Smith, Cambridge, Cambridge University Press.

Douglas, M. and ISHERWOOD, B., 1979, The World of Goods. Towards an Anthropology of Consumption, London, allen Lane.

Elson, D, 1992, "Male Bias in Structural Adjustment", in H. Afshar and C. Dennis, eds. Women in Adjustment Policies in the Third World, London, Macmillan.

--- 1993, "Structural Adjustment with Gender Awareness: 'Vulnerable Groups', 'Gender based Distortions'", University of Manchester, Gender Analysis and Development Economics, Working Paper Number 2.

Eurad/Wide, 1994, World Bank Structural Adjustments and Gender Policies.Strangers passing in the night fleeting acquantainces or best friends?, Brussel.

Federici, S., 1976, Counterplanning from the kitchen, Bristol, Falling Wall press.

Fisher, J., 1993, Out of the Shadows: Women, Resistance and Politics in South America, London, Latin America Bureau.

Folbre, N., 1994, Who pays for the kids?, London, Routledge.

Frye, N., 1957, Anatomy of Criticism, Princeton, Princeton University Press.

Garegnani, P., 1984, "Value and Distribution in the Classical Economy and Marx", in Oxford Economic Papers, vol 36, pp. 291-325.

Harcourt, W., ed., 1994, Feminist Perspectives on Sustainable Development, London, Zed Books.

Keynes, J.M., 1930, "On the Question of High Wages', in Political Quarterly, vol. 1, pp. 110-24.

Maher, V., 1984, "Possession and Dispossession: Maternity and Mortality in Morocco", in Medick, H., and Sabean, D., eds., Interest and Emotion. Studies in Kinship and the Family, Cambridge, Cambridge University Press.

Mies, M., and Shiva, V., 1993, Ecofeminism, London, Zed Books.

Moser, C., 1993, Gender Planning and Development: Theory, Practice and Training, London, Routledge.

Nussbaum, M. C., 1990, "The Discernment of Perception: An Aristotelian Conception of Private and Public Rationality", in Love's Knowledge: Essays in Philosophy and Literature, Oxford, Oxford University Press.

Pateman, C., 1988, The Sexual Contract, Cambridge, Polity Press.

Picchio, A., 1992, Social Reproduction: the Political Economy of the Labour Market, Cambridge, C.U.P.

Polanyi, K., 1977, The Livelihood of Man, New York, Academic Press.

Room, G., 1990, New Poverty in the European Community, London, Macmillan.

Ruddick, 1990, Maternal Thinking, New York, Valentine Press.

Sen, A, K, 1983, "Poor Relatively Speaking", in Oxford Economic Papers, vol. 35, pp. 153-69.

--- 1985a, Commodities and Capabilities, Amsterdam, North Holland.

--- 1985b, Resources, Values and Development, Oxford, Basil Blackwell.

--- 1987, "The Standard of Living", in G. Hawthorn, ed., The Tanner Lectures, Clare Hall College, Cambridge, Cambridge University Press.

---- 1990, "Gender in Cooperative Conflicts", in I. Tinker, ed., Persistent Inequalities: Women and World Development, Oxford, Oxford University Press

Sparr, P., 1995, "From Nairobi to Beijing: Globalization,

Women and Poverty in the U.S.', in Development, n.1, pp.14-19.

Sraffa, P., 1951, "Introduction", in Sraffa, P. and Dobb, M., eds., Ricardo, D., On the Principles of Political Economy and Taxation, Cambridge, Cambridge University Press.

--- 1960, Production of Commodities by Means of Commodities, Cambridge, Cambridge University Press.

Townsend, P., 1985, "A Sociological Approach to the Measurement of Poverty- A Rejoinder to Professor Amartya Sen", in Oxford Economic Papers, vol 37, pp. 659-68.

--- 1993, The International Analysis of Poverty, Harvester, Wheatsheaf.

Walker, R., Lawson, R., Townsend, P., 1984, Responses to Poverty: Lessons from Europe, London, Heineman.

World Bank, 1994, Enhancing Women's Parrticipation in Economic Development, Policy paper, Washington.

World Bank (Blackden, C.), 1994, Paradigm Posponed: Gender and Economic Adjustment in Sub-African Africa, Washington.

World Bank, 1994, Eurad/Wide position paper, World Bank Structural Adjustment and Gender Policies, Sept., Washington.

Measures of unrecorded Economic Activities in Fourteen Countries*

Luisella Goldschmidt-Clermont**
Elisabetta Pagnossin-Aligisakis

Introduction

Part of the goods and services consumed by the population are produced and consumed without undergoing monetary transactions; this non-monetised consumption and the corresponding productive activities go unrecorded in labour statistics and in the national accounts. This is so, for instance, for the goods and services provided to the household by unpaid household members ; S. Kuznets already pointed out in the 1930s, that "housewives' services" (as they were called at the time) constituted the largest single item left out of the national accounts. Other unrecorded economic activities include repairs of household premises and equipment, basket making, weaving, knitting, sewing, etc. for own-consumption . The data presented in this paper show the order of magnitude of the unrecorded economic activity : measured in hours of work, it is, in industrialised countries, as large as the recorded activity.

How does this non-monetary sector of the economy compare with the recorded economy? How does it compare in size, in value, in contribution to human welfare? How do the monetary and non-monetary sectors interact ; in other words, how, why and when do production and manpower leave the household for the market, and vice-versa. What do these transfers mean in terms of personal welfare and of the nation's "extended income" (monetary plus non-monetary income)? How are these transfers affected by labour-market factors such as market rigidities, shortage of manpower in periods of economic growth or concern for unemployment or underemployment in periods of recession? Should we account for the non-monetary sector in economic statistics, in

economic analysis, in economic and social policy formulation? What is the impact of economic development and of increased monetisation on household production, on the distribution of the nation's manpower between the market and non-market sectors? In industrialised economies, what would the impact be, for instance, of a major reduction of working hours on the labour supply, on the production of goods and services for self-consumption, on the consumption of market goods, on time available for personal activities such as education, leisure and so on? Most of these questions cannot be answered in the present state of the art. The non-monetary sector, historically the oldest, is new from the point of view of economic studies: it was until recently almost totally neglected.

The world over, women are responsible for the major part of domestic activities ; this is why the 1995 Human Development Report puts some emphasis on this aspect of women's activity. Domestic activities must, however, be seen in context: the context of other non-monetised activities and the broader context of all economic activities. This perspective is adopted in the most recent studies assessing the economic dimension of unrecorded economic activities in industrialised countries : they try to capture not only domestic activities but all non-market production performed by households, including the "do-it-yourself" activities largely performed by men as well as unpaid work for the community ("voluntary" work) and market-oriented activity.

Boundaries

Human activities can be grouped into three main categories :
   (a) personal activities (non-economic) ;
   (b) productive non-market activities (mostly for own-consumption) ;
   (c) productive market-oriented activities.

The boundary between (a) and (b) is drawn by means of the "third-person criterion" which states that an activity is to be deemed productive if it may be delegated to a person other than the one benefiting from it. For instance, to listen to music is a personal activity because no one else can do it for me ; to prepare a meal is productive because some one else can do it for me.

The boundary between (b) and (c) roughly corresponds to the "production boundary" defined in the United Nations System of National Accounts (SNA). The presently available national accounts are constructed along the recommendations of the 1968 SNA . The 1993 revision of the SNA, only introduced minor changes to the production boundary ; as a result, a few items (goods produced by households for

---

*   Tables referred to in this text are to be found at the end of the chapter.

**   Please refer end of chapter.

own-consumption and water-carrying) will eventually be added to the national accounts, but the bulk of domestic activities remains outside the realm of the accounts. A similar situation prevails in labour statistics.

In this report, we call "SNA activities" those falling within the production boundary of the 1968 SNA. (At least as a first approximation, because there are minor points of overlap which still need to be sorted out. For instance, labour inputs into own house construction appear in time-use studies as production for own consumption and are therefore accounted for among non-SNA activities, thus filling a gap of official labour statistics. However, the output of this activity is accounted for in the SNA production account. These problems will have to be sorted out ; however, they do not affect the orders of magnitude which are our concern in this report).

While leaving domestic and related activities (non-SNA activities) outside the main framework, the 1993 SNA proposes to record households' non-market production in a "satellite account", i.e. in a supplementary system of the accounts.

The product of the non-SNA sector can be measured in physical units. For instance, so many millions of meals prepared by households, so many tons of clothes washed, so many siblings or aged persons cared for at home, and so on. Such data would be useful for studying trends in consumption of goods and services ; they would permit comparisons showing the relative share of the monetised and non-monetised sectors in the provision of a specific good or service.

Physical units however have serious limitations: for instance, amounts of washed clothes cannot be compared to, or aggregated with, number of children taken care of. In order to overcome this kind of difficulty, it is customary in economics to aggregate the corresponding monetary values ; by convention, the value of a commodity is the price at which it is exchanged. However, in non-SNA activities there are no prices: labour is unpaid and the product is not sold; here lies the difficulty of accounting for these activities.

In the studies presented in this report, the measurement of labour inputs is the first step: labour inputs are measured in physical units of time (section 2). A limited number of countries pursues the measurement in monetary units, measuring the value of labour inputs and, sometimes, the value of household production (section 3).

TIME-USE

The study presents time-use data from fourteen countries for which relatively recent measurements are available, representative of the total national population:

Australia, Austria, Bulgaria, Canada, Denmark, Finland, France, Germany, Great-Britain, Israel, Italy, Netherlands, Norway and United States.

This sample is not exhaustive : similar data may be available from other countries. What is provided here is an illustration of the economic magnitude of non-SNA activities, and in particular of domestic activities.

Time use : Methodology

There are many differences between the available time-use studies. In order to interpret their results, one has to be aware of the factors bearing on the averages, such as, for instance, the demographic structure of the population. However, there are also important differences deriving from surveys' methodology. As we were working, post factum, with existing data, we tried to eliminate some of these differences by a standardisation exercise ; other differences cannot be eliminated once the study is finished.

Differences which cannot be eliminated are, for instance, those relating to :
- data collection methods (diary, yesterday recall or other);
- handling of seasonal variations ;
- degree of representativeness of the sample, among which, handling of non-response ;
- handling of transportation time ;
- etc.

Differences which it was possible to eliminate, at least in part, were those relating to :
- time units ;
- age groups under observation ;
- categorisation of activities.

Time units. We adopted hours and minutes per day because they are closer to the readers' daily experience than the other units we encountered in the national studies (minutes per day, per week, per year; hours and decimals).

Age. We had requested data for the population aged 15 and above. Most of our correspondents were able to meet this requirement. Others however could only give data for the population aged 10 and above, or only for the total population (i.e. aged 0.1 year and above), while still others had at their disposal only data with an upper age limit (74 or 79 years).

The Finnish and German data were available for ages above both 10 and 15 (See appendix 2). This enabled us to evaluate the impact of this single factor on the results : the inclusion of the 10 to 15 years age group decreases the average proportion of economic time of 1 to 2 percentage points for the 24 hours break downs ; it modifies of less than 1 percentage point the break down of non-SNA activities. We therefore decided to present the data of the studies dealing with age 10 and up along with the other studies.

Categorisation of activities. In the different national studies, diverse categorisations have been adopted for non-SNA activities, making very difficult the assessment of common orders of magnitude. For the present review, we therefore proposed to use standardised categories largely based on the European Time Use Survey proposals (See appendix 1). It was thus possible to achieve an acceptable degree of homogeneity for the categorisation of activities thanks to the willingness of our national correspondents, either to re-allocate their own categories in order to meet our standardised classification, or at least to provide the necessary information for us to perform the re-allocation.

However non-negligible differences remain ; for instance, the inclusion or exclusion in SNA time of breaks or even of meals taken at the work-place, etc. One important difference lies in the handling of transportation time : in some studies, it is pooled with the related activity ; in other studies, it is associated with the related activity, but it can be isolated from it ; in others still, it is pooled into one large transportation category. French data show that transportation time for non-SNA and personal activities amounts to 3 per cent of the 24 hours day ; the inclusion of transportation time in one or another category of activities has therefore a non-negligible impact on the presentation of the time-use structure. (See appendix 3).

The fundamental differences between time-use studies have been analysed in detail by researchers in the field ; the consensus is now that, in order to ensure cross-national comparability, the forthcoming projects ought to be coordinated from the start and should use compatible methodologies.

Meanwhile, in this report, **we absolutely have to refrain from making cross-national comparisons with the available data.** The only permitted exercise, given the differences mentioned above, is to analyse, within the single countries, the structure of time-use and to determine the orders of magnitude and trends over time when available.

Time-use : Recent measurements

Basic structure of time-use

TABLE A shows the distribution of time between economic and non-economic activities, for all persons, in the fourteen countries.

In all of these countries, on average for the seven days of the week, **economic activities require less than one third of the 24 hours day** while over two thirds of the day are spent on non-economic activities. Economic time ranges, from country to country, **between 6:16 and 7:34 hours and minutes per day.**

Economic activities include SNA and non-SNA activities ; non-economic activities include physiological and recreational activities and education. The latter is an investment in human capital, as are also investments in health ; they produce returns in all activities, SNA, non-SNA and personal. Although they may have economic consequences, they do not meet the third person criterion (nobody can learn for someone else) and are therefore to be classified as personal activities.

It is important to stress that these are arithmetic averages calculated over the population under observation (see 2.1, age) and over 365 days ; they document orders of magnitude which are relevant from the macro-economic point of view.

From the social point of view, studies performed in different countries document the very large impact of many variables on the actual time-use structure of population sub-groups : household composition (number of adults in the household, number of children, age of the youngest child), life-cycle stage, occupational and employment status, male or female, urban or rural, day of the week, season of the year, etc. An unfavourable combination of these factors leads some sub-groups to a time structure quite different from the overall averages given above. Although we do not have at our disposal statistical data documenting the combined impact of all these variables, it is likely that the most stressed time-use structures (those with the smallest amount of personal time) would be found among men and women, employed full-time, raising at least one child below school age.

TABLE B gives the distribution of time between economic and non-economic activities, by gender, in the fourteen countries.

In five countries, gender equality is achieved, on average, in amount of economic time and, thus, in amount of time available for personal activities. In all other countries but one, women work more than men, the largest difference amounting to 1:45 hours and minutes per day (6:07 hours and minutes per day, for men ; 7:50 for women).

Average economic time ranges, from country to country,

*   for men, **between 6:07 and 7:38** hours and minutes per day ;
*   for women, between 6:15 and 7:50 hours and minutes per day.

TABLE C shows the distribution of economic time between SNA and non-SNA activities, for all persons, in the fourteen countries.

The time absorbed by non-SNA activities ranges, among the 14 countries, between 32 and 65 per cent of total economic time. For 12 of the countries, non-SNA time amounts to 50 ± 6 per cent of total economic time. Considering the reservations made in section 2.1 on the differences between national time-use studies, one may say that grosso modo non-SNA time amounts to half total economic time, or, in other words, that **non-SNA activities absorb as much labour time as SNA activities.**

TABLE D gives the distribution of economic time between SNA and non-SNA activities, by gender, for the fourteen countries.

In all of these countries, **men spend a larger share of their economic time in SNA activities**, the proportions differing from country to country, SNA activities absorbing between 55 and 79 per cent of men's economic time; **women spend more time in non-SNA activities**, the proportions differing in a wider range than for men, from 42 to 81 per cent of women's economic time.

TABLE E shows the overall distribution of time among non-SNA activities, in thirteen countries.

In all but one of the thirteen countries, **food related activities consume the largest proportion of non-SNA time**, the proportions ranging, from country to country, between 19 and 44 per cent and the amount of time ranging between 0:48 and 1:43 hours and minutes per day. (It should be remembered that these large ranges may be explained by differences in survey methodology as well as by

cultural differences).

In second position, depending from the countries, we find either child care, or upkeep of dwelling and surroundings, or management and shopping (with ranges from 13 to 24 per cent of non-SNA time).

TABLE F gives the distribution of time among non-SNA activities, by gender, in thirteen countries.

Gender differences in amount and proportion of time allocated to the various non-SNA activities illustrate cultural values about women's and men's roles. In all countries women spend appreciably more time than men on food related activities, textiles, upkeep of dwelling and surroundings and care of persons (adults and children), while men spend more time than women on construction and maintenance; all these are gender specific activities.

Time-use : Historical perspectives

TABLES G: We have data on the distribution of the 24 hours day between SNA, non-SNA and non-economic activities, at different points in time, for three countries:

Great-Britain: 1961, 1974 and 1985
Norway: 1971, 1981 and 1991
Bulgaria: 1977 and 1988.

Trans-temporal comparisons should however be handled with extreme caution because even small methodological differences between the successive surveys, may cause the apparent differences not to be significant. We shall therefore limit our comments to the larger changes.

TABLE G1. In Great-Britain, between 1961 and 1985, SNA and non-SNA time both decreased, causing a decrease of total economic time from 33 to 29 per cent of the 24 hours day. This global decrease is due to a drastic decrease of men's SNA time (minus 8 percentage points) and to a sizeable decrease of women's non-SNA time (minus 4 percentage points).

TABLE G2. In Norway, between 1971 and 1991, the stability of the overall SNA time (15 per cent of the 24 hours day) hides in fact a major change in the distribution by gender : a decrease of 4 percentage points for males and an increase of 4 percentage points for females. A decrease of 7 percentage points in females' non-SNA time, only partly compensated by an increase in males' non-SNA time, results in a general decline in total economic time.

The relative proportion of non-SNA time to SNA time decreases.

In these two industrialised countries, Great-Britain and Norway, one thus observes:

- a decrease in total economic time and in the economic time of each gender;
- an equalisation of genders' contribution to total economic time ;
- a trend pointing in the direction of an equalisation of genders' contribution to SNA and non-SNA activities respectively.

TABLE G3. In the Bulgarian data, the average amounts of time per person are not comparable for the two years because the averages are calculated on two different population bases : ages 6 and above for 1977, ages 0.1 and above for 1988. The age group 0.1 to 6 (males and/or females) does not contribute any labour time (Time Use Studies World Wide, 1990, pp. 496-499) ; its inclusion, in the averages, results in a decrease of average labour time and in an increase of non-economic time. It is therefore not possible to compare amounts of time in the two years. However, in a given year, we may calculate the ratio male/female for different activities. It is then possible to compare these male/female ratios for 1977 and 1988, as they are unaffected by the age group 0.1 to 6.

In Bulgaria, between 1977 and 1988, the male/female ratio for total economic activity decreases from 0.85 to 0.83 . (In other words, males were already contributing less total economic time than females in 1977 ; by 1988, the difference is further aggravated). This decrease is the result of :

- a decrease in the male/female ratio for SNA activities, where males' contribution remains higher than females: but the difference between genders decreases from 1:55 in 1977 to 1:39 in 1988 ;
- a decrease in the male/female ratio for non-SNA activities, where females' contribution remains higher than men's, but the difference between genders is further aggravated : 0:52 in 1977, 0:49 in 1988.

In the gender perspective, the trend points thus in the opposite direction than the one observed in Norway and Great-Britain. In Bulgaria, women's work-load relative to men's increased in total economic time, in SNA time and in non-SNA time.

TABLES H. We have data on the distribution of time among non-SNA activities, for three countries at several points in time :

Canada:	1961, 1971, 1981, 1986 and 1992
Great-Britain:	1961, 1974 and 1985
Norway:	1971, 1981 and 1991

For Norway, the data are presented according to our standardised categorisation ; for Canada and Great-Britain, the categorisation is the original national one.

The same reservations about trans-temporal comparisons apply as for tables G ; we therefore limit again our comments to the larger changes.

TABLE H1. In Canada, between 1961 and 1992, the average time in non-SNA activities, in hours and minutes per day,

- remained stable overall, between 3:15 and 3:12(-0:03)
- increased for men from 1:41 to 2:14 (+0:33)
- decreased for women from 4:49 to 4:08(-0:42)

Women's time in females' traditional activities decreased, mostly in meal preparation (-0:37) and clothing care (-0:15), but also in cleaning and child care. For these activities, there is essentially no increase in men's contribution.

Both genders' contribution increased in marketing (+0:11 each) and in repairs/maintenance (+0:09 for women; +0:23 for men).

During this period,
- meal preparation
  - : consumes less time in 1992 (0:47) than in 1961 (1:04),
  - : remains one of the two largest time-consuming categories of non-SNA activities (24 per cent in 1992, while it was the single largest one with 33 per cent in 1961);
- marketing
  - : consumes more time in 1992 (0:45) than in 1961 (0:33)
  - : rises to ex-aequo with meal preparation (24 per cent in 1992; 17 per cent in 1961) ;
- repairs/maintenance

: consumes more time in 1992 (0:35) than in 1961 (0:18),

: rises in third time-consuming position (18 per cent in 1992; 9 per cent in 1961) ;

- cleaning, child care and clothing care time decrease ;
- the largest decrease is in meal preparation (-0:17);
- the largest increase is in repair/maintenance (+0:17).

The increase in repair/maintenance occurs mostly between 1986 and 1992, counteracting the steady 1961-1986 decline in non-SNA time.

TABLE H2. In Great-Britain, between 1961 and 1985, the daily average time in non-SNA activities, in hours and minutes per day,

- decreased overall from   3:26 to 3:15   (- 0:9),
- increased for men from   1:38 to 2:12   (+ 0:34),
- decreased for women from   5:14 to 4:18   (- 0:56).

The trend however was not continuous, a large fluctuation appearing in the 1975 data, due to a time-lag between women's sharp decrease (- 0:48 in 1975) and men's sharp increase (+ 0:41 in 1985).

The overall decrease between 1961 and 1985 was due to a sharp decrease of women's time in two of women's traditional gender-specific activities (cooking/washing up and housework) not compensated by men's increases in these activities.

During this period,
• cooking/washing up
: consumes less time in 1985 (0:58) than in 1961 (1:08),

: remains the largest time-consuming category of non-SNA activities (30 per cent in 1985; 33 per cent in 1961) ;

• housework (upkeep of dwelling and textiles)
: consumes less time in 1985 (0:44) than in 1961 (0:59),

: remains the second largest category of non-SNA time (23 per cent in 1985; 29 per cent in 1961) ;

• shopping and odd jobs
: witness slight increases and are in third position in 1985 (15 per cent each) ;

• child care

: consumes more time in 1985 (0:21) than in 1961 (0:13), i.e. slightly more than one-third of the time devoted to cooking/washing-up,

• the largest decline is in housework (- 0:15); the largest increase is in odd jobs (+0:11)

TABLE H3. In Norway, between 1971 and 1991, the daily average time in non-SNA activities

- decreased overall from   3:54 to 3:36 (- 0:18),
- increased for men from   1:54 to 2:28 (+ 0:34),
- decreased for women from   5:36 to 4:31 (- 1:05).

The overall decrease was due to a drastic reduction of women's time in women's traditional gender-specific activities (food, textiles, upkeep of dwelling), not compensated by men's slight increase in these activities. Half of men's increased contribution went into child care.

During this period,
• food related activities
: consume less time in 1991 (1:07) than in 1971 (1:24) ;

: remain the largest time-consuming category of non-SNA time (31 per cent in 1991 ; 36 per cent in 1971) ;

• child care
: consumes more time in 1991 (0:37) than in 1971 (0:24) ;

: becomes in 1991, the second largest time-consuming category, consuming a little more than half the time devoted to food related activities ;

• upkeep of dwelling, care of textiles and management/shopping each consumed in 1971 more time than (or as much time as) child care ; they are relegated behind it in 1991;

• the largest declines occur in textiles and upkeep of dwelling ; the larger increases, in child care and, to a lesser degree, in management and shopping. (It should be noted that child care would come in third position if, as in Great-Britain above, upkeep of dwelling and textiles were lumped together).

For these three countries, the common trends are :
• an overall decrease in women's time in traditional women-specific activities, not compensated by men's increase in these activities ;

- less time, and a smaller proportion of non-SNA time, for food, textiles and upkeep of dwelling;
- a larger amount, and a larger proportion of non-SNA time, for management/shopping.

The common trends thus seem to go towards :
- a decrease in production time for traditional household goods and services, with the exception of child care increasing in Great-Britain and Norway ;
- an increase in management/shopping time.

In Canada and Great-Britain ,
- an increase in construction/maintenance.

Time-use : Cross-national comparisons

The ESRC British Time-Use Project produced comparative data for seven of the countries included in our study. The national surveys were conducted independently in the first half of the 1980s ; in order to achieve the comparisons, all surveys were extensively re-weighted. The population base is aged 20 to 60.

A large project is now under way, under the auspices of the Statistical Office of the European Union (EUROSTAT), for the introduction of harmonised time-use surveys in the European Union. The pilot surveys are scheduled for the Winter 1996 and the main surveys for 1997 (European Union, Statistical Office, 1994b).

For this report, we decided to use data directly provided by 14 countries, based on recent representative national surveys of the second half of the 1980s and early 1990s. As explained in section 2.1, only a limited amount of standardisation could be achieved; some initial fundamental differences between the surveys could not be cleared out.

A small number of coordinated studies have been carried out on a bilateral basis. Among them, a comparative study between Bulgaria and Finland that we present here as an illustration of what results may be achieved by comparative studies (Kirjavainen, Anachkova, Laaksonen, Niemi, Pääkkönen and Staikov, 1992). The purpose of this cooperative research project was to generate comparative data on women's and men's housework time. Carried out in Bulgaria in 1988 and in Finland in 1987-88, it used compatible methodological solutions for the two countries ; it is close to the definitions set out in our report for national representativeness, age of population and categorisation of activities . In the next section, we draw heavily on the chapter by Iiris Niemi and Bistra Anachkova (1992).

Bulgaria / Finland
Basic structure of time-use

TABLE I. The basic structure of time-use (population aged 10 and above) shows that, compared to their Finnish counterparts, people in Bulgaria spend, on average,
- more time on economic activities ;
- more time on SNA activities ;
- more time on non-SNA activities ;

and, as a consequence, have less time at their disposal for personal activities.

When comparing women's and men's time, the usual pattern is apparent in the two countries : women invest more time in housework than men do, men spend more time in paid work.

For each gender, the work load is higher in Bulgaria than in Finland.

The total work load is higher for females than for males in both countries ; but the difference between genders is larger in Bulgaria.

The heaviest work load is carried by Bulgarian women : 35 per cent of the 24 hour day, compared to 28 per cent in Finland, that is, on average, 1.5 hours greater.

Analysing the gender issue from another perspective, Niemi and Anachkova point out that
- in Bulgaria, women contribute 55 per cent of the total amount of work,
- in Finland, women contribute 53 per cent.
- in Bulgaria , women contribute 42 per cent of SNA work,
- in Finland, women contribute 41 per cent.

TABLE J. From the point of view of housework, Bulgarians and Finns spend the same amount of time on food preparation. This was unexpected, because earlier comparisons between Finland and Eastern European countries such as Hungary, Latvia and Russia have shown that Finns tend to spend less time on preparing food (Babarczy, Harcsa and Pääkkönen, 1991 ; Niemi, Eglite, Mitrikas, Patrushev and Pääkkönen, 1991).

Bulgarians spend more of their time on washing up, laundry and clothes upkeep, as well as on gardening and preserving food, than Finns do. (Dish washers and automatic laundering machines are more prevalent in Finnish households).

Bulgarians spend a lot of time making and repairing clothes compared with their Finnish counterparts, who tend to buy clothes ready made rather than making their own. More time is spent on helping family members, neighbours, relatives and friends in Finland.

Compared with Finnish women, Bulgarian women spend more time on all housework activities except shopping; one hour more each day on total housework.

- in Bulgaria, women do 68 per cent of all housework ;
- in Finland, women do 64 per cent.

The comparative study presents analyses by family cycle, education, socio-economic status, day of the week, age, etc. which it is not appropriate to report in detail here. In addition, the study introduces an interesting perspective on sharing (gender perspective) that we shall briefly present in the next paragraphs.

Sharing housework

Full-time employment is almost as common among women as among men in both countries. This means that gainful work is more equally shared than in the average Western European country.

For housework, social norms seem to define the differentiation of activities into male and female activities. In order to measure the level of sharing, Niemi and Anachkova use a ratio expressing women's share as a percentage of the total time spent by both sexes on housework. A high percentage for a specific activity means that the activity is female-segregated and a low percentage means it is male-segregated. A medium percentage shows that the activity is equally shared between men and women.

TABLE K. Preparation of food and housekeeping are typical female jobs in both countries. Although the total time spent on cooking does not differ, the sharing differs considerably. Food preparation is more female-dominated in Bulgaria than in Finland. Washing up is shared more equally than food preparation in Bulgaria, but not so in Finland.

Niemi and Anachkova distinguish three categories of housework, grouped according to gender segregation :
- female-segregated housework : food preparation, dish washing, indoor cleaning, laundry and clothes upkeep and child-care ;

- male-segregated housework : maintenance in which the most strongly male dominated are house building and repairs, repair and maintenance of household equipment and vehicles, and do-it-yourself production of articles for the home;
- housework not segregated by gender : shopping and errands.

In conclusion, the authors notice that female-segregated housework is somewhat more equally shared in Finland in comparison with Bulgaria. As possible explanations, they offer existing differences in the type of housework : in Finland, the standard of household technology of the average home is higher and there are commercial services geared to the needs of private households. Another explanation is related to social norms associated with housework sharing : the debate on questions of equality may have contributed to a more equal sharing in Finland ; this view is supported by the fact that higher socio-economic status increases the probability of men's participation in female-segregated housework activities. Men's participation in housework activities is obviously dependent on the time available ; men are more likely to participate in housework when they have time off from paid work. That is why older men and men who are not employed tend to participate more in housework than men in their middle age and currently employed.

Sharing of male-segregated housework activities occurs on more equal terms in Bulgaria than in Finland. Women spend more time doing typically male tasks in Bulgaria than in Finland. Albeit that this seemingly enhances equality, it also means that Bulgarian women do a greater amount of all types of housework activities. They do more of both female-segregated and male-segregated tasks than their Finnish counterparts. This results in Bulgarian women carrying a greater responsibility for the total housework burden compared to women in Finland.

Time-use : Other analytical perspectives

Time-use studies performed **in Bulgaria** use additional approaches for the collection and analysis of time-use data (Staikov, 1982a and b).

Data on the use of time were collected, in 1988, on the entire resident population (0.1 year and above). Averages per resident are obtained by dividing the total time data by the total number of residents (all, or male or female).

TABLE L shows the basic structure of time-use. Considering the entire resident population, thus children included, in 1988 :

- 29 per cent of time was devoted to production, equally divided between SNA and non-SNA activities;
- 71 per cent was available for non-economic activities.

If these figures are compared to those of table A (population aged 10 and above), one sees that, as expected, the inclusion of chidren aged 0.1 to 10 lowers the average economic time from 32 to 29 per cent.

Expressed in absolute figures, one can say that the 1988 Bulgarian standard of living was achieved with an

average labour input of 7 hours per day per resident.

This method of averaging production time over the entire resident population has the advantage of placing "average production time" in a perhaps less misleading perspective than other arbitrarily chosen ages (above 10, 15, 18 and/or below 60, 65, 70, etc.). Its main advantage is however to draw attention to the consumption perspective.

TABLE M shows the average time required daily from and for the residents for several categories of non-SNA activities. For instance, food preparation requires, on average, from each resident 51 minutes of daily labour. Seen from the other end, for every resident fed, 51 minutes of labour are consumed. This is an illustration of what we may call **the double perspective : production/consumption.**

TABLE N gives the estimated time expenditures during an average human life, under the conditions (demographic and time-use structure) prevailing in the survey year. On average, over their life-span, 1988 Bulgarian males will dispose of 596731 hours and females of 654985 hours.

Over their life span,

females will thus dispose of 10 per cent more total time than males.

However

females will only have enjoyed 2 per cent more personal time,

because they work much more in non-SNA activities (120 per cent more than men) while carrying an important load in SNA activities (only 21 per cent less than men).

Over their life-span, the 1988 residents of Bulgaria, for every 1000 hours of life, will have spent
- 294 hours in economic activities, of which :
  - : 143 hours in SNA activities and
  - : 151 hours in non-SNA activities
- 706 hours in non-economic activities.

We recognise here, expressed differently, the proportions given in tables A and C for Bulgaria.

Time-use : Conclusions

Labour statistics are misleading

Time-use measurements clearly have a potential for assessing the economic dimensions of human labour. Perhaps the most important indication they give is that, on average, the labour inputs into non-SNA activities are of the same order of magnitude as the labour inputs into SNA activities. Labour statistics however record only the latter ; because of this enormous gap, labour statistics give a distorted image of how even industrialised societies utilise the available labour resources to achieve their standard of living.

At present, the comparison between the time invested in SNA and non-SNA activities can only be achieved by means of time-use data. Labour statistics provide data on "hours worked" (in SNA activities) which cannot be compared to time-use data because of entirely different data collection methods (sources, definitions, etc.). Labour statistics also provide data on the number of "homemakers", a residual category of non-employed women assumed to be working full-time in domestic activities. The work performed in non-SNA activities, by both women and men counted as "active" in labour statistics, is totally unrecorded.

Measurements in time units have the following characteristics which qualify them as a satisfactory tool for the economic assessment of non-SNA activities :
- they are the result of direct observations and do not require any theoretical assumptions;
- they are eminently fit for international comparisons, the time unit being the same around the world.

However they do not measure human effort, i.e. they make

no difference between one hour worked in harsh circumstances and one hour worked in more confortable circumstances: one hour of laundering in the cold water of a stream or the same amount of time spent in operating an electric washer-dryer are very different from the human point of view. To our knowledge these qualitative differences have never been measured on a large scale, neither for SNA nor for non-SNA activities.

Cross-national comparability : still some way to go

Time-use research is, at least in Eastern and Western Europe and in North America, a mature field of study. Researchers regularly exchange their experiences within the professional International Association for Time Use Research. In order to ensure cross-national comparability of time-use data, work was done on guide-lines for codification and classification of activities (Harvey and Niemi, 1994) and on joint (or at least comparative) cross-national studies. The European Time Use Study (ETUS) project of EUROSTAT will produce the valuable data necessary for the full performance of time-use studies in the economic assessment of non-SNA labour ; Eastern-European, North-American and Japanese researchers should not encounter major problems of integration with ETUS procedures.

In other countries, a certain number of time-use studies have been produced, although in dispersed order, mostly by anthropologists. INSTRAW is funding some research on the measurement of women's economic contributions. Connections with the research discussed in the preceding paragraph exist ; steps are being taken to develop them in order to avoid an excessive imprint of Western culture while preserving, for the future, world-wide comparability.

Amount of personal time : an indicator of human development ?

If cross-nationally comparable data were available, amount of personal time (i.e. non-economic time) could be used as an indicator of human development. It could be calculated as a national average over the entire population ("resident population", as we called it in section 2.5).

Within one country, personal time is unevenly distributed among sub-sets of the population. The indicator should therefore account for differences between genders, age groups, employment status, employment sector (agriculture, industry, trade, the services), etc. In addition, if the indicator is to be used for cross-national or trans-temporal comparisons, it should account for differences in the demographic structure

of the populations : a large proportion of children increases the average non-economic time ; a low life expectancy (i.e. a small proportion of people beyond working age) increases the average economic time.

Economic and social policy

Personal time indicators, calculated for sub-sets of the population, would throw light on population groups carrying a particularly heavy work load and in need of economic and social alleviative measures.

A series of such measures have already been considered and even enforced for alleviating the work load of population groups in the child-bearing ages, the ages presenting the heaviest work loads :

- for SNA economic activity : legal and contractual provisions effectively ensuring flexibility (exit and re-entrance, part-time, continuity of social security provisions, etc.) for both men and women in connection with child-birth and child-raising ;
- equal opportunities (education, employment, wages) for men and women, so that both can effectively choose to benefit from these provisions ; as long as males are paid higher wages and are the "main wage earners", households cannot give up the "main" monetary income, and neither males nor females can really choose between SNA and non-SNA economic activity, nor equally share them ;
- for non-SNA activities : provision of public or private alternative services.

In economic policy, employment creation has often been seen as a means to draw into "productive" activity, "inactive" population groups. Such statistical terminology is borrowed from economics schools of thought which consider as "economic" only the monetised (i.e. market-oriented) activities. This misleading concept and its related misleading terminology have been applied, in particular, to Third World women. With, in some cases, disastrous effects on their work load and on the quality of life of their households.

In order to avoid these pitfalls, it is necessary to **consider human work as a whole, SNA plus non-SNA**. Employment creation can contribute to an increase in the quality of life. At the micro level, it is perceived as giving access to monetary means for purchasing goods or services only available through market channels or produced at a lower human cost in the market rather than in the household. At the macro level, it should correspond to a division of labour and specialisation process towards increased labour productivity. However, the goal (increase in the quality of life) is not achieved and employment creation becomes counter-productive from the human development point of view, if it merely adds to the total work load (SNA plus non-SNA) of those who already carry a full work load. Employment creation (i.e. in SNA activities) should be parallelled by an innovative supply (private or public) of goods and services alleviating the non-SNA work load.

Such innovative supply initiatives are also sources of employment creation ; they amount to a transfer of production from non-SNA to SNA. This transfer can occur spontaneously but chaotically, with unnecessary human costs in the time-use structure of individuals. It could be smoother if two kinds of analysis were available:

- a thorough sociological analysis of aspirations and constraints bearing on individual choices between SNA, non-SNA and non-economic activities;
- a thorough analysis of economic requirements for supplying households with alternative, good quality, market commodities produced under higher productivity circumstances than in households and therefore at an accessible cost.

MONETARY VALUATION

Monetary valuation : Methodology

The physical output of households is not sold ; it therefore has no price. However it is necessary to express its value in monetary units so that the output of the various non-SNA activities can be aggregated and compared to the national accounts aggregates.

In order to ensure compatibility with national accounts procedures, non-SNA output should be valued at the market price of equivalent market products. However, in industrialised countries, **such output-based valuations** have only been performed occasionally and on a limited number of activities.

The available monetary valuations of non-SNA activities (and in particular of domestic activities), established on a national scale in industrialised countries, are **input-based**. All these studies first determine the value of the labour factor ; some studies stop there, while others pursue the valuation by adding the value of the other inputs, in order to obtain the value of household production at cost of inputs.

The value of the unpaid labour factor is obtained by imputing a market wage to the hours invested in household

production. Several kinds of market wages have been used, in earlier studies, for this imputation. The most frequently used are :

- wages for equivalent market functions, i.e. wages of workers producing, in *market enterprises*, the goods or services produced by unpaid household members ;
- wage averages, i.e. average wages of all market workers or average wages of subsets of workers (women, service enterprises, etc.) ;
- wages of substitute household workers, polyvalent, i.e. workers who could perform, *within the household premises*, all (or most) of the productive activities performed by unpaid household members.

In the present study, we decided to leave out the "wages for equivalent market functions" alternative because they correspond to productivity circumstances in market enterprises (mass production, streamlining, capital intensiveness, etc.) which are entirely different from those prevailing in households ; the wages paid in a market enterprise correspond to its productivity and the value of unpaid household labour is overstated, at least in the production of goods, if counted at this wage rate.

We decided to also leave out average wages of subsets of workers (subsets defined by characteristics commanding different wage levels) as used in some studies as a proxy for "opportunity cost of time". These average wages are inappropriate for macro-economic valuations for several reasons. The opportunity cost of time approach is derived from the micro-economic theory of time allocation ; it imputes to household work time the wage the unpaid household worker would earn in the market if he/she would choose to give up household work and take up employment. The micro-economic theory of household behaviour rests on a number of assumptions : rational behaviour of utility maximising well-informed individuals, having choices and choosing freely in a competitive market, reaching equilibrium conditions, etc. ; in practice these assumptions are rarely verified because of labour market and household functioning constraints. One disturbing result of evaluations based on opportunity cost of time is that a same household activity commands different values depending on who performs it ; for instance, the value of dish-washing is higher if the person performing the activity is a university graduate or only attended primary school.

The valuations, provided by the countries participating in the present HDR study, are based on the wages of substitute household workers.. They appear as the most appropriate for imputing a monetary value to unpaid household work because they correspond to the market value of labour performed in household productivity circumstances. The best wages (inclusive of payments in kind, paid holidays, fringe benefits, etc.) on which to base the imputation are those of polyvalent substitutes with household management responsibilities. Alternatively, the wages of housekeepers performing several different tasks may be used, adjusted in order to account for the additional responsibilities and for the continuous availability of unpaid household workers.

Net or gross wages ? There is no general agreement as to which are best. We think that the choice between the two depends on the use to be made of the valuation results: net wages reflect the economic fluxes actually generated by non-SNA activities; gross wages reflect which fluxes would be generated and how SNA aggregates would be affected, if production was transfered from households to the market. For inclusion in the household sector satellite account, the estimates based on net wages are therefore more appropriate ; they cannot, however, be compared to "compensation of employees"

Net wages are defined in the same way in our source studies while gross wages are defined in different ways : they always include income taxes, but sometimes they include, in addition, employers' social security contributions, which in some countries amount up to 40 per cent of the wages. (We call these all inclusive wages "extra gross" wages). In other countries social security is financed from public funds. The impact of these differences on the imputed value of labour is illustrated by data available from a few countries, using the same data set and more or less inclusive wage bases of polyvalent household substitutes (See table O). In the French and German data, the "extras" raise the estimates respectively of 3 and 9 percentage points compared to gross wages. In the Danish and German data, the estimates based on "extra gross" wages are respectively 16 and 23 percentage points higher than those based on net wages.

Other differences certainly exist from country to country in the way the hourly wages of substitute household workers are determined : for instance, on the basis of monthly rates, counting hours actually worked or contractual hours (Schäfer and Schwarz, 1994), or on an hourly basis where hours not worked are not counted .

All these examples illustrate the impact of certain choices made for the evaluation and thus contribute to partly explain the range of results obtained in the different countries.

Our standardisation efforts (choice of the same category of wages for the imputation, distinction between net, gross

and "extra-gross" wages) reduce the very large diversity of valuation methods previously used in the various studies ; the valuation picture is thus somewhat clarified. However, although the valuations of labour presented in this study are expressed in the same language, the language has not yet been codified : each study still uses its own dialect.

Because of differences in wage determination and because of differences in the basic time-use data (see section 2.1), the values of non-SNA labour thus obtained are not cross-nationally comparable; a fortiori, the same is true of the valuations of household production based on these labour factor valuations. Similar problems and differences characterise the measurement of capital consumption which enters into the calculation of value added. Different concepts of what should be included as capital consumption in household production yield different results ; one example is given by German estimates for 1992: the inclusion of imputed rents from owner-occupied dwellings raises the value of household production of four percentage points (Schäfer and Schwarz, 1994).

The same comment thus applies here as in chapter II: **we should absolutely refrain from making detailed cross-national comparisons.**

Monetary valuation : Recent measurements

TABLE O shows the value of labour and the value of production at cost of inputs, in non-SNA activities. Because of the reservations made in the preceding section, **the available data allow us only to situate orders of magnitude, or even only their lower bound.** We can define orders of magnitude when values appear to be in similar ranges ; this is the case of labour values. When values give very distant results, we have to "play it safe" and point at the lower bounds ; this is the case with production values.

a)   *Imputed market value of non-SNA labour, based on gross or "extra gross" wages*

The value of non-SNA labour is not an entity comparable to GDP ; we use here GDP merily as a measuring rod.

Six countries provide a total of eight estimates of the value of non-SNA labour based on gross or "extra-gross" wages ; they all are larger than one third of GDP. The estimates range between 33 and 72 per cent of GDP. The median values obtained with extra-gross wages in seven estimates from five countries situate the

value of non-SNA labour at 43 ± 10 per cent of GDP.

The value of non-SNA labour (at "extra-gross" wages) can be compared to the national accounts item "compensation of employees" (which is also calculated at "extra-gross" wages). In one country, the value of non-SNA labour inputs is higher than SNA labour inputs (compensation of employees) ; in the other countries, they are lower.

b) *Imputed market value of non-SNA labour , based on net wages*

The previous estimate, based on "extra-gross" wages, includes fluxes (taxes, social security contributions) which actually are not generated by household production. Two estimates of the value of non-SNA labour based on net wages are available, respectively at 21 and 31 per cent of GDP.

c) *Imputed value of non-SNA production, at cost of inputs, using extra-gross wages.*

Four estimates are available from four countries. The three lower ones yield values of 50 ± 5 per cent of GDP ; the two other ones, some 85 per cent.

We can therefore say that the lower bound estimates give a

value of non-SNA production close to half the value of GDP.

As said above, these estimates include fluxes which are not generated by household production ; however they use extra-gross wages, as do SNA calculations leading to GDP, our measuring rod.

d) *Imputed value of non-SNA production, at cost of inputs, using net wages.*

One estimate is available at 33 per cent of GDP. Depending on the use to be made of the valuation (see section 3.1), it can be considered an **underestimate** of the value of non-SNA production because it is calculated on net wages, while the measuring rod (GDP) is calculated on extra-gross wages.

We can say that the lower bound estimate yields a

value of non-SNA production equal to one third of GDP.

If one looks up from the table, these summarised results may appear contradictory, the lower bound value of non-SNA labour obtained in some studies being larger than the lower bound value of production obtained in other studies. This observation takes us back to the reservations made in 3.1 : different choices made during the valuation process may have a large impact on the results (Schäfer and Schwarz, 1994). The **range of values** is such that, in the present state of the art, one can only draw two rudimentary conclusions :

* the value of non-SNA production is very high ;
* the value of non-SNA production can be calculated, but in order to achieve cross-national comparability, methodological recommendations have to be developed internationally.

Monetary valuation : Historical perspectives

TABLE P. We have data on the value of labour or on the value of production in non-SNA activities at different points in time, for four countries :

Bulgaria:	1971, 1977 and 1988
Denmark:	1964, 1975 and 1987
Finland:	1979/82 and 1990
Norway:	1972, 1981 and 1990.

Keeping in mind the same reservations as for trans-temporal comparisons of time-use data, the value of labour in non-SNA activities, expressed as a percentage of GDP seems to have increased over time in Denmark and decreased in Finland and Norway. The value of non-SNA production seems to have increased in Bulgaria.

Monetary valuation : other perspectives

Extended private consumption

TABLE Q shows the contribution of non-SNA activities to extended private consumption. Three different aggregates are considered :

* "modified" SNA private consumption (i.e. minus goods and services consumed in non-SNA production: intermediate inputs and some

consumer durables) ;

- non-SNA contribution to private consumption (gross value added at the cost of inputs) ;
- "extended" private consumption : i.e. modified SNA plus non-SNA private consumption.

We have data from three countries ; their results are close:

non-SNA production contributes some 60 per cent of extended private consumption

If and when cross-nationally comparable data will become available, it will be possible to compare extended per capita consumption in the different countries, expressed in US $ at purchasing power parity (PPP).

TABLE R shows the contribution of non-SNA activities to per capita extended private consumption in Bulgaria. Although the data are based on a rule of thumb estimate of PPP, they provide an **illustration** of the comparisons such data would permit ; in this case, the comparison is trans-temporal.

Keeping this and the earlier reservations in mind, the contribution of non-SNA production to extended private consumption per capita in Bulgaria, appears to have decreased from 65 to 58 per cent between 1971 and 1988.

Standardised extended per capita consumption

Data on per capita extended private consumption can be integrated to data on total economic time, in order to achieve more meaningful cross-national comparisons. The reasoning is as follows : a given consumption level may be achieved in one country with more labour inputs than in another. The country achieving this consumption level with lower labour inputs may be considered to be in a more favourable position from the human point of view, because less economic time means availability of more personal time. In order to achieve such integrated comparisons it is necessary to standardise labour time and to calculate what we call standardised extended per capita consumption. The procedure consists of choosing a common labour time for all countries (for instance, a median labour time) and calculating what per capita extended consumption would have been in each country if total economic time had been equal to the chosen standard. This procedure was used in Malaysia by Kusnic and Da Vanzo (1980).

TABLE S presents data integrating per capita extended private consumption in US $ and per capita total economic time. Bulgaria provided the data enabling us to make the calculations on a trans-temporal basis in order to **illustrate** the procedure. We arbitrarily chose to standardise total economic time to 8 hours, i.e. to approximately the median length of economic time for the period 1971 to 1988. The same reservations apply as to table R on PPP estimates and monetary fluctuations.

Between 1971 and 1988, in Bulgaria,
> per capita extended consumption declined of 22 percentage points
> (from US $ 2736 to US $ 2137)

During the same period,
> total economic time decreased from 8:40 to 7:03 hours and minutes per day.

The standardised data indicate that the decline in consumption is strongly related to the decrease in economic time : if Bulgarians had worked the same amount of time (8 hours) in both years, the decline in consumption would only have been of 3 percentage points.

In other words, extended per capita consumption does not tell the whole story ; it has to be related to the amount of labour required for achieving it. The same procedure could be applied to cross-national data and would permit a more integrated appraisal of levels of living.

Monetary valuation : Conclusions

Extended production accounting

The revised SNA (1993 SNA) has formally recognised that non-SNA activities are productive and that they contribute to the "well-being" (we prefer the term "consumption") of the population. It recommends to handle the measurement of these activities in a satellite account, which is a flexible frame where monetary units can be presented alongside physical units, for instance time units. However, in order to be compatible with measurements of SNA activities, a different measurement methodology than the one presented in this report will have to be used : the valuation will have to be output-based, that is it will have to start with the physical measurement of household output and then value it at market prices. (Goldschmidt-Clermont, 1987, 1989, 1993). Unfortunately very little experience is available, as yet, with this approach at the national levels ; it should, however, not be more difficult to develop than the refined strategies developed for the traditional sectors of the national accounts.

At the national level, interesting results are already appearent : for instance, the information yielded by trans-temporal data or by the data gathered for the construction of the German satellite account of household production, the first of its kind. They illustrate the feasibility of constructing such monetary data, which would provide an important contribution for economic and social analysis purposes.

Once data will be available, measurements of **the contribution of non-SNA activities to extended private consumption** will provide an important missing element for the understanding of national economies. In the meantime, cross-nationally, we have to satisfy ourselves with indications (upper and lower bounds) of the orders of magnitude. Clearly, the values are not negligible.

Cross-national comparability: still a long way to go

There is still a long way to go before monetary valuations of non-SNA production can be used in a human development index.

Some monetary valuations were performed in different countries since already many years, but the field lacks coordination : it progresses in dispersed order. The first and (to our knowledge) only international conference on the subject was held in 1993 in Ottawa at the initiative of Statistics Canada.

As we saw in this chapter, data are definitely not comparable cross-nationally even for the valuation of unpaid labour which is the item on which most of the valuation efforts have been concentrating.

Standardised consumption: an indicator of human development ?

Comparisons between countries or between sub-sets of a population will be further enhanced by the integration of consumption figures and time-use data into a measure we called *"standardised private consumption"*. At equal consumption levels, two countries or population categories may have expanded different amounts of labour ; the purpose of this measure is to account for this difference in the

comparisons.

Agenda for the future

This chapter should probably conclude on an agenda for the future :

- increased contacts, systematic exchange of information and coordination between those involved in the monetary valuation of household production, in a similar way and in contact with those involved in time-use measurements ;
- development of the output-based approach ;
- allocation of the necessary financial resources for this new sector of economic accounting which was neglected until now.

The positive reaction of the national statistical offices, from which we requested data within short delays and at a time of year when they are involved with heavy routine work, shows that there is interest for the subject of non-SNA activities. We may therefore be hopeful for the future !

GENERAL CONCLUSIONS

This report is mostly based on statistical data contributed, at our request, by national sources from fourteen countries :

> **Australia, Austria, Bulgaria, Canada, Denmark, Finland, France, Germany, Great-Britain, Israel, Italy, the Netherlands, Norway and the United States.**

With the exception of a coordinated study by Bulgaria and Finland, the national surveys from which the data originate, were performed independently and it was therefore not possible to achieve, a posteriori, cross-national comparability. It was however possible to achieve a normalised presentation of results which revealed some common orders of magnitude and trends.

Because the time-use data presented here are not satisfactorily comparable cross-nationally and because the valuation data are not comparable at all, this report should be seen more as an illustration than as a compilation of results.

A fundamental approach adopted in our analysis is that human labour should be considered in its integrality, whether invested in SNA or in non-SNA activities ; a similar approach is adopted towards production. This position is a departure from traditional economic and statistical approaches which apply the concepts "economic", "labour" and "production" only to SNA activities.

Orders of magnitude

In all of the above-mentioned countries,

- total economic time, i.e. SNA plus non-SNA, averaged over all days and over the population aged 15 and above, amounts to less than one third of the 24 hours day, ranging, from country to country, between 6:16 and 7:34 hours and minutes per day ;
- non-SNA statistically unrecorded activities absorb as much labour time as recorded SNA activities ; by excluding non-SNA activities, official labour statistics present a statistical gap amounting to one half of human labour: for purposes of economic and social policy formulation, official statistics are misleading ;
- food related activities consume the largest proportion of non-SNA time.

Only a few of our national sources could provide monetary valuation data. The median values obtained with gross wages in seven estimates from five countries situate the

value of non-SNA labour at 43 ± 10
per cent of GDP.

The lower bound values obtained in three estimates from two countries situate the

**value of non-SNA production around
half the value of GDP.**

Data available from three countries indicate that

**non-SNA production contributes some 60 per cent of
extended private consumption.**

Gender perspective

In five countries, gender equality is achieved from the stand-point of average time in economic activities and, thus, of time available for personal activities. In all other countries but one, women work more than men, the largest difference amounting to 1:45 hours and minutes per day.

Men spend a larger share of their economic time in SNA activities than in non-SNA activities; the proportions vary, from country to country, between 55 and 79 per cent. Women spend a larger share of their economic time in non-SNA activities than in SNA activities ; the proportions vary more widely, from country to country, than men's, between 42 and 72 per cent.

In all countries, non-SNA activities are gender-specific : women contribute a larger proportion than men of the time required for food related activities, care of textiles, house-cleaning and care of persons; construction and maintenance are men-specific activities. The sharing ratio varies from one country to another.

With the valuation methods presently used which are based on the value of inputs, the only possibility for valuating separately genders' contribution would be to allocate the value of production to each gender proportionately to its labour time contribution. Not a meaningful exercise, which would not take us any farther than where we stand with time-use data alone.

The available data indicate that both SNA and non-SNA activities are necessary, even in industrialised countries, for meeting consumption requirements. The contributions of these two categories of activities are complementary. Non-SNA activities make possible the performance of SNA activities and vice-versa ; together they determine final extended consumption. The same is true of genders' contributions.

Gender specificity of activities may be seen as the equivalent, in the household, of specialisation in the market sectors of the economy. Sharing of activities, often considered a goal towards gender equality, is necessary as a means for ensuring inter-changeability and economic security, in the face of the changing position of women in society and of perturbations in the labour market.

Trends

In the industrialised countries for which we have data at different points in time, the trends over the last three decades seem to point in the direction of :

- a decrease of economic time, overall and for both genders ;
- an equalisation of genders' contribution to total economic time ;
- an equalisation of genders' contribution to SNA and to non-SNA time ;
- a large decrease of women's time in traditional women-specific activities, not compensated by men's increase in these activities ;

- a smaller amount of time, and a smaller proportion of non-SNA time, for food, textiles and upkeep of dwelling ;
- a larger amount and a larger proportion of non-SNA time, for management and shopping.

Without data on the physical output of households, it is not possible to determine whether the decreases in time inputs correspond to decreases in the amount or quality of household production or whether the time decreases correspond to higher labour productivity in the household.

A cross-national comparison is available between two countries having reached different levels of living. Some of the trends in the basic structure of time observed in the historical perspective presented above, also appear when comparing Bulgaria to Finland: in Finland, less time is devoted to economic activities and to non-SNA activities, and there is overall more sharing of non-SNA activities between genders. These differences are probably correlated to a pattern of economic development ; however, the Finnish data indicate that economic factors interplay with social factors in influencing time allocation.

Looking at the future

In order to progress in our understanding of unrecorded non-SNA economic activities, the first priority is ...to record them. We thus need cross-nationally comparable data sets on time-use, permitting the analysis of labour allocation. We also need monetary valuations of households' output compatible with national accounting data. These two data sets, combined in the household production satellite account, would enable us to understand the inter-face between the monetised market sector and the households' non-market sector. These data would also constitute a precious basis for economic and social policy formulation.

Time-use methodology is progressing rapidly towards coordination and comparability ; this is not the case of households' product accounting methodology. Although still susceptible of improvements, time-use is, for the time being, the best available tool for the economic assessment of non-SNA activities and for their comparison with SNA activities.

Three kinds of measures were identified, in this report, as potential indicators of human development :
- average amount of personal time and its di tribution among the population;
- average extended (i.e. generated by SNA plus

non-SNA activities) per capita consumption;
- standardised consumption, i.e. a measure integrating extended labour time and extended consumption in order to relate consumption levels with the labour input required for achieving them.

The first one may hopefully materialise in a not too distant future. The two other ones may take much more time, ... unless statistical bodies are prepared to invest, in the measurement of presently unrecorded activities, staff and financial means commensurate with the economic weight (labour time and consumption value) of these activities.

LIST OF TABLES

TIME-USE: RECENT MEASUREMENTS

Table A. Distribution of time between economic and non-economic activities, all persons (14 countries).

Table B. Distribution of time between economic and non-economic activities, by gender (14 countries).

Table C. Distribution of economic time between SNA and non-SNA activities, all persons (14 countries).

Table D. Distribution of economic time between SNA and non-SNA activities, by gender (14 countries).

Table E. Distribution of time among non-SNA activities, all persons (13 countries).

Table F. Distribution of time among non-SNA activities, by gender (13 countries).

TIME-USE: HISTORICAL PERSPECTIVES

Tables G. Distribution of time between SNA, non-SNA and non-economic activities, all persons and by gender:

> Table G1. Great-Britain: 1961, 1974 and "1985".
> Table G2. Norway: 1971, 1980 and 1990.
> Table G3. Bulgaria: 1977 and 1988.

Tables H. Distribution of time among non-SNA activities, all persons and by gender:

> Table H1. Canada: 1961, 1971, 1981, 1986 and 1992.
> Table H2. Great-Britain: 1961, 1974 and 1980s.
> Table H3. Norway: 1971, 1980 and 1990.

TIME-USE: CROSS-NATIONAL COMPARISONS

Table I. Bulgaria and Finland, 1988.
Distribution of time between SNA, non-SNA and non-economic activities, all persons and by gender.

Table J. Bulgaria and Finland, 1988.
Distribution of time among housework activities, all persons and by gender.

Table K. Bulgaria and Finland, 1988.
Sharing of housework activities by gender: equality ratios.

TIME-USE: OTHER ANALYTICAL PERSPECTIVES

Table L. Bulgaria 1988.
Distribution of time between SNA, non-SNA and non-economic activities, all residents and by gender.

Table M. Bulgaria 1988.
Distribution of time among non-SNA activities, all residents and by gender.

Table N. Bulgaria 1988.
Distribution of time, over the life-span, between SNA, non-SNA and non-economic activities, all residents and by gender (1988 structure).

MONETARY VALUATION: RECENT MEASUREMENTS

Table O. Value of labour and value of production at cost of inputs, in non-SNA activities (seven countries).

MONETARY VALUATION: HISTORICAL PERSPECTIVES

Table P. Historical perspective. Value of labour and value of production, in non-SNA activities. (Bulgaria, Denmark, Finland and Norway).

MONETARY VALUATION: OTHER PERSPECTIVES

Table Q. Contribution of non-SNA activities to extended private consumption. (Bulgaria, Finland and Germany).

Table R. Contribution of non-SNA activities to per capita extended private consumption, in U.S.$. (Bulgaria, 1971, 1977 and 1988).

Table S. Integrated per capita extended private consumption in U.S.$ and per capita total economic time. (Bulgaria 1971, 1977 and 1988).

APPENDICES

Tables T1 and T2. Effect of age lower limit adopted for the study: the Finnish and German data. (Appendix 2).

Table U. Effect of categorisation of transportation time: the French data. (Appendix 3).

Table A.
Distribution of time between economic and non-economic activities, all persons (14 countries)

Average time per person.
Hours and minutes per day (h.:m.)

(pop.aged)	Australia 1992 (15 +)	Austria 1992 (10 +)	Bulgaria 1988 (10 +)	Canada * 1992 (15 +)	Denmark 1987 (16-74)	Finland 1987/8 (15 +)	France 1985/6 (15 +)	Germany 1991/2 (16 +)	Great Britain * "1985" (15 +)	Israel 1991/2 (14 +)	Italy 1988/9 (15 +)	Netherlands 1987 (12 +)	Norway * 1990/1 (16-79)	USA 1985 (15 +)
Time in economic activities (SNA plus non-SNA)														
h.:m.	7:24	6:59 (a)	7:40	7:05	7:34	7:01	6:51(a)	7:21	6:52	6:16	7:01	6:01	7:13	7:20
%	31	29	32	30	32	29	29	31	29	26	29	25	30	30
Time in non-economic activities														
h.:m.	16:36	17:01	16:19	16:49	16:25	17:00	17:09 (b)	16:39	17:08	17:44	17:03	17:59 (a)	16:47	16:38
%	69	71 (b)	68	70	68	71	71	69	71	74	71	75	70	70
Total time														
h.:m.	24	24	24	24	24	24	24	24	24	24	24	24	24	24
%	100	100	100	100	100	100	100	100	100	100	100	100	100	100

SOURCES:
Australia: Australian Bureau of Statistics (1994).
Austria: Austrian Central Statistical Office (1994).
Bulgaria: Niemi and Anachkova (1992).
Canada: Statistics Canada (1993).
Denmark: Bonke (1994).
Finland: Statistics Finland (1994).
France: Grimler and Roy (1991).
Germany: [Germany]. Federal Statistical Office (1994).
Great Britain: ESRC Research Centre of Micro-social Change, British Time-Use Project (1994).
Israel: [Israel.] Central Bureau of Statistics (1995).
Italy: [Italy.] National Statistical Institute (1994).
Netherlands: Statistics Netherlands (1994).
Norway: Statistics Norway (1994).
United States: Maryland, University of (1994).

NOTES:
*: Our calculations.
Because of rounding off and because of transformation of time units, percentages may not totalise to 100 and time to 24 hours.
Austria: (a) Including travel time for SNA activities and excluding travel time for non-SNA activities. (b) Including travel
time for non-SNA activities (0:25, 2%).
France: (a) Excluding travel time for non-SNA activities. (b) Including travel time for non-SNA activities.
Italy: Time in SNA activities without work travels is 2:51.
Germany: Time in SNA activities: of which: paid work (2:54), travel time (0:18), other job related time (job seeking, etc.) (0:04). Lunch break is not included.
Great Britain: "1985", actually 1983/7.
Netherlands: (a) Including "reading, talking with children; indoor and outdoor playing with children".

Table B.
Distribution of time between economic and non-economic activities, by gender (14 countries)

Average time per person.
Hours and minutes per day (h.:m.)

	Australia 1992		Austria 1992		Bulgaria 1988		Canada * 1992		Denmark 1987		Finland 1987/8		France 1985/6		Germany 1991/2		Great Britain * "1985"		Israel 1991/2		Italy 1988/9		Netherlands 1987		Norway * 1990/1		USA 1985	
(pop.aged)	(15 +)		(10 +)		(10 +)		(15 +)		(16-74)		(15 +)		(15 +)		(16 +)		(15 +)		(14 +)		(15 +)		(12 +)		(16-79 +)		(15 +)	
	M	F	M	F	M	F	M	F	M	F	M	F	M	F	M	F	M	F	M	F	M	F	M	F	M	F	M	F
Time in economic activities (SNA plus non-SNA)																												
h.:m.	7:23	7:23	6:33a	7:18a	6:58	8:24	7:10	7:09	7:38	7:29	6:50	7:10	6:28a	7:09a	7:21	7:20	6:51	6:53	6:17	6:15	6:07	7:50	5:45	6:17	6:52	7:25	7:08	7:33
%	31	31	27	31	29	35	30	30	32	31	28	30	27	20	31	31	29	29	26	26	25	32	24	26	28	30	30	32
Time in non-economic activities																												
h.:m.	16:37	16:37	17:27	16:42	17:02	15:50	16:50	16:51	16:23	16:29	17:09	16:50	17:32	16:51	16:39	16:40	17:09	17:07	17:43	17:45	17:57	16:14	18:15	17:43	17:13	16:43	16:52	16:26
%	69	69	73 b	70 b	71	66	70	70	68	69	71	70	73 b	70 b	69	69	71	71	74	74	75	68	76 a	74 a	72	70	70	68
Total time																												
h.:m.	24	24	24	24	24	24	24	24	24	24	24	24	24	24	24	24	24	24	24	24	24	24	24	24	24	24	24	24
%	100	100	100	100	100	100	100	100	100	100	100	100	100	100	100	100	100	100	100	100	100	100	100	100	100	100	100	100

SOURCES: see table A.

NOTES:
*: Our calculations.
Because of rounding off and because of transformation of time units, percentages may not totalise to 100 and time to 24 hours.
Austria: (a) Including travel time for SNA activities and excluding travel time for non-SNA activities. (b) Including travel
time for non-SNA activities and non-economic activities (M = 0:25, 2%; F = 0:23, 2%).
France: (a) Excluding travel time for non-SNA activities. (b) Including travel time for non-SNA activities.
Italy: Time in SNA activities without work travels is, respectively, 4:14 and 1:36.
Germany: Time in SNA activities: including paid job, travelling because of work, other job related time.
Excluding lunch break.
Great Britain: "1985", actually 1983/7.
Netherlands: (a) Including "reading, talking with children; indoor and outdoor playing with children".

Table C.
Distribution of economic time between SNA and non-SNA activities, all persons (14 countries)

Average time per person.
Hours and minutes per day (h.:m.)

(pop.aged)	Australia 1992 (15 +)	Austria 1992 (10 +)	Bulgaria 1988 (10 +)	Canada * 1992 (15 +)	Denmark 1987 (16-74)	Finland 1987/8 (15 +)	France 1985/6 (15 +)	Germany 1991/2 (16 +)	Great Britain * "1985" (15 +)	Israel 1991/2 (14 +)	Italy 1988/9 (15 +)	Netherlands 1987 (12 +)	Norway * 1990/1 (16-79)	USA 1985 (15 +)
Time in SNA activities														
h.:m.	3:17	3:25 (a)	3:50	3:41	5:10	3:33	3:03	3:16	3:29	3:11	3:08	2:06 (a)	3:37	3:38
%	44	49	50	52	68	51	45	44	51	51	45	35	50	50
Time in non-SNA activities														
h.:m.	4:07	3:34 (b)	3:50	3:24	2:24	3:28	3:48 (a)	4:05	3:23	3:05	3:53	3:55 (b)	3:36	3:42
%	56	51	50	48	32	49	55	56	49	49	55	65	50	50
Total time in all economic activities														
h.:m.	7:24	6:59	7:40	7:05	7:34	7:01	6:51	7:21	6:52	6:16	7:01	6:01	7:13	7:20
%	100	100	100	100	100	100	100	100	100	100	100	100	100	100

SOURCES: see table A.
NOTES:
* Our calculations.
Because of rounding off and because of transformation of time units, percentages may not always totalise to 100 and time to 24 hours.
Austria: (a) Including travel time for SNA activities (b) Excluding travel time for non-SNA activities.
France: (a) Excluding travel time for non-SNA activities.
Germany: Time in SNA activities: including paid work, travelling because of work, other job related time.
Excluding lunch break.
Great Britain: "1985", actually 1983/7.
Italy: Time in SNA activities without work travels 2:51.
Netherlands: (a) Excluding "travelling because of work". (b): Including "travelling because of work". Excluding
"reading, talking with children; indoor and outdoor playing with children".

126

Table D.
Distribution of economic time between SNA and non-SNA activities, by gender (14 countries)

Average time per person.
Hours and minutes per day (h.:m.)

	Australia 1992		Austria 1992		Bulgaria 1988		Canada * 1992		Denmark 1987		Finland 1987/8		France 1985/6		Germany 1991/2		Great Britain * "1985"		Israel 1991/2		Italy 1988/9		Netherlands 1987		Norway * 1990/1		USA 1985	
(pop.aged)	(15 +)		(10 +)		(10 +)		(15 +)		(16-74)		(15 +)		(15 +)		(16 +)		(15 +)		(14 +)		(15 +)		(12 +)		(16-79)		(15 +)	
	M	F	M	F	M	F	M	F	M	F	M	F	M	F	M	F	M	F	M	F	M	F	M	F	M	F	M	F
Time in SNA activities																												
h.:m.	4:29	2:06	4:40a	2:17a	4:34	3:22	4:39	2:46	6:00	4:19	4:21	2:48	4:00	2:10	4:28a	2:12a	4:39	2:34	4:40	1:50	4:41	1:45	2:58a	1:13a	4:24	2:44	4:31	2:47
%	61	28	71	31	66	40	65	39	79	58	64	39	62	30	61	30	68	37	74	29	77	22	52	19	64	38	63	37
Time in non-SNA activities																												
h.:m.	2:54	5:17	1:53b	5:01b	2:24	5:02	2:31	4:23	1:38	3:10	2:29	4:22	2:28a	4:59a	2:53	5:08	2:12	4:19	1:37	4:25	1:26	6:05	2:47b	5:03b	2:28	4:31	2:37	4:46
%	39	72	29	69	34	60	35	61	21	42	36	61	38	70	39	70	32	63	26	71	23	78	48	81	36	62	37	63
Total time in all economic activities																												
h.:m.	7:23	7:23	6:33	7:18	6:58	8:24	7:10	7:09	7:38	7:29	6:50	7:10	6:28	7:09	7:21	7:20	6:51	6:53	6:17	6:15	6:07	7:50	5:45	6:17	6:52	7:25	7:08	7:33
%	100	100	100	100	100	100	100	100	100	100	100	100	100	100	100	100	100	100	100	100	100	100	100	100	100	100	100	100

SOURCES: see table A.
NOTES:
* Our calculations.
Because of rounding off and because of transformation of time units, percentages may not always totalise to 100 and time to 24 hours.
Austria: (a) Including travel time. (b) Excluding travel time.
France: (a) Excluding travel time.
Germany: Time in SNA activities: including paid work, travelling because of work, other job related time.
Excluding lunch break.
Great Britain: "1985", actually 1983/7.
Netherlands: (a) Excluding "travelling because of work". (b): Including "travelling because of work". Excluding:
"reading, talking with children; indoor and outdoor playing with children".

Table E.
Distribution of time among non-SNA activities, all persons (13 countries)

Average time per person.
Hours and minutes per day (h.:m.)

(pop.aged)	Australia 1992 (15 +)	Austria 1992 (10 +)	Canada * 1992 (15 +)	Denmark 1987 (16-74)	Finland * 1987/8 (15 +)	France 1985/6 (15 +)	Germany 1991/2 (16 +)	Great Britain * "1985" (15 +)	Israel 1991/2 (14 +)	Italy 1988/9 (15 +)	Netherlands 1987 (12 +)	Norway * 1990/1 (16-79)	USA 1985 (15 +)
Time in Non-SNA activities (a)													
food related activities h.:m.	0:48	1:16	1:04	(a) 1:10 (b) 0:50	1:04	1:08 (a)	0:59	1:01	0:55 (a)	1:43	1:01 (a)	1:07	1:16
%	19	35	31	49 35	31	30	24	30	30	44	26	31	34
child care h.:m.	0:32	0:19	0:26	0:13	0:20	0:18 (b)	0:23 (a)	0:24	0:42 (b)	0:15	0:14 (b)	0:37	0:23
%	13	9	13	9	10	8	9	12	23	6	6	17	10
adult care h.:m.	0:11	0:07	0:02		0:09	0:04	0:05 (a)	0:03	0:04 (c)	0:05	0:02	0:11	0:04
%	4	3	1		4	2	2	1	2	2	1	5	2
textiles h.:m.	0:19	0:26	0:19	0:07	0:19	0:25	0:23	0:13	0:07	0:28	0:11 (c)	0:20	0:17
%	8	12	6	5	9	11	9	6	4	12	5	9	8
upkeep of dwell./surr. h.:m.	0:26	0:43	0:33	0:21	0:35	0:42	0:33	0:39	0:44 (d)	0:46	0:43 (d)	0:28	0:35
%	11	20	16	15	17	18	14	19	24	20	18	13	16
construction maintenance h.:m.	0:12	0:12	0:11	0:28	0:12	0:14	0:21 (a)	0:12	0:02	0:03	0:21	0:13	0:09
%	5	6	6	19	6	6	9	6	1	1	9	6	4
management/ shopping h.:m.	0:56	0:06	0:27	(c) 0:03 (d) 0:23	0:36	0:30 (c)	0:47 (a)	0:41	0:22 (e)	0:11	0:38 (e)	0:27	0:34
%	23	3	13	2 16	17	13	19	20	12	5	16	13	15
gardening h.:m.	0:26	0:19	0:13	0:02 (e)	0:03	0:24	0:25	0:09	0:03	0:13	0:19	0:13	0:07
%	11	9	6	1	1	11	10	4	2	6	8	6	3
unpaid work (community) h.:m.	0:17	0:06	0:16		0:10	0:03	0:09 (a)	0:05	0:05 (f)	0:10	0:25	0:00	0:17
%	7	3	8		5	1	4	2	3	4	11	0	8
Total time in non-SNA activities													
h.:m.	4:07	3:34 (a)	3:24	2:24	3:28	3:48 (d)	4:05	3:27	3:05	3:53	3:55	3:36	3:42
%	100	100	100	100	100	100	100	100	100	100	100	100	100

SOURCES: see table A.

NOTES:
* Our calculations.
Because of rounding off and because of transformation of time units, percentages may not always totalise to 100 and time to 24 hours.
(a) For the detailed content of these categories, see Appendix 1.
Austria: (a) Excluding travel time.
Denmark: (a) Including shopping (i.e. all kinds of shopping. (b) Excluding shopping. (c) Excluding shopping.
(d) Including shopping. (e) Data sampled in february.
France: (a) Excluding "purchasing everyday consumer goods". (b) Excluding: "accompanying children to their
clubs". (c) Including: "purchasing everyday consumer goods" and excluding "phone calls to institutions". (d) Excluding travel time.
Germany: (a) Including travel time.
Great Britain: "1985", actually 1983/7.
Israel: (a) Excluding travels related to everyday shopping. (b) Including related travels.
(c) Excluding related travels. (d) Including vehicle maintenance. (e) Including related travels and travels relating to everyday shopping.
(f) Including travels related to adult care.
Netherlands: (a) Excluding: "daily shopping (groceries, etc.)". (b) Excluding: "reading, talking with children;
indoor playing with children", "outdoor playing with children". (c) Excluding: "doing/ hanging out laundry"; "ironing/folding
putting away laundry". (d) Including: "doing/ hanging out laundry"; "ironing/folding/putting away laundry ".(e) Including: "doing daily shopping (groceries, etc.)".

Table F.
Distribution of time among non-SNA activities, by gender (13 countries)

Average time per person.
Hours and minutes per day (h.:m.)

	Australia 1992 (15 +)		Austria 1992 (10 +)		Canada * 1992 (15 +)		Denmark 1987 (16-74)		Finland * 1987/8 (15 +)		France 1985/6 (15 +)		Germany 1991/2 (16 +)		Great Britain * "1985" (15 +)		Israel 1991/2 (14 +)		Italy 1988/9 (15 +)		Netherlands 1987 (12 +)		Norway * 1990/1 (16-79)		USA 1985 (15 +)	
(pop.aged)	M	F	M	F	M	F	M	F	M	F	M	F	M	F	M	F	M	F	M	F	M	F	M	F	M	F
Time in Non-SNA activities (a)																										
food related activities																					(a)	(a)				
h.:m.	0:24	1:11	0:27	1:58	0:39	1:33	0:45	1:36	0:32	1:34	0:27	1:45	0:26	1:28	0:32	1:31	0:19	1:27	0:25	2:53	0:30	1:33	0:41	1:32	0:42	1:50
%	14	22	24	40	26	35	46(a)	50(a)	22	36	18	35	15	29	31	45	20	33	29	47	18	31	28	34	25	38
child care													(a)	(a)							(b)	(b)				
h.:m.	0:14	0:49	0:08	0:32	0:14	0:36	0:08	0:19	0:11	0:28	0:07	0:28	0:12	0:32	0:12	0:36	0:21	1:02	0:07	0:22	0:06	0:22	0:23	0:48	0:17	0:35
%	8	15	7	11	9	14	8	10	7	11	5	9	7	10	12	18	22	23	8	6	4	7	16	18	11	12
adult care													(a)	(a)												
h.:m.	0:11	0:11	0:07	0:06	0:03	0:03			0:11	0:07	0:03	0:04	0:04	0:06	0:02	0:04	0:04	0:04	0:03	0:08	0:02	0:03	0:12	0:13	0:04	0:04
%	6	3	6	2	2	1			7	3	2	1	2	2	2	2	4	2	3	2	1	1	8	5	3	2
textiles																										
h.:m.	0:04	0:34	0:02	0:48	0:03	0:20	0:01	0:12	0:02	0:34	0:02	0:45	0:03	0:41	0:03	0:24	0:01	0:13	0:00	0:53	0:01	0:21	0:02	0:37	0:05	0:28
%	2	11	2	16	2	8	1	6	1	13	1	15	2	13	3	12	1	5	0	15	1	7	1	14	3	10
upkeep of dwell./surr.																					(d)	(d)				
h.:m.	0:09	0:42	0:18	1:07	0:16	0:48	0:07	0:34	0:25	0:45	0:22	1:01	0:15	0:49	0:19	0:59	0:13	1:12	0:10	1:28	0:13	1:14	0:17	0:39	0:25	0:45
%	5	13	16	22	11	18	7	18	17	17	15	21	9	16	18	29	13	27	12	21	8	24	11	14	13	16
construction maintenance													(a)	(a)												
h.:m.	0:20	0:04	0:22	0:03	0:19	0:04	0:31	0:25	0:22	0:02	0:26	0:02	0:36	0:08	0:19	0:05	0:04	0:01	0:06	0:00	0:29	0:13	0:24	0:03	0:15	0:04
%	11	1	19	1	12	1	32	13	15	1	18	8	21	3	19	2	4	0	7	0	17	4	16	1	8	1
management/ shopping																										
h.:m.	0:46	1:07	0:04	0:04	0:27	0:31	0:02	0:03	0:33	0:38	0:26	0:34	0:40	0:53	0:33	0:49	0:23	0:21	0:10	0:11	0:30	0:45	0:14	0:28	0:34	0:35
%	26	21	4	1	15	12	2 (b)	2 (b)	22	14	18	11	23	17	32	24	24	8	12	3	18	15	10	10	21	12
gardening																										
h.:m.	0:30	0:22	0:19	0:19	0:18	0:10	0:04	0:01	0:03	0:04	0:31	0:17	0:26	0:24	0:14	0:05	0:04	0:02	0:16	0:10	0:23	0:16	0:15	0:11	0:08	0:07
%	17	7	17	6	12	4	4 (c)	1 (c)	2	1	21	6	15	8	14	2	4	1	19	3	14	5	10	4	5	2
unpaid work (community)													(a)	(a)												
h.:m.	0:16	0:17	0:06	0:04	0:16	0:18			0:10	0:10	0:04	0:03	0:11	0:07	0:05	0:05	0:07	0:03	0:09	0:11	0:34	0:17	0:00	0:00	0:15	0:20
%	9	5	5	1	11	7			7	4	3	1	6	2	5	2	7	1	10	3	20	6	0	0	10	7
Total time in non-SNA activities																										
h.:m.	2:54	5:17	1:53a	5:01a	2:31	4:23	1:38	3:10	2:29	4:22	2:28a	4:59a	2:53	5:08	2:19	4:38	1:37	4:25	1:26	6:05	2:47	5:03	2:28	4:31	2:37	4:46
%	100	100	100	100	100	100	100	100	100	100	100	100	100	100	100	100	100	100	100	100	100	100	100	100	100	100

SOURCES: see Table A.

NOTES:
* Our calculations.
Because of rounding off and because of transformation of time units, percentages may not always totalise to 100 and time to 24 hours.
(a) For the detailed content of these categories, see Appendix 1.
Austria: (a) Excluding travel time.
Denmark: (a) Including shopping (i.e. all kinds of shopping). If shopping is excluded, time is, respectively: 0:28 (28%) and 1:12 (38%).
(b) Excluding shopping. If shopping is included, time is, respectively: 0:20 (20%) and 0:28 (14%).(c) Data sampled in February.
France: (a) Excluding travel time.
Germany: (a) Including travel time.
Great Britain: "1985", actually 1983/7.
Israel: (a) Not including travels related to everyday shopping. (b) Including related travels.
(c) Not including related travels. (d) Including vehicle maintenance. (e) Including related travels and travels relating to everyday shopping.
(f) Including travels related to adult care.
Netherlands: (a) Excluding daily shopping. (b): Excluding: "reading, talking with children";
"indoor playing with children"; "outdoor playing with children". These categories are included in the non-economic activities. (c) Excluding: "doing, hanging out laundry"; ironing / folding/ putting away laundry". (d) Including: "doing, hanging out laundry; "ironing / folding / putting away laundry".

Table G1.
Distribution of time between SNA, non-SNA and non-economic activities, all persons and by gender
Great Britain : 1961, 1974/5 and "1985"

Population aged: 15 +.
Average time per person.
Hours and minutes per day (h.:m.).

	1961 *	1974/5 *	"1985" *	1961 *		1974/5 *		"1985" *	
	All			M	F	M	F	M	F
Time in economic activities									
SNA									
h.:m.	4:23	4:02	3:29	6:34	2:24	5:42	2:30	4:39	2:34
%	18	17	15	27	10	24	10	19	11
non-SNA									
h.:m.	3:32	3:02	3:23	1:37	5:16	1:31	4:25	2:12	4:19
%	15	13	14	7	22	6	18	9	18
Total time in economic activities									
h.:m.	7:55	7:04	6:52	8:11	7:40	7:13	6:55	6:51	6:53
%	33	29	29	34	32	30	29	29	29
Time in non-economic activities									
h.:m.	16:05	16:56	17:08	15:49	16:20	16:47	17:05	17:09	17:07
%	67	71	71	66	68	70	71	71	71
Total time, all activities									
h.:m.	24	24	24	24	24	24	24	24	24
%	100	100	100	100	100	100	100	100	100

SOURCE: ESRC Research Centre of Micro-social Change, British Time-Use Project (1994).

NOTES:
1985": Actually 1983/7
All survey formats adjusted to match the time recorded in the 1961 diaries.
* Our calculations.
Because of rounding off and because of transformation of time units, percentages may not always totalise to 100 and time to 24 hours.

Table G2.
Distribution of time between SNA, non-SNA and non-economic activities, all persons and by gender
Norway : 1971/2, 1980/1 and 1990/1

Population aged: 16-79 years.
Average time per person.
Hours and minutes per day (h.:m.).

	1971/2 *	1980/1 *	1990/1 *	1971/2 *		1980/1 *		1990/1 *	
	All			M	F	M	F	M	F
Time in economic activities									
SNA (a)									
h.:m.	3:38	3:29	3:37	5:29	1:56	4:40	2:23	4:30	2:49
%	15	15	15	23	8	20	10	19	12
non-SNA(b)									
h.:m.	4:09	3:39	3:31	2:13	5:55	2:26	4:46	2:36	4:22
%	17	15	15	9	25	10	20	11	18
Total time in economic activities									
h.:m.	7:47	7:08	7:08	7:42	7:51	7:06	7:19	7:06	7:11
%	32	30	30	32	33	30	30	30	30
Time in non-economic activities									
h.:m.	16:13	16:52	16:52	16:18	16:09	16:54	16:41	16:54	16:49
%	68	70	70	68	67	70	70	70	70
Total time, all activities									
h.:m.	24	24	24	24	24	24	24	24	24
%	100	100	100	100	100	100	100	100	100

SOURCE: [Norway.] (1992).
N.B. Data in this table are slightly different from those in all other tables because of differences in data sources.
NOTES:
* Our calculations.
Because of rounding off and because of transformation of time units, percentages may not always totalise to 100 and time to 24 hours.
(a) "Income producing work (ordinary work in main occupation; overtime work in main occupation; agriculture, forestry and fishing on own property/boat; work in secondary occupation; meals at the work place; time spent at place of work before and after working hours, breaks and journey to work".
(b) "Housework; maintenance; family care; purchase of goods and services; other household work and family care; travels in connection with household work and family care".
(c) "Personal needs; education; leisure time; other, unknown".

Table G3.
Distribution of time between SNA, non-SNA and non-economic activities, Bulgaria : 1977 and 1978

(pop. aged)	1977 (6 +)			1971/2 (0.1 +)		
	M	F	M/F *	M	F	M/F *
Time in economic activities						
SNA						
%	18.4	11.8	1.55	16.7	12.0	1.39
non-SNA						
%	13.4	25.6	0.52	9.9	19.9	0.49
Total time in economic activities						
%	31.8	37.4	0.85	26.6	31.9	0.83
Time in non-economic activities						
%	68.2	62.6	1.08	73.4	68.1	1.07
Total time, all activities						
%	100	100	1	100	100	1

Sources: [Bulgaria.] Central Statistical Office (CSU) (1994a and 1994b).

Notes:
* Our calculations.

Table H1.
**HISTORICAL PERSPECTIVE: DISTRIBUTION OF TIME AMONG NON-SNA
ACTIVITIES, ALL PERSONS AND BY GENDER
CANADA: 1961, 1971, 1981, 1986 AND 1992**

Population aged: 15 +.
Average time per person.
Hours and minutes per day (h.:m.).

	1961 *	1971 *	1981 *	1986 *	1992 *	1961 *		1971 *		1981 *		1986 *		1992 *	
	All					M	F	M	F	M	F	M	F	M	F
Time in non-SNA activities (a)															
meal preparation h.:m.	1:04	0:56	0:50	0:44	0:47	0:20	1:47	0:18	1:32	0:20	1:19	0:17	1:11	0:22	1:10
%	33	30	28	25	24	20	37	17	35	17	33	14	30	17	28
cleaning h.:m.	0:32	0:31	0:31	0:30	0:29	0:13	0:52	0:13	0:49	0:20	0:41	0:16	0:43	0:11	0:46
%	17	17	17	17	15	13	18	12	19	17	17	14	18	8	19
clothing care h.:m.	0:20	0:14	0:10	0:10	0:11	0:05	0:34	0:02	0:26	0:02	0:17	0:01	0:17	0:02	0:19
%	10	8	6	5	5	5	12	3	10	2	7	1	8	1	8
repairs/ maintenanc h.:m.	0:18	0:17	0:22	0:17	0:35	0:22	0:14	0:23	0:12	0:28	0:14	0:23	0:11	0:45	0:23
%	9	10	12	10	18	21	5	22	4	24	6	21	5	35	9
marketing h.:m.	0:33	0:40	0:42	(b) 0:53	0:45	0:26	0:40	0:34	0:47	0:35	0:49	(b) 0:45	(b) 0:58	0:37	0:52
%	17	22	24	30	24	26	14	32	18	29	21	39	25	28	21
child care h.:m.	0:29	0:26	0:24	0:23	0:25	0:15	0:42	0:14	0:37	0:14	0:35	0:12	0:33	0:16	0:27
%	14	13	13	13	14	15	14	14	14	11	16	11	14	11	15
Total time in non-SNA activities															
h.:m.	3:15	3:04	2:59	2:56	3:12	1:41	4:49	1:45	4:22	1:58	3:56	1:55	3:55	2:14	4:08
%	100	100	100	100	100	100	100	100	100	100	100	100	100	100	100

SOURCES: ch. Jackson (1992 and 1994)

NOTES:
The estimates for 1961 are "backcasts" from the 1971, 1981 and 1986 data.
* Our calculations
Because of rounding off and because of transformation of time units, percentages may not always totalise to 100 and time to 24 hour
(a) Activity categories are those of the Canadian source and therefore differ from our standardized categorization:
 "Food preparation: meal preparation; meal clean-up
Cleaning: indoor cleaning; outdoor cleaning.
Clothing care: laundry, ironing, folding; mending.
Repairs/maintenance: home repairs and maintenance; gardening and pet care; other housework (bills).
Marketing/shopping: travel-domestic; everyday shopping; shopping for household durable goods; shopping for
personal care services; shopping for government/financial services; adult medical/dental care (outside home);
other professional services; repair services; waiting and queuing for purchases; other unencodeable services;
travel for goods/services.
Child care:
Physical child care: baby care; child care.
Tutorial child care: helping, teaching, reprimanding children; reading, talking, conversation with children; play with children.
Other child care: medical care; other child care; travel associated with children" (Jackson, 1992:8).
Unpaid work for the community not included.
(b) The 1986 time use survey was done in the two months prior to Christmas.

Table H2.
**HISTORICAL PERSPECTIVE: DISTRIBUTION OF TIME AMONG NON-SNA
ACTIVITIES, ALL PERSONS AND BY GENDER
GREAT BRITAIN: 1961, 1974/5 AND 1980s**

Population aged: 15 +.
Average time per person.
Hours and minutes per day (h.:m.).

	1961	1974/5	"1985"	1961		1974/5		"1985"	
	All			M	F	M	F	M	F
Time in non-SNA activities (a)									
cooking/ washing up h.:m. *	1:08	0:58	0:58	0:13	2:02	0:12	1:41	0:30	1:25
%	33	33	30	13	39	13	39	23	33
child care h.:m. *	0:13	0:13	0:21	0:04	0:22	0:05	0:21	0:11	0:32
%	6	7	11	4	7	5	8	8	12
housework h.:m. *	0:59	0:45	0:44	0:12	1:45	0:07	1:23	0:15	1:13
%	29	25	23	12	33	8	31	11	28
odd jobs h.:m. *	0:18	0:23	0:29	0:24	0:13	0:33	0:13	0:35	0:22
%	9	13	15	24	4	36	6	27	9
shopping h.:m. *	0:25	0:27	0:29	0:11	0:39	0:16	0:37	0:22	0:36
%	12	15	15	11	12	18	14	17	14
gardening h.:m. *	0:18	0:09	0:09	0:28	0:09	0:14	0:05	0:14	0:05
%	9	5	4	29	3	15	2	11	2
community service h.:m. *	0:05	0:04	0:05	0:06	0:04	0:04	0:04	0:05	0:05
%	2	2	2	6	1	4	2	4	2
Total time in non-SNA activities									
h.:m. *	3:26	2:59	3:15	1:38	5:14	1:31	4:26	2:12	4:18
%	100	100	100	100	100	100	100	100	100

SOURCE: ESRC Research Centre on Micro-social Change, British Time-Use Project (1994).

NOTES:
"1985": actually 1983/1987.
(a) Activity categories are those of the British Time-Use Project.
* Our calculations.
Because of transformation of time units, time may not always totalise to 24 hours.

Table H3.
HISTORICAL PERSPECTIVE: DISTRIBUTION OF TIME AMONG NON-SNA ACTIVITIES, ALL PERSONS AND BY GENDER
NORWAY: 1971/2, 1980/1 AND 1990/1

Population aged: 16-79 years.
Average time per person.
Hours and minutes per day (h.:m.).

	1971/2 *	1980/1 *	1990/1 *	1971/2 *		1980/1 *		1990/1 *	
	All			M	F	M	F	M	F
Time in non-SNA activities (a)									
food related activities h.:m. %	1:24 36	1:18 34	1:07 31	0:30 26	2:24 43	0:42 29	2:10 41	0:41 28	1:32 34
child care h.:m. %	0:24 10	0:31 13	0:37 17	0:06 5	0:36 11	0:18 13	0:36 11	0:23 16	0:48 18
adult care h.:m. %	---	0:11 5	0:11 5	---	---	0:12 8	0:12 4	0:12 8	0:13 5
textiles h.:m. %	0:36 16	0:25 11	0:20 9	0:00 0	1:00 18	0:00 0	0:42 13	0:02 1	0:47 14
upkeep of dwell./surr. h.:m. %	0:42 18	0:36 15	0:28 13	0:12 11	1:06 20	0:18 13	0:54 17	0:17 11	0:39 14
construction maintenanc h.:m. %	0:12 5	0:14 6	0:13 6	0:36 31	0:00 0	0:24 16	0:06 2	0:24 16	0:03 1
managemen shopping h.:m. %	0:24 10	0:23 10	0:27 13	0:18 16	0:18 5	0:18 13	0:24 8	0:14 10	0:28 10
gardening h.:m. %	0:12 5	0:13 6	0:13 6	0:12 6	0:12 3	0:12 8	0:12 4	0:15 10	0:11 4
unpaid work (community) h.:m. %	0:00 0	0:00 0	0:00 0	0:00 6	0:00 0	0:00 0	0:00 0	0:00 0	0:00 0
Total time in non-SNA activities									
h.:m. %	3:54 100	3:51 100	3:36 100	1:54 100	5:36 100	2:24 100	5:16 100	2:28 100	4:31 100

SOURCE: Statistics Norway (1994)
NOTES:
* Our calculations.
Because of rounding off and because of transformation of time units, percentages may not alwa totalise to 100 and time to 24 hours.

135

Table I. BULGARIA AND FINLAND, 1988
DISTRIBUTION OF TIME BETWEEN SNA, NON-SNA AND NON-ECONOMIC
ACTIVITIES, ALL PERSONS AND BY GENDER

Population aged: 16-79 years.
Average time per person.
Hours and minutes per day (h.:m.).

	BULGARIA 1988 (10 +)			FINLAND 1987/8 (10 +)		
	All	M	F	All	M	F
Time in economic activities						
SNA h.:m. * %	3:50 **16**	4:34 **19**	3:22 **14**	3:22 **14**	4:05 **17**	2:38 **11**
NON-SNA h.:m. * %	3:50 **16**	2:24 **10**	5:02 **21**	3:07 **13**	2:09 **9**	4:05 **17**
Total time in economic activities						
h.:m. * %	7:40 **32**	6:58 **29**	8:24 **35**	6:29 **27**	6:14 **16**	6:43 **28**
Time in non-economic activities						
h.:m. * %	16:19 **68**	17:02 **71**	15:36 **65**	17:31 **73**	17:45 **74**	17:17 **72**
Total time, all activities						
h.:m. * %	24 **100**	24 **100**	24 **100**	24 **100**	24 **100**	24 **100**

SOURCE: I. Niemi and B. Anachkova (1992).

NOTES:
* Our calculations.
Because of rounding off and because of transformation of time units, percentages
may not always totalise to 100 and time to 24 hours.

Table J. BULGARIA AND FINLAND 1988
DISTRIBUTION OF TIME AMONG HOUSEWORK ACTIVITIES,
ALL PERSONS AND BY GENDER

Average time per person.
Hours and minutes per day (h.:m.).

(pop. aged)	BULGARIA 1988 (10 +)			FINLAND 1987/8 (10 +)		
	All	M	F	All	M	F
food **%***	0:53 **24**	0:12 **9**	1:32 **30**	0:48 **25**	0:20 **15**	1:15 **31**
food preparation	0:36	0:07	1:02	0:37	0:16	0:56
washing up	0:18	0:05	0:30	0:12	0:04	0:19
housekeeping **%***	1:00 **27**	0:09 **6**	1:46 **15**	0:41 **22**	0:11 **8**	1:08 **28**
in.cleaning	0:22	0:08	0:35	0:23	0:10	0:35
laundry	0:16	0:01	0:30	0:08	0:01	0:14
clothes upk.	0:22	0:01	0:42	0:10	0:00	0:19
maintenance **%***	1:04 **28**	1:22 **58**	0:47 **35**	0:46 **24**	1:00 **45**	0:32 **13**
heat./water	0:06	0:08	0:04	0:06	0:09	0:04
home upkeep	0:12	0:22	0:03	0:11	0:21	0:02
garden./pres. (a)	0:32	0:37	0:28	0:05	0:04	0:07
out. cleaning	0:03	0:04	0:03	0:05	0:06	0:04
other dom. (b)	0:02	0:02	0:03	0:15	0:14	0:15
dom. travel (a)	0:08	0:10	0:06	0:04	0:06	0:02
child care **%***	0:19 **8**	0:08 **6**	0:30 **10**	0:18 **10**	0:10 **8**	0:25 **11**
shopping (c) **%***	0:30 **13**	0:30 **21**	0:31 **10**	0:37 **19**	0:32 **24**	0:41 **17**
total **%***	3:46 **100**	2:21 **100**	5:05 **100**	3:11 **100**	2:15 **100**	4:03 **100**

SOURCE: I. Niemi and B. Anachkova (1992).
NOTES:
* Our calculations.
(a) "Gardening" and "domestic travel" are not quite comparable between the two countries becaus
of codification differences.
(b) "Other domestic activities" includes helping family members, neighbours, relatives and friends.
(c) "Shopping and errands" includes acquisition of consumer goods and durables (including time
spent on queues), health care services, making calls on public and private services and private a
etc., as well as travels related to these activities.

137

Table K.   BULGARIA AND FINLAND, 1988
SHARING OF HOUSEWORK ACTIVITIES BY GENDER: EQUALITY RATIOS

Activity	Equality ratios (a)	
	BULGARIA	FINLAND
food	**88**	**79**
food preparation	90	78
washing up	86	83
housekeeping	**92**	**86**
indoor cleaning	81	78
laundry and clooth upkeep	97	97
maintenance	**36**	**35**
heating/ water	33	31
home upkeep	12	9
gardening/ preserving	43	64
outdoor cleaning	43	40
other domestic	60	52
domestic travel	38	25
child care	**79**	**71**
shopping/ errands	**51**	**56**
housework total	**68**	**64**

SOURCE: I. Niemi and B. Anachkova (1992).

NOTES:
* Our calculations.
(a) Time used by women expressed as a percentage of the total time used by men and women. A high percentage for a specific activity means that the activity is female-dominated, a low percentage means that the activity is male-dominated and a medium percentage shows that the activity is equally shared between men and women.

Table L. BULGARIA 1988.
DISTRIBUTION OF TIME BETWEEN SNA, NON-SNA AND NON-ECONOMIC ACTIVITIES, BY ALL RESIDENTS AND BY GENDER

Population aged: 0.1 +.
Average time per person.
Hours and minutes per day (h.:m.).

	1988		
	All	M	F
Time in economic activities			
SNA h.:m. %	3:26 14	4:00 17	2:53 12
NON-SNA h.:m. %	3:37 15	2:23 10	4:47 20
Total time in economic activities			
h.:m. %	7:03 29	6:23 27	7:40 32
Time in non-economic activities			
h.:m. %	16:57 71	17:37 73	16:20 68
Total time, all activities			
h.:m. %	24 100	24 100	24 100

SOURCE: [Bulgaria.]   Central Statistical Office (CSU) (1994b).

Table M. BULGARIA 1988.
DISTRIBUTION OF TIME AMONG NON-SNA ACTIVITIES,
ALL RESIDENTS AND BY GENDER
NORWAY: 1971/2, 1980/1 AND 1990/1

Average time per person.
Hours and minutes per day (h.:m.).

(pop. aged)	BULGARIA 1988 (0.1 +)		
	All	M	F
Time in non-SNA activities (a)			
food related activities h.:m.	0:51	0:14	0:86
%	24	10	30
child care h.:m.	0:17	0:07	0:27
%	8	5	9
adult care h.:m.	0:02	0:01	0:03
%	1	1	1
textiles h.:m.	0:33	0:02	0:63
%	15	1	22
upkeep of dwell./surr. h.:m.	0:28	0:17	0:37
%	13	12	13
construction maintenance h.:m.	0:11	0:19	0:03
%	5	13	1
management/ shopping h.:m.	0:24	0:24	0:24
%	11	17	9
gardening h.:m.	0:37	0:43	0:32
%	17	30	11
unpaid work (community) h.:m.	0:13	0:15	0:11
%	6	11	4
Total time in non-SNA activities			
h.:m.	3:36	2:22	4:46
%	100	100	100

SOURCE: [Bulgaria.] Central Statistical Office (CSU) (1994b).

NOTE:
(a) For the detailed content of these categories, see Appendix 1.

Table N. BULGARIA 1988.
DISTRIBUTION OF TIME OVER THE LIFE SPAN BETWEEN SNA, NON-SNA AND NON-ECONOMIC ACTIVITIES, BY ALL RESIDENTS AND BY GENDER (1988 STRUCTURE)

Population aged: 0.1 +.
Average time per resident.

	1988		
	All	M	F *
Longevity	71.33	68.12	74.77
Time in economic activities			
SNA h. %	89258	99414 100	78735 79
NON-SNA h. %	94118	59341 100	130587 220
Total time in economic activities			
h. %	183376	158755 100	209322 132
Time in non-economic activities			
h. %	441475	437976 100	445663 102
Total time, all activities			
h. %	624851	596731 100	654985 100

SOURCE: [Bulgaria.] Central Statistical Office (CSU) (1994b).

NOTE:
* : The female percentage is relative to a base of 100 for the male hours

Table O.
VALUE OF LABOUR AND VALUE OF PRODUCTION AT COST OF INPUTS, IN NON-SNA ACTIVITIES (SEVEN COUNTRIES)

Per cent of GDP.

	Value of labour inputs ##				Value of production				Sources
	SNA	Non-SNA			SNA	Non-SNA			
	C.o.E. # (i.e. gr. w +)	W. Sp ##			GDP	gross V.A. at cost of inputs (labour factor: W. SP##)			
		n.w.	gr.w.	gr.w. +		n.w.	gr.w.	gr.w. +	
Australia 1992 (age : 15 +)	51			72	100			86	Ironmonger (1994)
Denmark 1987 (age : 16-74)	56 *	21 (a) *		37 */**	100			43 (b) **	* Mollgaard and Rormose (1995) ** Bonke (1993)
Finland 1990 (age : 15 +)	56			45	100			46.4	Vihavainen (a) (1995)
France 1985 (age : 15 +)			33	36	100				Chadeau (1992)
Germany (a) 1992 (age : 16 +)	55	31	45	54 (b)	100	33	47	55 (c)	Schäfer and Schwarz (1994)
Norway 1990 (age : 16-79)				38	100				Dahle, Kitterod (1992)
Bulgaria (a) 1988 (age : 0.1 +)	85				100	47	71	84	Zachariev, Todorova, Tcsekova Mantchevska (1994, unpubl.)

NOTES:

\#: C.o.E : compensation of employees
\##: wage of a subsitute household worker, polyvalent
gr.w.: gross wages / n.w.: net wages
gr.w.+: gross wages including employers' social security contributions
Denmark: (a) Net wages are calculated as gross wages for unskilled menial workers minus the average tax paid by these workers.
        (b) Including gross value added for owner-occupied dwelling is 50.
Finland: (a) Plus additional unpublished calculations based on Statistics Finland (1990b).
Germany: (a) Old Länder only (former territory of the Federal Republic of Germany).
        (b) Paid leave, paid public holidays, paid absence because of sickness not included.
        (c) Including gross value added for owner-occupied dwelling, is, respectively: 37. 51, 59.
Bulgaria: (a) The value of labour inputs and therefore the value of production are calculated on a different population basis (age: 0.1 +) than in other studies (age: 15+). See details in section 2.4.

Table P. HISTORICAL PERSPECTIVE
VALUE OF LABOUR AND VALUE OF PRODUCTION, IN NON-SNA ACTIVITIES

Per cent of GDP.

Valuation methods	Value of labour inputs ##				Value of production				Sources
	SNA	Non-SNA			SNA	Non-SNA			
	C.o.E. # (i.e. gr. w .+)	W. Sp ##			GDP	gross V.A. at cost of inputs (labour factor: W. SP##)			
		n.w.	gr.w.	gr.w. +		n.w.	gr.w.	gr.w. +	
Denmark 1964 (age: 16+)				28 (a)					Bonke (1993)
1975 (age: 16+)				39 (a)					Bonke (1993)
1987 (age : 16-74)	56 *	21 (b) *		37 */**				43 (c) **	Molligaard and Rormose (1995) ** Bonke (1993)
Finland 1979/1982 (age: 16-75)			41.7 (a)						Finland, P.VIII (1982)
1990 (age : 15 +)	56		45		100			46.4	Vihavainen (b) (1995)
Norway 1972 (age : 16-79)				53 (a)					
1981 (age : 16-79)				41 (a)					
1990 (age : 16-79)				38 (a)					Dahle, Kitterod (1992)
Bulgaria (a) 1971 (age: 6+)	52 (b)				100	43	48	54	Zachariev, Todorova, Tcsekova Mantchevska (1994, unpubl.)
1977 (age: 6+)	42 (b)				100	27	38	42	
1988 (age : 0.1 +)	85				100	47	71	84	

NOTES:

#: C.o.E.: compensation of employees
##: Wage of a substitute household worker, polyvalent
gr.w.: gross wages / n.w.: net wages
gr.w.+: gross wages including employers' social security contributions
Denmark: (a) Wage substitute household worker, polyvalent, called "Market Alternative Housekeeper Cost" (Bonke, 1993).
  (b) Net wages are calculated as gross wages for unskilled menial workers minus the average tax paid by these workers.
  (c) Including gross value added for owner-occupied dwelling is 50.
Finland: (a) "Wages received by municipal home helpers" (p.17).
  (b) Plus additional unpublished calculations based on Statistics Finland (1990b).
Norway: (a) "Qualified municipal home helpers" including Employers' National Insurance Contribution" (p.7).
 "Purchasing goods and services and the pertaining travels: not included" (p.4). "Leadership and participation in community and voluntary public services...(are) not included in the Norwegian imputations for 1972, 1981 and 1990" (pp. 4-5).
Bulgaria: (a) The value of labour inputs and therefore the value of production are calculated on a different population basis (age: 0.1 +) than in other studies (age: 15+). See details in section 2.4.
(b) Percentage of GNP.

Table Q.

CONTRIBUTION OF NON-SNA ACTIVITIES TO EXTENDED PRIVATE CONSUMPTION
BULGARIA, FINLAND AND GERMANY

Per cent (%) of extended private consumption.

Valuation methods	Private consumption			Sources
	Extended SNA SNA + NON-SNA	SNA modified (a)	NON-SNA	
Finland 1990	100	37	63	Statistics Finland (a) (1994)
Germany (a) 1992	100	38	62 (b)	Schäfer and Schwarz (1994)
Bulgaria (a) 1988	100	42	58	Tcsekova (1994, unpublished)

NOTES:
(a): "Private consumption" as given in SNA minus goods and services used in non-SNA production (I.e. intermediate inputs and consumer durables).
Finland: (a) Unpublished calculations.
Germany: (a) Old Länder only (former territory of the Federal Republic of Germany).
(b) Value of production in non-SNA activities (labour factor calculated on net wages of substitute household workers, polyvalent).
Bulgaria: (a) The value of labour inputs and therefore the value of production are calculated on a different population basis (age: 0.1 +) than in other studies (age: 15+). See details in section 2.4.

Table R.
CONTRIBUTION OF NON-SNA ACTIVITIES TO PER CAPITA EXTENDED PRIVATE
CONSUMPTION, IN U.S. DOLLARS
BULGARIA: 1971, 1977 AND 1988

Valuation methods	Private consumption current PPPS U.S. $			Sources
	Extended SNA SNA + NON-SNA	SNA modified (a)	NON-SNA (b)	
1971 U.S.$ %	2735.8 **100**	963 **35.2**	1772.8 **64.8**	Time-use data: see section 2
1971 U.S.$ %	3198 **100**	1244 **38.9**	1954 **61.1**	Monetary valuation: Mantchevska and Ilieva (1994 unpubl.)
1971 U.S.$ %	2137 **100**	889 **41.6**	1248 **58.4**	

NOTES:
PPP U.S. $ is not calculated, but estimated by Mantchevska and Ilieva:
1971: 1 BGL = 1.170 U.S.$
1977: 1 BGL = 1.075 U.S.$
1988: 1 BGL = 0.410 U.S.$
(a): "Private consumption" as given in SNA minus goods and services used in non-SNA production (i.e.
intermediate inputs and consumer durables).
(b) Value of production in non-SNA activities (labour factor calculated on net wages of substitute household workers, polyvalent).
Time-use data were collected in 1971 and 1977 on the population aged 6 years and over; in 1988, on the entire resident population (0.1 year and over).
The value of labour inputs is essentially not affected by these differences because the labour contribution of children aged 6 and below
is negligible (Time use studies world wide, 1990, pp.496-499).

Table S.
INTEGRATED PER CAPITA EXTENDED PRIVATE CONSUMPTION (U.S. DOLLARS)
AND PER CAPITA TOTAL ECONOMIC TIME (hours and minutes per day)
BULGARIA: 1971, 1977 AND 1988

Current PPP U.S.$ and average time per person in hours and minutes per day (h.:m.)

	Per capita extended private consumption (SNA + NON-SNA) (a) (b) U.S.$ (PPP)	Total economic time per person (SNA + NON-SNA) h.:m.	Standardized extended per capita consumption (c) U.S.$ (PPP)	Sources
1971 h.:m.		8:40		Time-use data:
U.S.$	2736		2516	see section 2
1977 h.:m.		8:19		
U.S.$	3198		3075	Monetary valuation:
1988 h.:m.		7:03		Mantchevska and Ilieva (1994 unpubl.)
U.S.$	2137		2440	

NOTES:
PPP U.S. $ is not calculated, but estimated by Mantchevska and Ilieva:
1971: 1 BGL = 1.170 U.S.$
1977: 1 BGL = 1.075 U.S.$
1988: 1 BGL = 0.410 U.S.$
(a): "Private consumption" as given in SNA minus goods and services used in non-SNA production (i.e. intermediate inputs and consumer durables).
(b) Production value in non-SNA activities (labour factor calculated on net wages of substitute household workers, polyvalent).
(c) Standardized at 8 hours total economic time per person, per day.

REFERENCES

Australian Bureau of Statistics, 1994. Special elaboration of How Australians Use Their Time. Canberra: Australian Bureau of Census and Statistics, 1994. Table 2, pp. 8-9.

Austrian Central Statistical Office, 1994. Special elaboration of "Time Use Survey 1992". Private communication.

Babarczy, A.; Harcsa, I. and Pääkkönen, H. 1991. Time use trends in Finland and in Hungary. Helsinki: Central Statistical Office of Finland, Studies, No. 180. 65 p.

Bonke, Jens. 1993. "Household Production and National Accounts". Discussion papers, No. 93-07, Institute of Economics, University of Copenhagen, August. 25 p.

Bonke, Jens. 1994. Special elaboration of "The Danish Time-Budget Survey 1987". The Danish National Institute of Social Research. Private communication.

British Broadcasting Corporation. 1965. The people's activities. Audience Research Department. London: BBC.

British Broadcasting Corporation. 1976. The people's activities and the use of time. Audience Research Department. London: BBC.

[Bulgaria.] Central Statistical Office (CSU). 1994a. Special elaboration of "Time budget of the people's Republic of Bulgaria". 1978. Sofia: Kessi. Private communication.

[Bulgaria.] Central Statistical Office (CSU). 1994b. Special elaboration of "Time budget of the population of Bulgaria". 1990. Sofia. Partly published in Time use studies world wide. pp. 364-367.

Chadeau, Ann. 1992. "What is households' non-market production worth?", in OECD Economic Studies (Paris), No. 136, Sept. pp. 29-55.

Dahle, Anne Berit; Kitterød, Ragni Hege. 1992. "Time use studies in evaluation of household work", Paper presented at the 19th Nordic Statistics Meeting, Reykjavik, July 22-25 1992. 11 p.

ESRC Research Centre on Micro-social Change, University of Essex. 1994. Special elaboration of the "British Time-Use Project". Private communication.

European Union, Statistical Office (EUROSTAT). 1994a. Coding proposal for the European time use survey. April.

European Union, Statistical Office (EUROSTAT). 1994b. 15th Meeting of the Statistical Programme Committee, Luxembourg, 1 and 2 December. Item 8 of the agenda. Time use surveys; Project and action programme for the introduction of harmonised time-use surveys in the European Union. (CPS 94/15/8).

[Finland.] Ministry of Social Affairs and Health, Research Department. 1980-1986. Housework study, Fourteen parts, Special Social Studies. Part VIII, Säntti, Riitta; Otva, Ritva-Anneli; Kilpiö, Eila. 1982. "Unpaid housework: Time use and value". Helsinki: Official Statistics of Finland.

[Germany] Federal Statistical Office. 1994. Special elaboration of "The time use survey 1991/1992". Private communication.

Gershuny, J.; Miles, I.; Jones, S.; Mullings, G.; Thomas, G.; Wyatt, S.. 1986. "Time budgets: Preliminary analysis of a national survey", in Quarterly Journal of Social Affairs. Vol. 2, No. 1. pp. 13-39.

Goldschmidt-Clermont, Luisella. 1987. "Assessing the economic significance of domestic and related activities", in Statistical Journal of the Economic Commission for Europe (Geneva), Vol. 5. pp. 81-93.

Goldschmidt-Clermont, Luisella. 1989. "Valuing domestic activities", in Bulletin of Labour Statistics (Geneva), No.4. pp.ix-xii.

Goldschmidt-Clermont, Luisella. 1993. "Monetary valuation of non-market productive time: Methodological considerations", in Review of Income and Wealth (New-Haven), Series 39, No. 4, December. pp 419-433.

Grimler, Ghislaine; Roy, Caroline. 1991. "Les emplois du temps en France en 1985-1986", Document de travail de la Direction des Statistiques Démographiques et Sociales, No. F9114. INSEE, novembre.

Harvey, Andrew S. 1990. Guidelines for time use data collection. Ottawa: Statistics Canada. General Social Survey, Working Paper No.5. May. 38 pp.

Harvey, Andrew S. and Niemi, Iiris. 1994. "An International Standard Activity Classification (ISAC): Toward a framework, relevant issues", in (Proceedings of the) Fifteenth Reunion of the International Association for Time Use Research, Amsterdam, June 15-18, 1993. NIMMO: Amsterdam. pp. 226-245.

Ironmonger, Duncan S. 1994. "The value of care and nurture provided by unpaid household work", in Family Matters, No. 37, April, pp. 46-51.

Israel, Central Bureau of Statistics. 1995. Time use in Israel, Time Budget Survey, 1991/2, Special Publication. Series No. 996. Jerusalem.

[Italy] Istituto Nazionale di Statistica (ISTAT). 1993. L'uso del tempo in Italia; Indagine multiscopo sulle famiglie, anni 1987-1991. Roma: ISTAT, No. 4.

[Italy] National Statistical Institute (ISTAT). 1994. Special elaboration of "Time Use Survey in Italy: June 1988 - May 1989". Private communication.

Jackson, Chris, 1992. "Trends in the value of household work in Canada, 1961-1986". Paper presented at the 1993 Meeting of the Canadian Economics Association, June 4-6, Carleton University, Ottawa, Ontario, 27 p.

Jackson, Chris. 1994. Special elaboration of data (Canadian surveys: 1961 to 1992). Private communication.

Kirjavainen, Leena M.; Anachkova, Bistra; Laaksonen, Seppo; Niemi, Iiris; Pääkkönen, Hannu and Staikov, Zahari. 1992. Housework time in Bulgaria and Finland. Helsinki: Statistics Finland, Studies, No. 193. 132 p.

Kusnic, Michael W. and Da Vanzo, Julie. 1980. Income inequality and the definition of income: The case of Malaysia. Santa Monica, California: Rand Corporation (R-2416-AID). June. 121 pp.

Mantchevska (V.T. Bank) and Ilieva, Jana (National Statistical Office). Consultants for tables R. and S. Private communication.

Maryland, University of. 1994. Special elaboration of the "American's Use of Time Project, 1985", Department of Sociology. College park, MD. Private communication.

Møllgaard, Elisabeth; Rørmose Jensen, Peter. 1995. "On the Measurement of a Welfare Indicator for Denmark 1970-1990", Rockwool Foundation Research Unit. Danmarks Statistik (forthcoming).

Niemi, Iiris, 1983. The 1979 time use study method. Helsinki: Central Statistical Office of Finland, Studies, No. 91.

Niemi, Iiris; Anachkova, Bistra. 1992. "Sharing of housework", in Housework time in Bulgaria and Finland. Statistics Finland, Studies, No. 193, pp. 12-41.

Niemi, I.; Eglite, P.; Mitrikas, A.; Patrushev, V.D and Pääkkönen, H. 1991. Time use in Finland, Latvia, Lithuania and Russia. Helsinki: Central Statistical Office of Finland, Studies, No. 182.

[Norway] 1992. "The time budget surveys 1970-1990". in Norges Offisielle Statistikk C 10. Oslo-Konsvinger: Statistik Sentralbyra.

Petrova, Lili, 1994. Special elaboration of Bulgarian time-use data (personal archives). Private communication.

Robinson, John P.; Andreenkov, Vladimir and Petruchev, Vassily. 1988. The Rhythm of Everyday Life. Boulder Co: Westview Press.

Robinson, John P.; Bostrom, Ann. 1994. "The Overestimated Workweek", in Monthly Labor Review, August, pp. 11-23.

Schäfer, Dieter; Schwarz, Norbert. 1994. "Wert der Haushaltsproduktion 1992" ("Value of household production in 1992"), in Wirtschaft und Statistik (Wiesbaden), No. 8. pp 597-612.

Staikov, Zahari. 1982a. "Problems of the comparison of time-budgets", in "It's about Time", Proceedings of the Reunion of the International Association for Time Use Research, Sofia, 1982, pp. 54-65.

Staikov, Zahari. 1982b. "Magnitude and structure of aggregate and generation time use budgets; indicators of social progress", in "It's about Time", Proceedings of the Reunion of the

International Association for Time Use Research, Sofia, pp. 349-362.

Statistics Canada. 1993. Overview of the 1992 General Social Survey on Time Use (GSS-7), General Social Survey Working Paper #9, August.

Statistics Finland. 1990a. Household Expenditure Survey. 1990.

Statistics Finland. 1990b. National Accounts. 1990.

Statistics Finland. 1990c. Wage Statistics. 1990.

Statistics Finland. 1994. Special elaboration of "Time Use Survey 1987/8".

Statistics Netherlands. 1994. Special elaboration of "De tijdsbesteding van de Nederlandse bevolking; kerncijfers 1989" ("A Survey on time use in the Netherlands, 1987"). Voorburg/Heerlen.

Statistics Norway. 1994. Private communication.

Tcsekova, Nikolina. 1994. Consultant for table Q. Private communication.

Time Use Studies World Wide, 1990. A collection of papers presented at the 1989 Varna conference of the International Association for Time Use Research. Sofia: Socioconsult Ltd.

Vihavainen, Marjut. 1995. "Calculating the value of the household production in Finland 1990". Working Papers. Helsinki: Statistics Finland (forthcoming).

Zachariev, Peter. 1994. Special elaboration of Bulgarian time-use data (personal archives). Private communication.

Zachariev, Peter; Todorova, Boyka and Tcsekova, Nikolina. 1994. Consultants for table O. Unpublished data derived from Statistical Reference Book, Economics of Bulgaria, 1993, p.6.

APPENDIX 1. CATEGORISATION OF ACTIVITIES

Derived from the Coding Proposal for ETUS, the European Time Use Survey (European Union, Statistical Office, 1994a)[1]

ETUS codes	
	SNA ACTIVITIES:
1	Gainful employment
	NON-SNA ACTIVITIES:
	(See below)
	NON-ECONOMIC ACTIVITIES:
0	Personal care
2	Study
5	Social life and entertainment
6	Sports participation
7	Arts, hobbies and games
8	Mass media
	PARTICIPATIVE ACTIVITIES
421	Meetings (participation in social, political, etc. organizations)
422	Religious activities (religious practice and ceremonies)
429	Unspecified
	NON-SNA ACTIVITIES:
1)	**DOMESTIC AND RELATED ACTIVITIES** Work done for own or another household
	FOOD RELATED ACTIVITIES:
311	Preparing meals
312	Preparing snacks (including preparing coffee, tea or drink)

---

[1]   Work is still in progress for ETUS. At the time this report goes to press (August 1995) this coding proposal of April 1995 is not any more up to date.

313	Setting the table
314	Meal cleanup, dish washing
315	Baking
316	Preserving, freezing, canning, gathering of wild food
341	Tending edible plants
361	Purchasing everyday consumer goods
319	Unspecified

CHILD CARE:

381	Physical care
382	Supervision of the child (including babysitting)
383	Reading or playing with the child
384	Talking to the child
385	Learning with the child (help with homework, guiding in doing things)
386	Outdoors with children
387	Accompanying children to their clubs (waiting at a sport centre, musician lesson, etc.)
388	Visiting school/nursery (including parents' meeting)
366 (part)	Medical/dental services for children
389	Unspecified

390	ADULT CARE (except housework):

Physical care of a sick or elderly adult
Visits to hospitals
Washing, cutting hair, massaging
Help with another person's his/her gainful employment
Mental help, information and advice

MAKING AND CARE OF TEXTILES:

331	Laundry (loading and unloading washing machine, hanging out, putting away)
332	Ironing (including mangling, tasks connected with ironing and mangling, e.g. folding)
333	Mending and care of clothes and shoes
334	Producing textiles (productive activities included in the 1993 SNA, weaving cloth, dress making, tailoring, making shoes)
335	Handicrafts (knitting, needlework, embroidery)

339	Unspecified

UPKEEP OF DWELLING AND SURROUNDINGS:

321	Cleaning dwelling (vacuuming, washing/waxing floors, washing windows, making beds, tidying, tending flowers, arranging the home)
322	Cleaning cellar, garage, shed
323	Cleaning yard, pavement, shovelling snow
324	Separating and disposal of waste
325	Forestry, woodcutting and collecting firewood (productive work included in 1994 SNA)
326	Heating and water supply
327	Other household upkeep (packing for a trip, move etc., looking for lost items)
329	Unspecified

CONSTRUCTION, REPAIRS AND MAINTENANCE:

351	House construction and renovation (including major changes to the house, including major extension and alteration)
352	Repairs to dwelling (replastering walls, repairing roofs, painting, papering, carpeting, decoration, repairs to fittings etc.)
353	Repairing household equipment and appliances
354	Vehicle maintenance
355	Production of household goods (making furniture, furnishing, production of pottery, utensils and durables, etc.)
356	Other
359	Unspecified

HOUSEHOLD MANAGEMENT, SHOPPING AND SERVICES:

362	Purchasing durable consumer goods (including half-durable consumer goods, buying clothes, shoes, furniture, household appliances, dwelling, books, etc., purchasing for maintenance and repair)
363	Administrative services (visiting post office, bank, municipality authorities)

364	Laundry, shoemaker
365	Garage, maintenance vehicle
367	Personal services (haircut, etc.)
370	Household management (planning and arranging, budgeting, paperwork, making shopping list, arranging and supervising outside services at home. Phone calls to institutions, correspondence with authorities, etc.)
369	Unspecified

GARDENING AND PET CARE:

342	Tending ornamental plants (also graves), flowers, mowing the lawn
343	Tending domestic animals (when not on a farm)
344	Feeding and caring for pets
345	Walking the dog
368 (part)	Veterinary services, etc.
349	Unspecified

2)   **UNPAID WORK FOR THE COMMUNITY**

WORK FOR ORGANIZATION

411	Work for the organization itself (including work for groups and associations, as well as work for school and kindergarten, and neighbourhood groups, etc., work as committee member, administrative work, preparing activities, work for events, baking etc. for the organization, working in the canteen, repairs and other odd jobs for the organization, giving information, distributing leaflets)
412	Work for people via organizations Non-profit organizations Delivering meals; Teachers or course instructor; Coach, referee etc. in sport and gymnastics; Leader of a youth group, e.g. scout leader; Work in a child care group;
419	Unspecified work for organization

Appendix 2

Table T1.
EFFECT OF AGE LOWER LIMIT ADOPTED FOR THE STUDY
FINLAND 1987/8

Average time per person.
Hours and minutes per day (h.:m.).

(pop. aged)	All persons		by gender			
			M		F	
	15 +	10 +	15 +	10 +	15 +	10 +
Time in economic activities						
SNA h.:m. %	3:33 15	3:22 * 14	4:21 18	4:05 * 17	2:48 12	2:38 * 11
NON-SNA h.:m. %	3:28 14	3:07 * 13	2:29 10	2:09 * 9	4:22 18	4:05 * 17
Total time in economic activities						
h.:m. %	7:01 29	6:29* 27	6:50 28	6:14 * 26	7:10 30	6:43 * 28
Time in non-economic activities						
h.:m. %	17:00 71	17:31 * 73	17:09 72	17:45 * 74	16:50 70	17:17 * 72
Total time, all activities						
h.:m. %	24 100	24 100	24 100	24 100	24 100	24 100

SOURCES: Statistics Finland (1994); I. Niemi and B. Anachkova (1992).

NOTE:
* Our calculations.

Table T2.
EFFECT OF AGE LOWER LIMIT ADOPTED FOR THE STUDY
GERMANY, 1991/2

Average time per person.
Hours and minutes per day (h.:m.).

	All persons		by gender			
			M		F	
pop.aged	16 +	12 +	16 +	12 +	16 +	12 +
Time in economic activities						
SNA h.:m. %	3:16 14	3:08 13	4:28 19	4:17 18	2:12 9	2:07 9
NON-SNA h.:m. %	4:05 17	3:56 16	2:53 12	2:48 12	5:08 21	5:00 21
Total time in economic activities						
h.:m. %	7:21 31	7:04 29	7:21 31	7:05 30	7:20 31	7:07 30
Time in non-economic activities						
h.:m. %	16:39 69	16:56 71	16:39 69	16:55 70	16:40 69	16:53 70
Total time, all activities						
h.:m. %	24 100	24 100	24 100	24 100	24 100	24 100

SOURCES: [Germany.] Federal Statistical Office (1994).

Appendix 3

Table U
EFFECT OF CATEGORISATION OF TRANSPORTATION TIME
FRANCE, 1985/6

Average time per person.
population aged: 15+
Hours and minutes per day (h.:m.).

	France 1985/6					
	All	All	M	M	F	F
Time in economic activities						
SNA h.:m.	3:03	3:03	4:00	4:00	2:10	2:10
%	13	13	17	17	9	9
NON-SNA h.:m.	4:31 a	3:48 b	3:14 a	2:28 b	5:40 a	4:59 b
%	19	16	13	10	24	21
Total time in economic activities						
h.:m.	7:34 a	6:51 b	7:14 a	6:28 b	7:50 a	7:09 b
%	32	29	30	27	33	30
Time in non-economic activities						
h.:m.	16:26 c	17:09 d	16:46	17:32 d	16:10	16:51
%	68	71	70	73	67	70
Total time, all activities						
h.:m.	24	24	24	24	24	24
%	100	100	100	100	100	100

SOURCE: Grimler and Roy (1991).

NOTES:
(a) Including travel time for non-SNA and non-economic activities.
(b) Excluding travel time for non-SNA activities.
(c) Excluding travel time for non-economic activities.
(d) Including travel time for non-SNA and non-economic activities.

**   Luisella Goldschmidt-Clermont*(1,2) and Elisabetta Pagnossin-Aligisakis(2); Free University of Brussels(1) and University of Geneva(2); in cooperation with Karen Blanke, Manfred Ehling, Dieter Schaefer and Norbert Schwarz, Federal Statistical Office of Germany; Jens Bonke (1) and Peter Rormose(2), Danish National Institute of Social Research(1) and Danmarks Statistik (2); Jonathan Gershuny (1) and Sally Jones(2), ESRC Research Centre on Micro-social Change, University of Essex (1) and School of Social Sciences, Univ. of Bath (2); Ghislaine Grimler, France; Inge Gross, Austrian Central Statistical Office; Eeva Hamunen, Hannu Pääkkönen and Marjut Vihavainen, Statistics Finland; Duncan Ironmonger, Department of Economics, University of Melbourne; Ragni Hege Kitterød and Julie Aslaksen, Statistics Norway; Gina Koslov, Central Bureau of Statistics, Israel; Iiris Niemi, European Time Use Survey, Statistical Office of the European Union; John P. Robinson, University of Maryland; Leonarda Roveri, National Statistical Institute, Italy; Zahari Staikov (1), Bistra Anachkova(1), Lili Petrova (2), P. Zahariev (3), Jana Ilieva (3), Boyka Todorova (3), Nikolina Tcsekova (3) and Mantchevska (4), Institute of Sociology, Bulgarian Academy of Sciences (1), Sofian Sociological Society (2), National Statistical Institute (3) and V.T.Bank (4); Statistics Canada; Statistics Netherlands. who kindly supplied the data. Responsibility for the statistical data lies with the national contributors as quoted in the table sources, while the commentary and opinions expressed herein are, unless otherwise indicated, the responsibility of the two authors. January 31, 1995

93306-September-1996-10M